Contents at a Glance

Table of Contents

Helping Kids with Coding

by Camille McCue, PhD
Sarah Guthals, PhD

for
dummies®
A Wiley Brand

Helping Kids with Coding For Dummies®

Published by: **John Wiley & Sons, Inc.**, 111 River Street, Hoboken, NJ 07030-5774, www.wiley.com

Copyright © 2018 by John Wiley & Sons, Inc., Hoboken, New Jersey

Published simultaneously in Canada

For general information on our other products and services, please contact our Customer Care Department within the U.S. at 877-762-2974, outside the U.S. at 317-572-3993, or fax 317-572-4002. For technical support, please visit https://hub.wiley.com/community/support/dummies.

Wiley publishes in a variety of print and electronic formats and by print-on-demand. Some material included with standard print versions of this book may not be included in e-books or in print-on-demand. If this book refers to media such as a CD or DVD that is not included in the version you purchased, you may download this material at http://booksupport.wiley.com. For more information about Wiley products, visit www.wiley.com.

Library of Congress Control Number: 2018935055

ISBN 978-1-119-38067-2 (pbk); ISBN 978-1-119-38066-5 (ebk); ISBN 978-1-119-38058-0 (ebk)

Manufactured in the United States of America

10 9 8 7 6 5 4 3 2 1

Introduction

Welcome to the world of computer programming! Whether you're an expert at programming or you've never written a line of code in your life, you can coach young people in learning the basics of coding. Just like learning to read, cook, or drive, basic principles define the discipline of coding, and the broader discipline from which coding is derived: computer science. This book coaches you step-by-step through the concepts and commands you need to help the kids in your life learn to program!

About This Book

Coding is fast becoming a skill that every child needs to be educated for in the 21st Century. Knowing how to code means possessing a skill that allows the children you're coaching to create things that are highly useful in modern society — apps, websites, analysis tools, and more. Helping kids learn how to code also means you're assisting them in developing a skill that is highly marketable and sets them apart from peers at school and later, in their careers.

But coding is taught at only a small fraction of schools, and often only at the high school level. This book offers you an easy-to-understand, but comprehensive, overview of all the coding fundamentals you need to teach. We largely avoid a theoretical approach to the material, instead offering you hands-on, practical content and methods of instructing your kids in coding. Like content in all *For Dummies* titles, this book is clear, concise, and organized in an easy-access format.

Helping Kids with Coding For Dummies is structured in a progressive sequence, with introductory topics preceding more challenging topics. The book builds in complexity, but you can dive straight in to any chapter, to discover more about that topic at any time. You already know about variables but need a bit of guidance in assisting your kid with loops? Then head straight to Chapter 10 for help.

As you explore each chapter, keep in mind the following structure:

>> Each chapter begins with hands-on, away-from-computer activities. These games and "act-it-out" skits get you and your coders thinking about the big ideas before you dive into the code.

>> Each chapter has guidance in writing code snippets in pseudocode, followed by many popular programming languages. *Pseudocode* is literally "fake code" that stands in conceptually for real code but doesn't really run on a computer.

>> Each chapter ends with a small project that features the theme of the chapter. Projects are written in a variety of languages, but you can adapt them to any language in which you want to write them. You don't need to buy any software to use the featured programming languages.

>> Programming code is shown in monofont.

>> Command sequences using onscreen menus use the command arrow. For example, when working in Scratch, you can open a new project as follows: From the menu bar, choose File ⇨ New.

Foolish Assumptions

In this book, we make some assumptions (possibly foolish assumptions!) regarding you getting started in your role as a coding coach:

>> You are a parent, a teacher, an after-school guide, a summer mentor, a tutor, a coach, or other guide who is interested in helping youth learn to code.

>> You have patience, a sense of humor, or both! Learning coding yourself — and helping young coders develop and improve their own skills — requires some of these.

We've also made some assumptions with regard to the coding work you'll be doing:

>> You possess at least a little experience in typing on a computer keyboard, navigating a computer interface, and using a trackpad or mouse. Your background may be in using a Windows-based PC, a Macintosh, or both.

>> You're capable of using a web browser such as Safari, Chrome, or Firefox, and you can type a URL to access a website such as Scratch.com and Code.org.

>> You're comfortable with performing basic math, such as adding and subtracting, and performing basic logical operations, such as comparing two numbers.

» You can spell reasonably well, and you can locate and correct misspellings in your code. Programming languages often provide error messages as clues to help you track down misspellings, so you're not entirely on your own here! But you have to spell everything in your code correctly to get your program to run as you want.

Icons Used in This Book

The Tip icon indicates tips and shortcuts that you can use to make your work easier. These tips may apply to away-from-computer activities or to actual coding. Tips applying to issues that pop up often may be repeated in several places through the book.

The Remember icon calls your attention to important ideas you want to keep in mind while performing a task.

The Warning icon advises you to watch out, informing you of critical information that helps you steer clear.

The Technical Stuff icon marks slightly more in-depth nuts and bolts of programming, some of which might be helpful in achieving coding success.

Where to Go from Here

The programming concepts you use and coach are mostly universal. Because each concept features hands-on activities and pseudocode, you can teach these ideas to children as young as early elementary. But really, any age is the right age to start working on programming concepts, and there's never any wrong age to learn something new!

Progressing from away-from-computer concepts and pseudocode to at-the-computer coding can be done at any time when your young coder expresses interest. The programming snippets in this book are presented in some of the most popular languages used by novice coders, used from kindergarten through high school. All the languages are free, and all have stood the test of time with regard to their ease-of-use. Scratch is a popular way to get started, but for many programming purists, Scratch's drag-and-drop puzzle pieces are inauthentic — their preference is any text-based language such as Python, JavaScript, or Java. Samples of all these languages are included in each chapter.

Don't forget to check out the cheat sheet that goes with this book. You can find what programming languages we recommend for each age group, all the projects we've created for this book, and more. Go to www.dummies.com and search by this book's title.

Regardless of which activities and programming languages you explore with your young coders, remember to cultivate curiosity, praise achievement, and encourage leveling up. And above all, have fun!

1
Getting Started with Coding

Find out why kids are coding and how you fit into their journey.

Get the big picture of coding.

Find out which languages are the best for kids you're teaching.

Meet Steve Jobs, Steve Wozniack, Ada Lovelace, and Guido van Rossum.

Chapter **1**

Welcome To (Or Back To) Coding

Who are you and where do you fit into the brave new world of coding? You may be a newbie programmer who wants to learn or "level up" coding skills to coach the next generation of kiddos to programming success. Or perhaps you're a seasoned programmer who wants to "dial it down" and explore a good starting point for kid coders. Or perhaps you're someone in between — you've coded in a past school or career experience — maybe in a language that's lost steam — and now you're returning to the practice to learn the newest tricks of the trade.

Whoever you are and whatever your goal, we're excited to welcome you to (or back to) coding!

In this chapter, you find out why kids are coding and why so much attention is currently focused in education on the discipline of computer programming. We also talk about the range of roles you can play in the teaching and learning of computer science, and identify strategies you can employ when working as a coding teacher, parent, or coach.

Why Kids Are Coding

Literacy has been a societal goal for centuries, with conscientious parents and teachers working to ensure that the children in their charge learn the skills necessary to succeed in their careers and in life. Until the 1970s, literacy meant mastering the traditional three "R's" of "reading, 'riting, and 'rithmetic" (spelling was considered less necessary). As technology started becoming commonplace, computers started appearing in educational settings, and tech literacy became viewed as the fourth literacy.

Fast-forwarding to the 21st century, technology has become so ubiquitous that not only is tech literacy a skill that makes you educated, it's a skill that makes you highly marketable in the workplace. While tech literacy can include general skills such as word processing, generating spreadsheets, and creating slideshow presentations, the real skills lie in computer programming, or coding. That's because coding allows people to be not just users of technology, but producers of it (at least on the software end of things).

Schools are recognizing that to prepare kids for their futures, a good education must include coding instruction. In some countries, including the United Kingdom and Canada, coding instruction is a national directive. In others, such as the United States, fewer than 10 percent of schools teach coding. To fill in the gaps, many online courses, after-school programs, and summer camps are providing kids instruction in coding. Just like learning to ski or learning a foreign language, learning the basics of coding is best accomplished at a young age: Every learning experience is "new and different" and it's easy to get back up when you fall down. Regardless of who is delivering the instruction, kids everywhere are coding — and you can help facilitate that learning with the kids in your life using the guidance provided in this book!

What are they learning?

Kids are learning more than just coding. They're devising solutions to problems, building games, and creating programs that do the routine and redundant work humans don't want to do. There's a lot kids have to learn to perform those tasks. Here's a quick rundown of what they're learning:

>> **Computational thinking:** Computational thinking is the reasoning and planning you perform "in your head" when translating a problem and solution into a process that a computer can perform.

- **»** **Algorithmic thinking:** Algorithmic thinking is mapping out an organized, efficient set of steps, which you can use and reuse to perform a task.

- **»** **Communicating in a foreign language:** No, not an international language that's native to a country or people on Earth. But they are learning to communicate in a language that's not their native tongue — the language of computers. And they have to learn new words, new punctuation, and new rules for establishing successful communication.

- **»** **Patience and resilience:** No matter what you're making — a computer program, a musical performance, or a gourmet meal — patience is required to learn a new skill, and resilience is required to bounce back from challenges to master that skill.

- **»** **Creativity:** Contrary to popular belief, coding is not the cold, calculating discipline you may think it is. From inventing novel solutions to a problem, to inventing new video games, creativity is inherent in the coding process.

- **»** **Troubleshooting:** Troubleshooting, or debugging code, means tracing and retracing your steps — sometimes by isolating and testing smaller sections of code, sometimes by tracing through the syntax, and sometimes by testing sample data to example the output — to find and fix problems.

How are they learning?

Kids are coding on their tablets, laptops, and desktops, using a variety of widely available software tools, many of which are free! They are using books, online resources, and tutorials in web and video formats, and discussions with friends to guide them.

Unlike the early days of coding, many of the programming languages and environments kids are using are visual in nature. Many offer tile or block-based formats in which kids can drag and assemble code blocks together like interlocking puzzle pieces to create programs. This type of structure allows kids to tinker without worrying about spelling commands correctly, syntax (grammar), or punctuation. Modern, introductory languages often feature built-in "assets" such as character costumes and sound effects. And they usually provide some sort of error reporting to help kids in their debugging.

If you tried coding before the 21st century, you probably learned text-based, also known as "line" coding; the new, visual ways of coding are most likely foreign to you. You may have used languages such as Basic, Pascal, COBOL, or FORTRAN. While these languages have mostly faded away in popularity, they were powerful tools and popular in their heyday. Other "older" languages you may have used which are still around today include C, Python, Visual Basic, Ruby, Lua, and R. If you had the opportunity to tackle some serious coding, you may have worked with C++, Java, or JavaScript — some of the past and current heavy hitters in the coding world. The main kid-friendly language of yesteryear was Logo, what you may recall as the "turtle" language. Invented by MIT professor Seymour Papert, Logo and its derivatives were popular in schools, and still exist in several modern incarnations today. "Turtle" languages were about as close as most kids got to non-text based coding prior to Y2K. Fortunately, the more kid-friendly coding environments now available provide a lower floor for entering easily into the world of programming.

WARNING

Some purists are not fond of "kid" computer languages, especially those that are block-based, expressing concerns that this structure is not realistic, nor professional. They worry that these types of environments are not sufficiently authentic to lay proper foundations for future coding. However, research indicates that exploration in these languages still build the desired programming skills cultivated by working in more traditional, text-based, coding environments.

What does it mean down the road?

Your efforts in helping kids get started with coding lay the foundations for them to pursue more challenging programming activities in the future. You can help them build content skills, confidence, and the mindset required to succeed at coding. Whether they choose a career in computer science, or just dabble in writing small programs for various projects, your positive guidance and support contributes to developing an educated and confident young person. Who knows, you might even be responsible for cultivating the next Grace Hopper or Bill Gates!

COMPUTERS IN SCHOOLS

Kids have been coding since the first computers appeared in schools in the 1970s. Camille's school, Boone Elementary in San Antonio, Texas, received a teletype computer on which she had a 15-minute rotation once a week (although she often found ways to obtain additional time on the device). Operating essentially as a dumb terminal, the computer sent and received information over a simple telephone line, issuing drill-and-practice style math problems printed on giant rolls of form feed paper. Students would press the resistant, plastic buttons to input their answers. Following the completion of a problem set, the computer would respond with a score — at which time you would leap with joy if you earned 100%, or finagle more time to attempt another set if you had failed to reach the magical perfect score. Those were the days!

Why You Need to Know Coding

You have this book in hand, but you may still be asking yourself why you need to know coding. Why should you learn to code when your young coder has a teacher or a camp instructor or a YouTube video guide?

You should learn to code for many reasons:

» **The more you know, the better you can help.** More content knowledge and more relevant experience on your end leads to better ability to coach your young coder. This is especially true when it comes to troubleshooting code: kids make the same mistakes you make; if you've "been there, done that," you can help them find and fix their errors.

» **The more you code, the more you can empathize with your coder.** Sharing the joy and frustration of coding is part of being a good coach. The more you experience these emotions yourself, the better you are at understanding and appreciation the mindset and affective disposition of your kid.

» **It's the fourth literacy.** Maybe coding was offered when you were in school. Maybe it wasn't. Either way, it's here now and it's here to stay — and as the "fourth literacy," you need to learn it to be fully educated and a full participant in today's world.

» **It's quality time with your kids.** If you're a parent, you do a lot with your kids, but sometimes that "doing" is spent more passively than you'd like (driving to soccer practice, buying school supplies at Walmart). Learning something new (coding!) and working together on an app or website provides a great opportunity for you to spend quality time with your kids.

» **Doing so allows you to practice what you preach.** You're a teacher, a parent, a coach. . . and you're also a role model. If you don't already know how to code, it may be a challenge to encourage someone else to do so. As they say at Nike, Just Do It!

Fear and loathing (of coding)

One of your biggest challenges in learning to code may be your own fear and self-doubt. Perhaps you think you're "not smart enough." Another challenge may be a genuine dislike or disinterest in code. Like any new endeavor, there is often a sense of concern that you won't be capable of learning something new. Maybe you won't like it. Maybe it's too much work.

It may be worthwhile to note that a lot of other people who came before you shared the same fears (and loathing, of course) of coding. Like learning any new field — playing piano, ice-skating, speaking Mandarin, cooking, gardening, sewing — there is a learning curve in which the introductory phases are not especially fun or rewarding. But hopefully the experiences leading up to adulthood have shown you that, over time, sticking to the process of learning a new skill eventually results in elevated abilities and satisfaction in a job well done.

Computer programmers are not smarter than you are; they've just been at it longer! Like you, they started with introductory coding, building their skills a bit at a time, learning new programming languages and writing many programs until they built a solid base of coding knowledge and skills. Congratulations on taking the first step of learning to code and coaching the next generation to early successes in the world of computer science.

You may already know more than you think

If you're panicking that you suddenly need a degree in computer science to learn coding to successfully help the kids in your life. . . don't! You may already know more about coding and its underlying principles than you think. Just ask yourself a few questions:

» Are you good at learning new languages? Because coding uses its own languages featuring vocabulary, grammar, and syntax — you may find that learning to code is a snap!

» Are you good at planning and organizing? Because coding is about using concise, reusable instructions, start-to-finish — you may find that learning to code is familiar and easy!

» Are you confident about tinkering with your computer or mobile device to learn and use new features? Because coding is about commanding your technology devices to bend to your will — you may find that learning to code is easy and empowering!

» Are you excited by new challenges? Because coding energizes you to invent something tangible from nothing more than an idea in your head. You may find that learning to code is an exciting new adventure!

Sarah has taught hundreds of adults to code for the purpose of engaging the kids in their lives in coding. You can do it, too!

Where Do You Come In?

You come in by guiding and supporting young people in their coding endeavors, as a classroom teacher, a camp or after-school coach, or a parent/mentor. You do not have to be an expert coder — just an interested and caring adult who is willing to co-learn and support your kids in their pursuit of the computer science mission! Here are some ways you can accomplish these feats.

In the classroom

You can select a variety of coding experiences for a classroom setting depending on factors including grade level, available technology, and expected contact time. In the classroom setting — which is more formal than other settings — where you may meet with students multiple times over a quarter, semester, or full school year, you likely have time to work on developing both a breadth (covering many topics) and depth of programming skills among your students (providing students time to grow a greater complexity of skills within a topic of focus). You want to choose a programming environment, a curriculum, and appropriate technology tools for getting kids coding in your classroom.

Programming environments

You can choose several excellent programming environments for coding instruction. Most are free, but be sure to check online for the latest information and updates on each product.

>> **Everyone, away from the computer:** Not all computer programming work needs to occur on a computer. Both Computer Science Unplugged (csunplugged.org) and Code.org provide extensive, hands-on, away-from-the-computer activities to teach computational thinking concepts. These activities are superb lead-ins to their technology analogues, and are likely to be hits in their own right!

>> **PreK:** Daisy the Dinosaur and Bee-Bots are perfect for three and four year olds. Both feature a very limited set of commands, along with cute characters for the pre-reading crowd. Bee-Bots also has the advantage of providing a physical device for students to program and navigate around a playmat that you spread on the ground. The coding paradigm of both is drag-and-drop tiles. Daisy is available in the App Store for use on iPhone and iPad devices. Bee-Bots can be used on Mac and Windows platforms, as well as iPhones and iPads.

» **K-Grade 1:** Scratch Jr. and the Foos are both coding environments that visually pop and are extremely rich in pre-reader coding experiences. The Foos presents a series of puzzles that increase in complexity, while Scratch Jr. offers a more open-ended exploration space. The coding paradigm of both is drag-and-drop tiles. Both the Foos and Scratch Jr. run on mobile devices (iOS and Android) and in web browsers.

» **Grades 2–5:** Scratch and Tynker offer deep, exciting, coding experiences through which students can explore critical coding concepts, express their creativity, and share their work publicly. The coding paradigm of both is drag-and-drop tiles. Both run online and can also be downloaded and used in an offline environment.

» **Grade 6 and up:** Python, JavaScript, and GameSalad environments are all quite different, but they're a step up in complexity and offer real-world programming experiences to your young coder. Python is used in a variety of contexts, including commanding robots. JavaScript provides interactivity on websites, occupying a special place in web pages formatted using HTML and CSS. This book also addresses the use of Python and JavaScript in coding for the micro:bit electronics board — a great tool for applying your code to Internet of Things (IoT) devices. GameSalad facilitates creation of authentic game apps that can be sold in the App Store and Google Play store (but you have to pay to obtain a GameSalad license).

» **Grade 9 and up:** Java, C++, and Swift are considered professional coding languages that your coder can migrate to as she elevates her programming prowess. They are used for authentic programs and for writing software for IoT devices. Java is currently the language used on the AP Computer Science A exam — your coder is probably going to see this before she leaves high school. C++ is used in a variety of applications, such as databases and video gaming. Swift is Apple's powerful and easy-to-use programming platform.

App Inventor is a drag-and-drop teaching language for mobile devices. It provides a higher degree of complexity than other "easy to use" environments, while at the same time offering the use of Application Programming Interfaces (API), which are pre-written software that allows two applications to talk to each other. App Inventor permits your coder to do cool, "real" things such as integrate Google Maps and GPS location in apps.

Turn to Chapter 3 for more detailed information about each of these programming environnments and others that may be of interest to your young coders.

Choosing curriculum

The curriculum you select for your classroom depends on a variety of factors. You may be required to follow school or district guidelines created by educators other than yourself. Or perhaps you must adhere to standards set at the state level, or the national level by a group such as CSTA (Computer Science Teachers Association) or ISTE (International Society for Technology in Education).

Remember, coding is about creating authentic products that perform real tasks. Crafting your curriculum in a project-based model helps ensure students are doing the type of work that professional computer programmers perform. Try to create and customize activities in which students make real products, producing products including websites, online games, and apps. Encourage and support their innovations in crafting inventive graphics, multiple levels, and other customizations that make each child's program stand apart from her peers.

Most curriculum is shaped by a scope and sequence that ensures learners grow in their coding skills to meet key goals, with short-term benchmarks established along the way. Classroom teachers still have the opportunity, and the responsibility, to differentiate instruction for students of varying ability levels to appropriately challenge each student to rise above his current level. Create tiered options in which each student can create programs that match his skill set. Your coding experience and understanding of each individual child can help you customize the coding experience to create a successful learning environment for your entire classroom community. For specific coding curricula and associated grade level designations, check out Part 5.

TIP

Training and professional development (PD) for specific curricula are offered by organizations and universities. For example, the University of Texas at Austin (Camille's alma mater!) provides online and in-person PD for its UTeach AP Computer Science Principles course. The College of St. Scholastica offers an all online, four-course certification in CS Education. Such PD can result in credit to educators for things like raises or certifications.

Camp or after-school coach

With the increased attention on coding, more and more after-school programs and summer camps are popping up everywhere. If you're an instructor in such a program, you have a unique role in helping the young coders in your charge. You probably don't see the kids as consistently as a classroom teacher. And there may be greater variation in the experience and ability level of your kid community. But it's also probable that you're not locked into a highly structured curriculum.

Whatever the content and format of your workplace, remember to teach students first and coding second. Take time to learn each coder's interests, experience, and programming goals. Ideally, take a few notes on each participant, update them following each coding session, and review them prior to your next meeting.

Reminding yourself regularly of how each coder is progressing can help you to assist him in moving forward and reaching his goals.

As frequently as possible, communicate progress to your coder's parent or guardian. Include samples of the work product, especially links to completed programs the coder's family can view online!

Mentor

Mentors foster and grow coding abilities in youth through a variety of informal contexts. Perhaps you're a parent, friend, or co-worker of someone with a child who wants to learn coding. Or perhaps you're the teacher whom "everyone comes to see" when students need assistance on special projects they're tackling. Maybe you're a professional programmer who volunteers your time at Girl Scouts or Boys Scouts workshops. (Both groups have coding badges that kids can earn!) Mentors often work on an as-needed basis helping kids grow their coding skills or track down an extra-hard-to-find-bug. They typically maintain a long-term partnership with the kids they mentor, suggesting new projects, languages, and courses to pursue. As a mentor, you may also be asked to write letters of recommendation about the coders in your charge, attesting to their coding interests and abilities, to help them gain admittance to special programs in high school or university.

STEVE WOZNIAK AND STEVE JOBS: STARTING THE PERSONAL COMPUTER REVOLUTION

Commonly known as the Apple Guys, Steve Wozniak and Steve Jobs started the personal computer revolution, working on a great idea out of a garage. The products they designed and brought to life made home computing possible, easy, and relatively inexpensive for the first time in human history.

Both men were born in the 1950s and grew up during the decade when several electronics and computing firsts occurred: The first integrated circuit and the first computer modem were invented, the programming language FORTRAN was developed, and the first transistor radio was produced by Texas Instruments. These advancements set the stage for the work Wozniak and Jobs initiated in the early 1970s.

Introduced by a common friend who knew they liked electronics and loved pranks, Wozniak and Jobs initiated a working relationship with their creation of a digital tone generator. Known as the Blue Box — a rather illegal device — when connected to a telephone, it allowed users to make free phone calls, even internationally! More importantly, Jobs and Wozniak found that they enjoyed collaborating on technology projects, and both had a vision that computers weren't just for big businesses. They believed that an affordable, desktop-size computer could exist in every home, and that it could be used for everything from creating artwork, to managing budget spread-sheets, to playing games. The two men began designing and building their initial home computers, with Jobs focusing on the business and marketing side of the venture, and Wozniak (or "Woz" as he is called) focusing on the engineering design and technology.

Once Jobs and Woz realized there was demand for the first personal computers they built and sold, they landed an investor and the Apple Computer Company was launched! Known for their exceptional design qualities including an easy-to-use graphical user interface (GUI) and simple, elegant casings, Apple computing devices quickly established a permanent foothold in the world of home computers. As new versions of Apple's computing products emerged, the company grew and spawned new products — iPods, iPads, and iPhones — as well as exciting Mac stores where people, young and old, can purchase Apple products and learn how to use them.

When Jobs and Woz started the computer revolution, they envisioned having a computer on every desktop. If you have a Mac desktop, a MacBook laptop, or an Apple mobile device, then you've helped make their dream a reality! As Steve Jobs once said, *"The people who are crazy enough to think they can change the world are the ones who do."*

Photo credit: https://alumni.berkeley.edu/california-magazine/spring-2015-dropouts-and-drop-ins/silicon-valley-s-merry-prankster-put-his

Working with Young Coders

There are wide range of dispositions when it comes to kids getting started with coding. . .here are a few of the personality types you may encounter:

>> **The skydiver type:** This type of kid wants to dive right in, trying every line of code, without any specific plan of action associated with his efforts. While we applaud confidence and creativity at the computer, we would encourage you to steer this kid towards thinking and planning prior to coding and executing. A few years ago, a new child at Camille's school was very proud of his Scratch "expertise" — which turned out to be dragging hundreds of Scratch tiles and assembling them in nonsensical ways in the program workspace. It took several months to help him learn how to evolve from chaotic habits to conceptualizing an idea and translating it into functional code. Helping this type of child to work procedurally and incrementally, taking pride in completing a project start-to-finish, are behaviors you want to foster.

>> **The rational actor:** This kiddo wants to learn a new concept and then try out the associated code at the computer, one step at a time. This type of learner usually experiences success, but may struggle when confronted with an information gap in which she needs a command that she hasn't previously encountered. Helping this child to branch out and research on her own, employing a bit of grit in finding a solution, is a habit you want to coach and develop.

>> **The happy passenger:** This child is a bit tentative to try coding — even if he is a game-player or social media guru! He may seem in command of tech until he has to pop the hood and get into the mechanics of writing actual code. He has some tech-savvy, but until this point, he was just happy to be along for the ride. You need to help him understand that you're going to support his efforts to transitioning from a tech user, to a tech maker — through learning to code.

>> **The next Bill Gates:** This kid loves coding, knows everything about coding, wants to do more coding, watches Silicon Valley, has built her own computer, and has already applied to the Stanford Computer Science undergrad program. Continue to cheer for this kid, help clear the runway for her by removing trivial obstacles (which often exist in school settings), and actively seek projects, competitions, and peer programmers (who may be older) as partners for her.

Regardless of which kids and which coder personalities you encounter (likely all of them!), meet them where they are, and help lift them up to the next level. You have an important role in fostering their coding foundations and building both the hard and soft skills of a coder. Onwards!

Chapter **2**

Understanding the Big Ideas

his chapter helps you better understand the big concepts in coding, or computer programming: giving instructions to a computer so that it can perform a task. You see the big picture of writing a program before you focus on the specific details of writing lines of code.

Seeing the Big Picture in Coding

Learning to program a computer is similar in many ways to playing football. You have to first think about the goal of the program. Then you focus on the big picture, or game plan, to develop the key parts of the program.

For example, the goal of football is outscoring your opponent. The big picture of football may include kicking the football, running with the football, avoiding getting tackled, and moving the football to the end zone. Drilling down into special plays and perfecting fancy footwork comes after players cement their understanding of the goal and the big picture.

In coding, the goal is to complete a process that would not easily be accomplished without a computer. This may be providing an airplane simulation game or a tool for searching for a home overseas. The big picture involves all the large parts of the program that contribute to achieving the goal. Creating an airplane simulation may consist of providing a user a virtual airplane, giving controls to fly the plane, providing environments for the plane to fly in, and making the plane react according to user input. Creating a tool for searching for a home overseas may consist of providing the user a map, building areas onscreen to enter information about the desired attributes of the home, and creating a search mechanism based on user-input attributes.

How can you represent the big picture? You can act it out, or draw pictures, or write words to describe the important parts. Each of these activities is *unplugged* — they don't require the use of a computer — and each one helps you plan out your computer program before you sit down to begin coding.

TIP

Ask your young coders to think of something they're good at, such as baking cookies, playing Minecraft, or taking care of the family pet. Then ask them to think about their special skill and how they would explain it, in very simple terms, to an alien who has just stopped in to visit Earth. What are the most important parts of understanding how to go from ingredients to yummy baked cookies? What are the big picture ideas you need to know to complete a successful dog walk?

Acting Out the Big Picture, Unplugged

Too many times, people dive into a project by focusing on the details before mapping out the big picture. Camille once had a scary assignment in fifth grade in which she made this mistake! When asked to write a summary of *The Red Badge of Courage,* she panicked and tried to write a detail from every page of the book, somehow stitching them together, but not making any sense at all. It was an awful three hours of tears at the dinner table. What she should have done was take a step back and write a 30-second movie trailer version of the book, hitting the highlights and the most important parts that captured only the main ideas.

WARNING

Thinking about coding in terms of typing commands on a computer without stepping back to consider the big picture of what you want the program to do is a recipe for disaster. Plan before you code!

Dramatizing a noncoding process

One way of understanding the big picture of a computer program is to act it out, without any computer at all. Invite your young coder to try acting out an everyday activity that is not computer related.

One possibility is dramatizing the process of washing socks (as if asking a kid to wash her own socks wouldn't be drama enough!). For example:

1. **Ask your young coder to take off her socks (or dig them out of the laundry basket!).**

2. **Put the socks in the washing machine and pretend to wash them.**

3. **Take them out of the wash and move them to the dryer where you pretend to dry them.**

4. **Remove the socks from the dryer (all clean and dry!) and ask her to put them on her feet.**

Although you call this process "doing laundry" or "washing socks," you can have her act it out so that she can see the process actually involves more steps (see Figure 2-1).

"Drive to the intersection and turn right" is an example of a similar task you may perform when writing code for a car race video game. Although this single phrase describes the big picture, you need to drill down to more specific steps in order to accomplish the bigger task. For example, you need to move forwards 150 pixels and then make a square turn (also called a 90 degree turn) to the right (or to the left). When coding these actions in a programming language, you can use a sequence of commands that looks something like `forward 150 right turn 90`.

Acting out a big picture doesn't have to involve props, but it's often helpful to use them with new programmers. Making concrete connections to everyday objects and processes can help your kid form a mental model that she can refer to when she writes a computer program.

Walking through some daily tasks

TIP

You can step through a number of daily tasks to help a young learner grasp the concept of process. Brainstorm a list of everyday processes with your child and then ask him to demonstrate the big picture of each process. Here are some you can try:

» **Get up in the morning.**

1. Alarm clock rings.

2. Wake up.

3. Swing legs over the side of bed.

4. Stand up.

» **Feed the dog.**

1. Call the dog.

2. Scoop the dog food from the bag.

3. Place food in the bowl.

» **Perform a cannonball.**

1. Stand at the edge of the pool with arms outstretched.

2. Leap up and out over the water while tucking legs into your chest.

3. Hit the water, tushie first.

4. Cheer with joy as displaced water booms into the air, splattering everyone in a 3-meter radius.

» **Make a smoothie.**

1. Gather the fruit.

2. Put fruit into the blender.

3. Add ice.

4. Mix.

5. Pour into a glass.

Get creative and see how many processes you can act out! Remember, you don't have to actually use the real materials to act out a process. As in charades, you can use your imagination!

Creating an Algorithm

Think about the steps you use to perform any type of process — for example, getting up in the morning, performing a layup in basketball, or washing socks in the laundry. You probably perform the same actions every time. That's because a specific set of steps, from start to finish, define that process. Anyone who performs the same process probably uses those same steps, or a series of steps, that are nearly identical. Those steps are called an *algorithm.*

An *algorithm* is a step-by-step set of instructions to be followed in completing a task, especially by a computer.

Computers are fast, and they don't get bored or annoyed with doing complicated math or performing the same tasks over and over again. But they aren't especially smart, and they don't think for themselves (yet!), so it's up to the human operator of the computer to give it an algorithm so that it knows how to perform a process.

Turning a picture into words

One algorithm kids have likely performed in the household (or that adult family members wish they would perform!) applies to vacuuming. Unless you are living with a random vacuumer — someone who uses no specific pattern when attacking the carpets with the household Hoover — then you probably see a pattern used to vacuum rooms. What does the vacuuming algorithm look like? As a picture, it probably looks something like Figure 2-2.

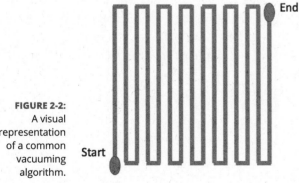

FIGURE 2-2:
A visual representation of a common vacuuming algorithm.

Turning the picture into words requires thinking about each step, from start-to finish, that the designated vacuumer needs to do to clean the room. These words, in order, may look like the following steps:

1. Position the vacuum in one corner of the room.

2. Plug in the vacuum.

3. Turn on the vacuum.

4. Push the vacuum in a straight line.

5. If you hit a wall, make a corner turn towards unvacuumed area.

6. Push forward a little.

7. Make a corner turn towards unvacuumed area.

8. Repeat Steps 4 through 7 until you reach the wall opposite your starting point.

9. If you've reached the wall opposite your starting point, then turn off the vacuum.

10. Unplug vacuum.

The step-by-step vacuuming process is a common algorithm for cleaning up your carpet, but the zigzag pattern isn't the only possible one. What other vacuuming patterns can you think of? What about patterns that start with the vacuum in the center of the room, such as a spiral pattern, or a pattern that looks like the spokes of a wheel?

What would the algorithm look like for each of these vacuuming patterns in Figure 2-3? Try to write them!

FIGURE 2-3: A spiral or a starburst pattern can be the basis for alternative vacuuming algorithms.

One possible vacuuming algorithm in code

Your young coder may already be asking, "So how can I turn this picture algorithm into code?" Here is a simple program in Scratch that shows one possible vacuuming algorithm. (For more on Scratch, see Chapter 3.)

The Scratch *stage* shows the room where the vacuuming takes place. On the stage are three objects: a front wall, a back wall, and a vacuum. The vaccum is initially positioned in the lower-left corner of the stage. Vaccuming progresses from the left wall (where the x-coordinate is large and negative) to the right wall (where the x-coordinate is large and positive). The front and back walls are used as indicators to know which direction to turn the vacuum. The vacuuming algorithm executes in a forever loop: If the vacuum touches the front wall, it turns right; if the vacuum touches the back wall, it turns left. The following command is used to find out whether the vacuum has reached the wall opposite the starting point:

```
if x position of vacuum > 220
```

When it does, the vacuuming process is complete, and the program ends by executing a `stop all` command, as shown in Figure 2-4.

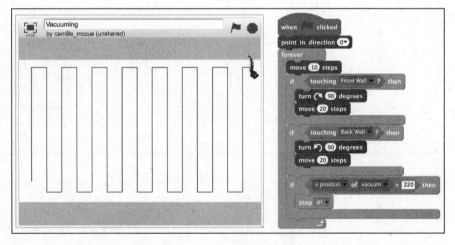

FIGURE 2-4:
The vacuuming algorithm written in Scratch.

Don't worry about the details of how to write the code; just see whether you can trace the algorithm. Notice at the start of the program that the vacuuming event begins when the green flag is clicked and that the starting conditions of the vacuum are also set at the start of the program: The vacuum points in the direction of 0 degrees — the front of the room — and (outside of the program) the user manually positions the starting point of the vacuum.

In later chapters, you can work more on translating algorithms into code. This chapter focuses on helping your coder assemble different types of commands together into a larger program that performs a task.

THE PURPOSEFUL CHAOS OF A ROOMBA

Manufactured by iRobot, Roomba (see figure) is a robotic vacuum that operates *autonomously*, meaning it does vacuuming chores so that you don't have to! Humans often use an up-and-back vacuuming algorithm, but the Roomba uses its own special computer program to move, rotate, and remove dirt from your floors and carpets.

The Roomba algorithm consists of spiraling, crossing the room, following a wall, and bouncing off at a random angle after bumping into an obstacle. Its sensors help it detect when it's headed for a collision or a drop-off, and its algorithm adjusts accordingly.

While the overall behavior of the Roomba may appear a bit chaotic, the device is an amazing example of how computer programming can offload humans from a truly repetitive and mundane task!

Photo credit: https://en.wikipedia.org/wiki/Roomba#/media/
File:Roomba_time-lapse.jpg

Representing Algorithms

Constructing an algorithm is an important step in creating a program that can run on a computer. As you work out the steps of an algorithm, you need to have some organized way of writing it down.

You can represent an algorithm before you translate it into code for use on a computer in many different ways, including

» Acting it out

» Drawing a picture

» Creating a storyboard

» Building a flowchart

» Writing pseudocode

» Coding the bones and comments in a programming language

Acting it out

Getting up on your feet and acting out an algorithm as you plan it is a fun, physical way to work through each step. Some algorithms lend themselves better to this method than others. Anything dealing with motion naturally fits well with acting it out. For example, creating a vacuuming algorithm is easily done by moving your body (and a real or imagined vacuum) across a carpet.

TIP

Another algorithm that is well-suited to this method is planning the navigation of a maze: Pretend you're a mouse and then work through your options of moving forward; turning when you bump into a wall; and keeping your general heading aimed towards the cheese. You can act out these actions with or without props, determining how you must construct your algorithm as you try different possibilities you may encounter in the maze.

Drawing a picture

Drawing a picture is a good, visual method for working through the steps of an algorithm. This method works especially well when a fairly simple, start-to-finish path defines the algorithm. For example, the path followed by a roller-coaster is the same every time the riders board the coaster and participate in the ride. The coaster follows the same set of climbs, falls, loops, and twists every time — there are no conditions that determine a course that deviates from the same pattern on every run. A single picture, like the one in Figure 2-5, can depict the entire algorithm, as long as you identify the start and end points.

A simple vacuuming algorithm is also something you can represent well by drawing a picture. A single picture easily shows the structure of the up-and-down motion, moving across the room. Refer to Figure 2-2.

Creating a storyboard

Sometimes, drawing a single picture (see preceding section) isn't enough to show all the steps of an algorithm. An algorithm that has multiple paths may require more than one drawing to map all its steps. One way to map these paths is create a storyboard. A *storyboard* is series of pictures showing the different screens that appear in your program (usually an app) and the sequence in which they can appear. For example, a kid creating a Choose Your Own Adventure app needs several pictures to map the possible routes in a story he wants to create, similar to the example shown in Figure 2-6.

TIP

You can make your own version of the cool app shown in Figure 2-6. Code.org provides a free and easy-to-use interface, called App Lab, for kids to design and code (using JavaScript in both text and tile/block editors) their own Choose Your Own Adventure app! The interface allows you to add your own images and construct as many paths through the story as can be dreamt. Check out App Lab at https://studio.code.org/projects/applab.

Building a flowchart

A *flowchart* is a diagram that shows the steps of an algorithm, in order, including decisions that need to be made that lead to different paths through the algorithm. A flowchart has a few shapes, connected with arrows, that outline the program from start to finish. Figure 2-7 shows a simple flowchart your child may write for an after-school homework algorithm.

Unlike creating a list of steps using only text (see the section "One possible vacuuming algorithm in code," earlier in this chapter), most flowchart text goes into its own special shape, and each shape has a unique meaning. Shapes are also connected in special ways depending on what job they do. Table 2-1 shows some of the most common shapes and what they represent.

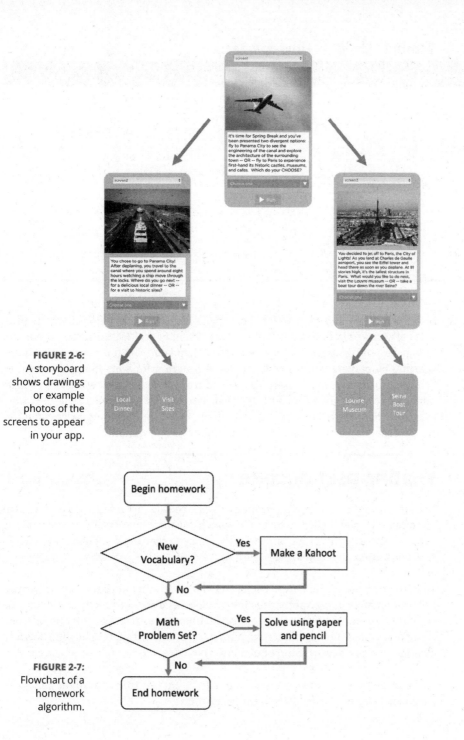

FIGURE 2-6:
A storyboard shows drawings or example photos of the screens to appear in your app.

FIGURE 2-7:
Flowchart of a homework algorithm.

TABLE 2-1   **Symbols Used In Flowcharts**

Flowchart Symbol	Example	What It Means
Arrow		Shows the order in which the program runs
Terminal		Starts or ends the program, or process in the program
Process		Performs a task or set of operations
Decision		Makes a decision, such as yes or no or true or false
Input/Output		Accepts input to or gives output from the program

TIP

Draw.io is a free and easy-to-use tool for drawing your own flowcharts. It provides all the symbols you need, along with a handy grid for arranging them and lining everything up just the way you want. Help your young coder practice flowcharting by playing with draw.io to plan a program for something fun, such as building a pizza. You can even ask him to work through how a pizza franchise might flowchart a pizza-building app: The app asks users for input regarding topping and crust choices and then gives output regarding cost. Your coder can make the flowchart activity as easy or as challenging as she wants!

Writing pseudocode

One strategy for planning a program is to write the big picture in a simplified form of computer code, called *pseudocode*, which means "fake code." Pseudocode is similar to shorthand for a computer. It's not code that the computer can actually run, but it is written similarly.

You can write pseudocode from the outset when working on your program, or you can write it after using another technique, such as drawing a picture. Pseudocode can often speed up the process of translating a program into functional code because it allows a programmer to think in code without getting bogged down in details, such as *syntax* (coding punctuation).

For example, if your coder is asked to add the numbers from 1 to 10, he can write pseudocode to represent this addition algorithm:

```
create variable total
create variable counter

set total to 0
set counter to 1

for counter = 1 to 10
    set total to the previous total + counter
    increase counter by 1
end for loop
```

Then, he can add print statements (in pseudocode) before and after the addition algorithm to create a complete program:

```
print "Adding up numbers from 1 to 10"

addition algorithm

print "The total is " + total
```

Pseudocode can appear in many different ways, so encourage your young coder not to worry about perfecting the language. Ultimately, it's only the code itself that must be perfect to execute.

Commenting the bones

Comments are special words you can include in computer code that aren't executable — they don't do anything. If comments don't do anything, why use them? Because they allow you to build the bones of a computer program — the structure that describes all the parts of the big picture — as part of the code itself. They also serve additional purposes, such as helping you remember later how you built the program and helping others (such as members of a team) understand the different sections of your program.

Commenting code in Scratch

In Scratch, each comment is attached to a code tile. Comments can be as short or as long as you want. Long comments can be collapsed to a single line. Scratch Comments appear light yellow in color when shown onscreen. Figure 2-8 shows comments for the complete vacuuming program in Scratch. (For an introduction to Scratch, see Chapter 3.)

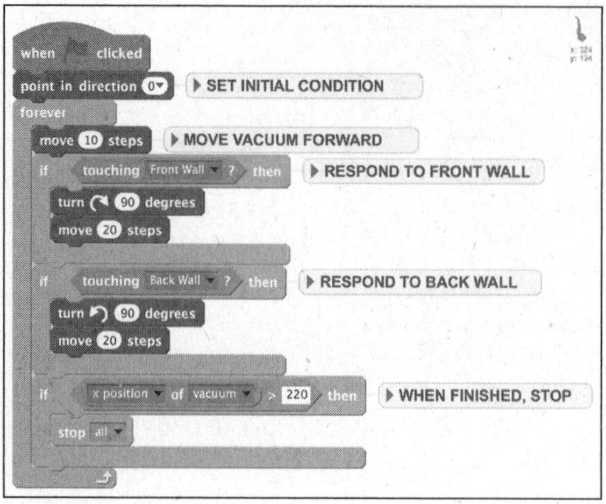

FIGURE 2-8:
Commenting code in a Scratch program.

Commenting code in JavaScript and Java

In JavaScript and Java, a short comment is indicated by two forward slashes. Everything that follows the two slashes (on the same line) is a comment and is not executed as code. A long comment is called a block comment. Every line begins with an asterisk. The first line precedes the asterisk with a forward slash, and the last line includes a slash after the asterisk.

In the Code.org Choose Your Own Adventure app shown in Figure 2-9, code lines 1 through 3 show a block comment, while line 5 and line 14 each show a short comment.

```
 1 - /*
 2    * This is a Choose Your Own Adventure App
 3    */
 4
 5    // When dropdown1 option is selected, show Panama City or Paris
 6 - onEvent("dropdown1", "change", function() {
 7 -   if ("Fly to Panama" == getText("dropdown1")) {
 8       setScreen("screen2");
 9     }
10 -   if ("Fly to Paris" == getText("dropdown1")) {
11       setScreen("screen3");
12     }
13  });
14    // When dropdown2 option is selected, show eat dinner or visit sites
15 - onEvent("dropdown2", "change", function() {
16 -   if ("Eat dinner" == getText("dropdown2")) {
17       setScreen("screen4");
18     }
19 -   if ("Visit historic sites" == getText("dropdown2")) {
20       setScreen("screen5");
21     }
22  });
23
```

FIGURE 2-9:
Commenting code in a JavaScript program.

TEACH COMMENTS WITH POP-UP VIDEO

Kids often resist commenting as they view it as extra stuff that doesn't contribute to getting their program up and running. But commenting is vital to help them structure their thinking and stay on track when programs become lengthy. In the professional world, comments also provide a way for teams of programmers to work collaboratively. The comments can serve as headings of sections that different people will write and as a means of communicating other descriptive information within the program.

To practice commenting, try doing so in a silly and simple context — play a game of Pop Up Video (made popular by VH1). Watch a fun video clip together and then view it a second time and shout comments that describe the sections. For example, "Now he's constructing a Pen-Pineapple-Apple-Pen!" "Now it's dance time!" For an example, see the figure.

Photo credit: YouTube/Pen–Pineapple–Apple–Pen

Organizing with Sequence, Selection, and Repetition

Infrastructure is something adults hear a lot in the grown–up world. *Infrastructure* is the physical plan of the world. It consists of the same components in any city on earth: roads, water pipes, electricity grids, and other items that give structure and organization to designed human habitats. Without infrastructure, daily life would appear chaotic!

Just like cities, computer programs possess infrastructure. At a very basic level, infrastructure consists of three key components:

>> Sequence

>> Selection

>> Repetition

These components provide the general plan for designing and executing a computer program.

Sequence

Sequence is the order in which a process is conducted. Every computer program must be organized so that steps are executed in a logical order. For example, ask your coder to order the steps in Figure 2-10 in a simple algorithm. The steps include answering Rocky; saying Rocky, roll over!; and asking What is the name of your dog?

FIGURE 2-10: Unsequenced steps in an algorithm.

Your coder should be able to recognize that you must first ask the name of the dog (*query*); then receive the answer (*input*); and then, remembering that Rocky is the name, say, Rocky roll over (*output*).

As a Scratch program, the algorithm looks something like Figure 2-11.

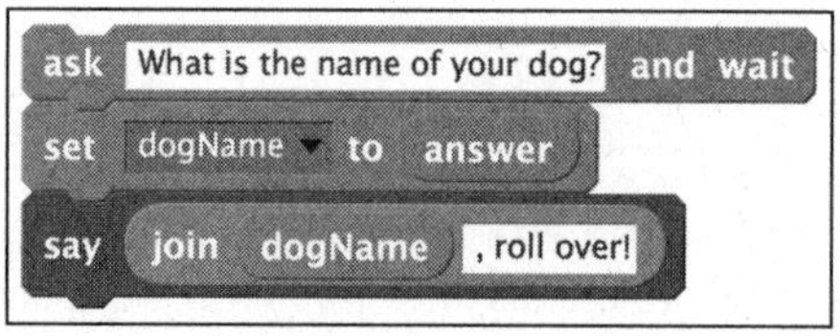

```
ask   What is the name of your dog?   and  wait
set   dogName ▼  to   answer
say   join   dogName   , roll over!
```

FIGURE 2-11: Steps sequenced in a logical order in a Scratch algorithm.

Understanding the order in which input and output must occur is just one example of sequence in a computer program. This books tackles many other sequences throughout the coding activities.

TIP

Invent some other sequencing tasks for your kid to try. What about gardening, baking brownies, or washing the car? What are the most important steps of each task, and how must they be sequenced?

Selection

Selection means choosing a path based on certain conditions. For example, when choosing a university to attend, you may decide between West Coast or East Coast. The decision you make then directs you to new sequences — and consequently, other selections — that relate to your choice. If you choose West Coast, then Stanford is on your list of potential universities, but not Harvard. Program commands associated with a decision that you didn't make aren't executed.

When coding, selection allows the programmer to create as many paths as needed to respond to the conditions of the program. Selection often involves conditional statements that are structured this way: if *[condition occurs]* then *[execute consequence]*. Conditional statements can be structured in different ways, depending on what the program needs to accomplish. Figure 2-12 shows three conditional command structures your coder can use in Scratch.

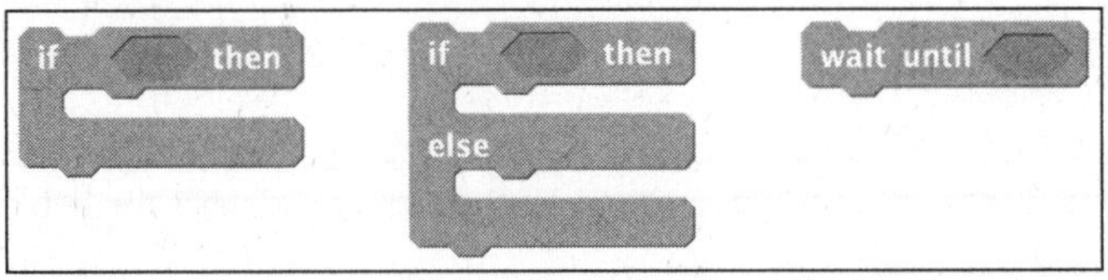

FIGURE 2-12:
Conditional
commands in
Scratch.

Here are some everyday examples, in standard English, that match the structure of the Scratch conditional commands:

if everyone completes homework by dinnertime then we'll eat at Olive Garden

if you eat oranges then you are a healthy pirate else you have scurvy

wait until countdown equals zero

Conditional statements that use an if-then-else statement evaluate whether the if condition is true or false: true determines the selection of one command sequence, while false determines the selection of a different command sequence. Conditional statements that use a wait until statement run when the condition (the statement following until) is true.

The Choose Your Own Adventure app makes frequent use of conditionals. Can you and your coder think of other examples in which conditional statements are used in everyday life?

Repetition

Repetition is the process of repeating something. You may have said to your kid, "How many times have I told you to take out the trash — I just keep repeating myself again and again, arrghh!" Unlike grownups, computers are happy to repeat themselves over and over. In fact, repetition is an important task when coding, and understanding how to write code blocks that repeat is critical to structuring your computer programs.

Using a `repeat` command is one way your coder can create a loop in his code. A *loop* is a structure that tells the computer to run the same commands multiple times, without writing those same commands over and over. Like a traffic circle (which we've all been stuck on many times!), you can continue looping around, again and again until there's a reason to eventually exit the loop. Creating a loop is similar to creating a chorus in a song: You can provide a notation that indicates a lyric should be sung eight times without writing it eight times:

```
repeat 8 ["Come on, be my baby, come on"]
```

Actually writing this bridge from Ed Sheeran's "Shape of You" requires eight lines, but using code, your kid can produce the same result in a single line. Repetition rocks!

Depending on the programming language your coder is using, loops are handled somewhat differently. Figure 2-13 shows some loop structures you use in Scratch.

FIGURE 2-13:
Loop commands
in Scratch.

Following are some examples, in standard English, that match the structure of the Scratch loop commands:

repeat 2 [apply shampoo, lather, rinse]

repeat 4 [drive to the end of the block, turn right]

forever [move forward 10 steps, wait 1 second, move backward 10 steps, wait 1 second]

repeat until [the value of the jackpot exceeds $100 million]

ADA LOVELACE AND CHARLES BABBAGE: THE FIRST "COMPUTER" AND COMPUTER PROGRAMS

Ada Lovelace, the daughter of a famed poet (Lord Byron) and a fierce, STEM-loving mother, was born in London in 1815. From an early age, Ada showed great passion for mathematics and engineering. She loved to examine diagrams depicting the revolutionary new machines emerging during the Industrial Revolution. At age 12, she imagined a design for an airplane, drawing her vision, "to make a thing in the form of a horse with a steamengine in the inside so contrived as to move an immense pair of wings, fixed on the outside of the horse, in such a manner as to carry it up into the air while a person sits on its back."

Photo credit: http://engineeringhistory.tumblr.com/
post/97568847004/tinted-photograph-
from-a-daguerreotype-of-ada

Ada was 17 when she met Charles Babbage, an inventor considered to be father of the computer. Babbage had designed a *difference engine*, a device that was a sort of mechanical calculator. He later evolved the design to a theoretical *analytical engine*, which was intended to use punch cards to convey a program for execution on the machine.

Babbage asked Ada to translate a description of the analytical engine and its operation from the original French text into English. In the process, she also added her own thoughts and ideas on the machine. Her notes, entitled, "Sketch of the Analytical Engine, with Notes from the Translator," ended up being three times longer than the original article. Her published work described how codes could be created for the device to handle letters and symbols along with numbers. She also theorized a method for the

(continued)

(continued)

engine to repeat a series of instructions, a process known as looping that computer programs use today. Ada also suggested other progressive concepts in her version of the article, including the idea that any content from music to text to pictures could be represented in a digital form and then handled by the machine. Babbage was so impressed with her work he dubbed Ada, the "Enchantress of Numbers." Some people have called her the "First Computer Programmer" as a result of programs she included in her publication, although there is some uncertainly about whether she wrote the programs or simply clarified Babbage's writings.

Unfortunately, Ada died early, at only 36 years of age. While her article gained little traction during her lifetime, the brilliance of Ada's ideas was eventually realized, and she received many posthumous honors for her work a century later. Best of all, in 1980, the U.S. Department of Defense named a newly developed computer language "Ada" in honor of Ada Lovelace. Her work has inspired a new generation of coders, especially young women, to enter the field of computer science.

In the first example, the `repeat` command indicates that the steps, "apply shampoo, lather, rinse" repeat two times. The second example demonstrates how to drive a square-shaped path in your neighborhood, ending up at your starting point. Example three shows a `forever` command that results in a bouncing motion that continues endlessly, until the program itself terminates or some other commands stop its execution. In the final example, the `repeat until` command is a hybrid command consisting of a `repeat` loop and an `until` conditional. The `until` conditional triggers a break out of the loop structure.

You can explore many other loop structures in Chapter 10. For this chapter, just remember that repetition is a fundamental structure that you're helping your young coder include in many programs.

TIP

Find some favorite songs or dances that include repeated sections. Work with your kid to identify the repeated lyrics or steps, as well as how many times the repetition occurs. Can you say, "Heyyyyyy, Macarena!"

Including Randomness in Your Coding

You and your coder may know that writing computer programs requires precision and attention to detail. But you both also know that the world is often imprecise and messy. So how can you write a precise program that models something in the imprecise world? The key is including some randomness in your program.

Randomness is found in a wide range of circumstances, from the outcomes of flipping coins to the path of a bug trekking across a wall. Using a random command in your programming is somewhat prevalent — keep this thought in mind every time you help your young coder get started on a program that involves variation or real-world problem-solving.

Here is a simple example of using a random command. This little program is created to work on a micro:bit electronics board (microbit.org). You don't need the actual board to write and test programs. You can see the programs function onscreen in an *emulator*, a digital version of how the program will work on the hardware.

In this tiny program, shown in Figure 2-14, `on button A Pressed` is the start event. Pressing button A causes two lines of code to run in sequence. The first line sets a `secret_number` variable to a random number: `pick random 0 to 9`. This second line shows the `secret_number` on the LED display.

FIGURE 2-14:
A micro:bit emulator and a simple JavaScript block program for generating and showing a random number.

Your coder could use this little sequence of commands as part of a larger program, perhaps a game, that requires a number to be pulled from a hat or a game piece to be moved according to the outcome of multisided dice roll. Ultimately, you and your coder can find that having some randomness is a good thing in your programs!

TECHNICAL STUFF

Recently, one of Camille's students was creating a program that models the number of people moving into and out of an apartment building. The student wanted to incorporate some randomness in the variables representing the number of people moving in each month and in the number of people moving out each month. Using a random number generation command and identifying a minimum and maximum value for each of her variables, the student produced a model that featured the randomness — and realism — that she hoped for.

Chapter **3**

Figuring Out Programming Languages

A *programming language* is the tool your kid uses to write code. A *programming environment* is the "place" (the interface on the computer) where your kid actually creates his code. Most programming languages look like a subset of the words, numbers, and symbols that exist in everyday written, human languages. In the same way that your child prints a sentence or solves a math problem on a piece of paper, the words and symbols he uses represent the language and the paper represents the environment.

Programming languages are called *high-level* because they allow human beings to use already familiar words to communicate with the computer. You may already know that the computer doesn't speak in a human language. A computer uses switches (similar to light switches in your house), set to off and on positions, to write and read information. Those off and on positions are represented by a special computer language, called *binary*, that uses only two symbols: 0 and 1. The binary language is a *low-level* language that is like the computer's mother tongue.

Special programs translate languages from high-level to low-level, so most programmers need only to focus on learning high-level languages. Your child has a wide variety of high-level programming language options available to him. We take a look at the most popular ones you're likely to encounter in this chapter.

What You Want in a Language

One of the biggest debates about selecting a programming language centers on what you hope to accomplish as a coding coach.

>> **Coding educators** often view the purpose of an introductory programming experience as an opportunity to build basic conceptual skills and confidence in the new coder. They often encourage the use of starter languages, such as Scratch, because they're easy to access and extremely forgiving. Starter languages are frequently tile-based (also called block-based) in format, providing the user puzzle-style pieces that can be snapped together in specific ways. This structure allows new coders to focus on ideas over syntax (which includes the details of punctuation in the code).

>> **Professional coders** typically view the purpose of an introductory programming experience as something that should mirror actual programming. They often encourage the use of an authentic language, such as Python, JavaScript, or Java, to ensure that new coders are learning and producing real code.

Each perspective has its advantages and disadvantages. Using a starter language may secure your children's interest, allowing them to ramp up to professional languages when they're ready. But using a professional language — if your children can understand it — means they don't have to switch early in their coding practice.

REMEMBER

Ultimately, kids are going to be expected to program in numerous coding languages throughout their lives. Whatever language you choose to get started will be "right" so long as you're willing to provide support and encouragement in their efforts to learn and apply it.

Free Languages for Tots and Kids

Getting started with coding can be accomplished as early as age four or five, even before a child can read! Programming languages that use symbols, instead of words, can be especially helpful in coaching young children to build fundamental programming concepts.

The Foos

The Foos is a free, fun, and instructionally excellent coding game for tots; see Figure 3-1. It's available at https://thefoos.com/webgl for desktop gameplay, as well as an app for both iOS and Android. The Foos are neighborhood buddies who live and work together in a colorful, animated city full of donut shops, construction sites, gourmet kitchens, and occasional visits to space! A pesky nuisance-maker, named Glitch, creates challenges for tots to solve, such as collecting crystals, or rescuing a puppy. To solve a puzzle, your tot uses simple programming commands, presented and demonstrated visually, to move her character onscreen. Tots don't need to be readers to engage in this coding game! Puzzles increase in difficulty, beginning with simple sequencing and directional orientation, to eventually requiring loops and conditionals to solve. An audio track and cute sound effects also provide clues to assist your young coder in solving each puzzle. An extensive collection of levels keeps kids busy, and learning, for hours.

FIGURE 3-1: The Foos is a symbol-based coding game, with hours of challenges. A great choice for tots!

Think & Learn Code-a-Pillar

Code-a-Pillar is a simple, fun, and free app that runs on iOS and Android devices. Its focus is encouraging young children to use directional command codes to navigate a caterpillar around a garden; see Figure 3-2. Visual tiles for forward, turn, and a small number of other commands help novice coders think sequentially to accomplish tasks. An audio track helps provide additional guidance to users. For those interested in making a concrete connection to a robotic toy, a physical code-a-pillar is available (at a price) to accompany the app.

Daisy the Dinosaur

Daisy the Dinosaur is an adorably fun and free coding game for tots; see Figure 3-3. It's available as an app for iPads. Daisy is a friendly dinosaur who responds to coding commands to move around in her world. Commands are text-based and presented as tiles, but the limited number of commands keeps this a doable app even for "nearly" non-readers. This app has limited use time, but it's a good entre to word-based tile coding.

FIGURE 3-2:
Code-a-Pillar trains tots to think sequentially, and offers a robotic toy option.

Photo credit: `http://www.fisher-price.com/en_US/ brands/think-and-learn/learning-apps/index.html`

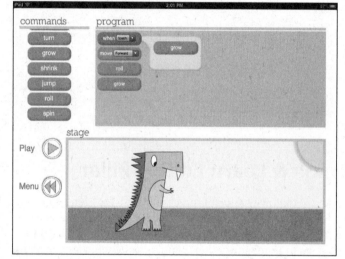

FIGURE 3-3:
Your tot can ease into simple, word-based code tiles to make Daisy dance in this free app.

Scratch Jr.

Scratch Jr. (`https://www.scratchjr.org`) is a fabulous, free, symbol-based coding environment for young children; see Figure 3-4. It's available for both iOS and Android devices. Scratch Jr, as the name states, is a junior version of the full Scratch coding environment. The app provides a full-featured, easy-to-use playground environment for creating animated stories, interactive toys, and simple games. It offers directional commands, loops, event handlers ("when Scratch Cat is touched, do this"), conditionals, messaging, and more. A large assortment of image and sound assets provides children a wide variety of options for character and scene creation. Scratch Jr. also permits sound recording and photo capture from your device! An additional bonus is that the interface can be switched to a handful of non-English versions, including Spanish.

Free Languages for Youth and Tweens

After your child begins reading, the door opens for additional programming languages and environments. Even the most basic of reading skills affords your beginner coder the ability to recognize code-based tiles, as well as type a few commands in text-based languages that require use of a QWERTY keyboard. As your young coder progresses into her tweens (pre-teen years), she can type more content to create longer programs in a text-based environment, as well as follow along with written tutorials that accompany some offerings.

Scratch

Scratch (https://scratch.mit.edu) is often considered the gold-standard for starter programming languages; see Figure 3-5. It's an intuitive, feature-rich, tile-based coding environment that's perfect for learning all the basics of coding — and having fun while doing so! Code tiles show words, but a huge number of language options are available (Mandarin, French, Spanish, Hebrew, Arabic, you name it!), and you can quickly switch the language display of the interface. Scratch is a web-based program that operates in your browser, so you can use any computer to access it. There is also an offline version available. If you have a spotty Internet connection, this is a great option.

Scratch offers an intuitive interface for building all sorts of programs. Young coders enjoy the built-in backgrounds, sprites (objects), animated costumes, sound effects, and music. They also find the categories of code tiles easy-to-navigate, and playground "code-and-test" workspace welcoming and forgiving. Scratch offers most critical command structures, including motion, loops, event handlers, math operations, logic operations, sensing, messaging, variables, and lists. The only "authentic" command it lacks is arrays, but most kids find that the list command comes close to meeting their programming needs.

There's no error reporting in Scratch; however, young coders understand that when code tiles don't snap together, they're not compatible. They can observe visually whether their programs function as they intend, and then make changes instantly, if needed.

One of the most exciting features of Scratch is its extensive, online community. Kids (and coders of all ages!) build, share, and comment on projects shared online. Every member of the Scratch community can "see inside" a shared project to learn from its code, and users can remix (with attribution) any shared project. Scratch is one of the key languages highlighted in this book. (For an in-depth book addressing Scratch, see *Scratch for Kids For Dummies* by Derek Breen.)

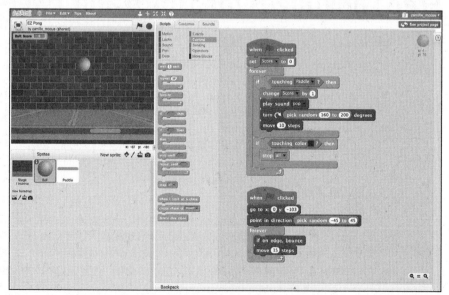

FIGURE 3-5:
Make (and share!) engaging games, simulations, and more using the feature-rich coding environment of Scratch.

Scratch is one of the languages used by some high schools in its AP Computer Science Principles course. It's also the language of choice in the Introduction to Programming course for undergraduates at the University of California, Berkeley!

Hopscotch

Hopscotch (https://www.gethopscotch.com) is a fun and full-featured new app development environment that's ideal for youth and tweens; see Figure 3-6. Available free for iOS device, Hopscotch uses a drag-and-drop interface that provides fabulous components including collisions, variables, and custom graphics. It also makes excellent use of mobile device sensors including the touch sensor, the microphone, and the accelerometer — features that really allow young coders to create inventive interactions that make their games pop! Hopscotch includes both tutorial and playground modes, and young coders love sharing their creations in the moderated online community.

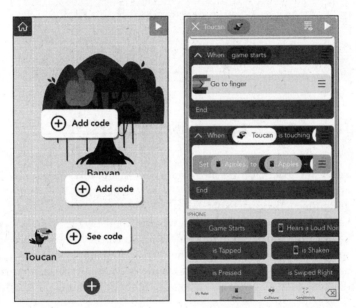

FIGURE 3-6:
Create nifty, full-featured apps and share them in the Hopscotch community!

Kodu

Kodu (https://www.kodugamelab.com) is a downloadable, desktop program for Windows PC devices and the Xbox; see Figure 3-7. Kodu provides a simple programming environment in which kids can use either a keyboard and mouse or game controller to develop their programs. Young coders can create elaborate 3D worlds, add characters, and then program those characters and their behaviors in the world. Kodu encourages its coders to share their creations in its online community, sparking new ideas for its audience. Parents, coding coaches, and teachers also appreciate the database of interdisciplinary curriculum materials available at the Kodu site.

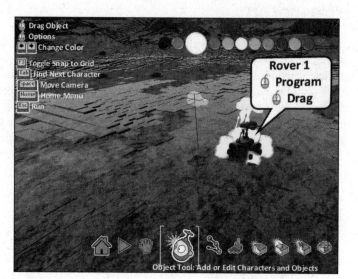

FIGURE 3-7:
Create awesome worlds for 3D games using Kodu.

Languages for Teens and Older

Teens and older learners likely want to dive into text-based coding languages that are used in real programming contexts. There are too many professional programming languages to list, but several preferred ones are ideal for getting started. Languages including Python, JavaScript, and Java are popular and doable, and have a wide range of circumstances in which they're used. Because of the widespread use of these languages, their use is highlighted extensively throughout this book. For those mature audiences who prefer a more visual approach, a handful of tile-based languages are available, including Alice and MIT App Inventor.

Alice

Alice (http://www.alice.org) is a teaching language developed at Carnegie Mellon University with the goal of helping new coders learn *object-oriented programming (OOP)* — the programming paradigm they need for professional programming endeavors. This environment is a downloadable, desktop program and is available for Windows, Mac OS, and Linux users; see Figure 3-8. Alice invites teens (and older) coders to create beautiful, animated, interactive stories using an extensive set of high-end graphics (including the Sims!) and audio assets. While the interface offers new coders the simplicity of working in drag-and-drop mode, it also shows a side-by-side view with the Java code it generates, helping transition users to text-based OOP coding. An extensive set of support "how-to" materials is available for download from the Alice site.

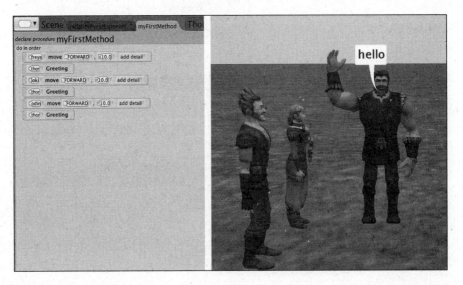

FIGURE 3-8:
Alice is a teaching language that introduces object-oriented programming (OOP).

REMEMBER

Alice is one of several languages used by high schools in the AP Computer Science Principles course. It's also taught to undergraduates at University of California, San Diego in its Introduction to Programming course.

MIT App Inventor 2

MIT App Inventor 2 (http://appinventor.mit.edu/explore) is a free, professional grade app development environment — which, surprisingly, is tile-based and relatively easy-to-use; see Figure 3-9. The environment is web-based, so there's nothing to download and you can operate it on both Windows and Mac OS platforms. Your coder can build real apps, in-browser, and then view the operation of those apps in a mobile device emulator on the computer screen. Via Wi-Fi, he can then connect to his mobile device and live test his app. Android mobile devices are currently supported, and MIT is in the process of implementing App Inventor for iOS (as of early 2018). MIT App Inventor 2 allows you to tap into a library of professional *application program interfaces* (APIs), which are code packages that allow two software programs to communicate. For example, you can build an app to locate where you parked your car by incorporating an API that employs geolocation from a mobile device, storing the location in your app, and allowing you to retrieve it later! Chapter 15 provides a complete tutorial on using MIT App Inventor 2 to make a mobile game.

FIGURE 3-9:
MIT App
Inventor 2 allows
coders to develop
real apps,
including APIs,
using a tile
paradigm.

Coders can upload and publish completed apps to the Google Play Store — but they need to participate in the Google Play Store Developer Program to do so. Once MIT implements App Inventor for iOS, coders will be able to also upload and publish apps to the Apple App Store (for those participating in the Apple Developer Program).

REMEMBER

High schools that prefer a mobile app approach to their introductory programming courses often choose MIT App Inventor 2 for their AP Computer Science Principles students.

Python

Python is a free, professional grade app programming language that has stood the test of time. Young coders find the text-based format of Python to be understandable and logical. The Python language uses a system called *dynamic type*, which means that coders don't have to declare variables before using them. Your coder can code something like num = 5, and Python knows that this statement means, "create a variable called num, of type integer, and give it a starting value of 5" — all in that one command! Also, Python has available a large standard library from which students pull code modules and incorporate the modules in their programs to perform more complex tasks.

Python uses an *interactive interpreter*, which means that your coder can run test code as he goes along, building his programs. Python is an excellent, general purpose language for your young coder as it's used in a wide range of applications in the real world. From testing microchips at Intel, to controlling robots, to powering Instagram, to creating scripts for graphical information systems (GIS), to building video games, Python is there! Like MIT App Inventor 2, Python coders can make use of a wide variety of APIs to increase the functionality of their programs quickly and easily.

Your coder needs an Integrated Development Environment (IDE) to type, edit, and run Python code. A good IDE is easy to use, and offers features such as code completion, automatic indenting, syntax highlighting, code cleanup, and access to an interactive interpreter during coding. One especially great Python IDE for beginners is Thonny (http://thonny.org); see Figure 3-10. Thonny is a downloadable program for Windows, Mac OS, and Linux, and comes with Python 3.6 built in. It takes only one quick install to get up and running! A wide variety of assistive teaching tools are built into Thonny, from limiting the interface view when you first begin, to stepping through expressions, to explaining variable scopes. Another excellent starter tool for learning and working with Python is Python Tutor (http://www.pythontutor.com), which offers quick-and-easy code creation, editing, and execution right in your web browser. Most examples of Python in this book are shown using Python Tutor.

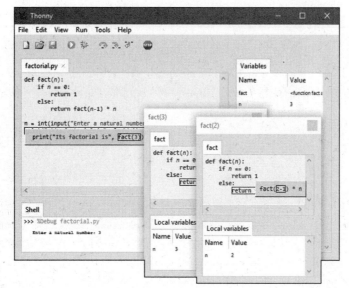

FIGURE 3-10:
Code, edit, debug, and execute Python code in a beginner-friendly IDE such as Thonny.

GUIDO VAN ROSSUM: CODE THAT IS UNDERSTANDABLE IN PLAIN ENGLISH

Commonly known as the "Benevolent Dictator For Life" in the Python community, Guido van Rossum created one of today's most popular programming languages while working on a hobby project over Christmas break in 1989, releasing it to the world in early 1991. He named his creation Python after the British sketch comedy series "Monty Python's Flying Circus." While this name was only supposed to be temporary, it became synonymous with an easy and intuitive programming language that is just as powerful as more complicated competitors like C++ and Java.

Python was developed when programming languages were actively diverging from "low-level" ancestors, like C and FORTRAN, which although optimized for efficient mathematic operations, were very clumsy for users of all experience levels. So called "high-level" languages were emerging to help computer users that were not formally trained software developers easily code common routines, such as reading a text file.

Guido van Rossum conceived Python after witnessing the limitations of other high-level languages that had their core functionality tightly controlled by their creators. He wanted an open-source high-level language that anyone could contribute to. This spawned a large community of contributors that were free to create their own Python modules for users of any profession, from physicists and biologists to social scientists and linguists.

Photo credit: www.flickr.com, photo by Ed Schipul

Rossum was able to maintain simplicity and readability by rejecting premature optimizations to core functionality that would only offer marginal improvements in execution speed at the cost of code clarity. Contributions were allowed as long as they adhered to the core tenants of readability, simplicity, and beauty, thus allowing for a fun coding experience — hence the Monty Python reference. One example of this philosophy is Python's pioneering file I/O interface, which allows users to read, modify, and write text files in any operating system with the same few (and only) lines of code.

Today, Python remains a unique high-level scripting language due to its rejection of exuberant syntax in favor of simple, less-cluttered grammar, while also providing an ever-expanding set of modules that make coding fun for users of all professions.

Though Rossum has continued to oversee the development and contributions to Python, he also has worked for Google from 2005 to 2012. He then moved over to the cloud file storage company, Dropbox, in 2012, where he continues to work today.

JavaScript

JavaScript is a free programming language that makes web pages pop! JavaScript works in coordination with HTML and CSS, the languages that format content for display on the web. But JavaScript is what allows your young coder to create interactive, dynamic web pages that do more than just show information and images. When your coder adds JavaScript to a webpage, she makes it possible to ask the user to type information into a form, respond to button clicks, display a Google Map or a Twitter tweet, or generate moving graphics for a game. The JavaScript language is considered untyped. While coders do have to declare a variable before using it (unlike Python), they don't have to declare its type, and the type can change throughout their program. So while `var pies; pies = 3;` may appear at the start of your coder's program, she can update the variable value later to `pies = 2.5;` and JavaScript won't care that she switched pies from being an integer to a decimal (or that she ate half a pie during the course of writing the program). Chapter 14 provides a complete webpage development project, including the use of JavaScript.

You can help your coder find an Integrated Development Environment (IDE) to type, edit, and run her JavaScript code. A great online IDE, as recommended by the authors of *JavaScript for Kids For Dummies*, Chris Minnick and Eva Holland, is JSFiddle (`https://jsfiddle.net`); see Figure 3-11. JSFiddle provides an interface consisting of four regions: one for HTML, one for CSS, one for JavaScript, and one for program output. JSFiddle serves as a great testbed for trying JavaScript code in a clearly organized and forgiving interface.

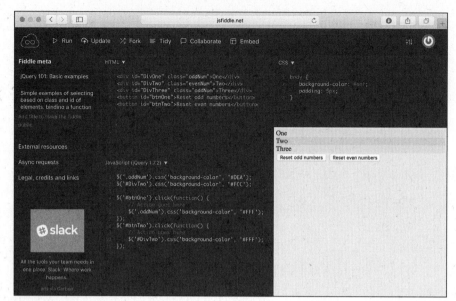

FIGURE 3-11:
Create and try out JavaScript, HTML, and CSS code in the JSFiddle IDE.

Another excellent way to learn JavaScript is using the free App Lab available at the Code.org website (`https://code.org/educate/applab`). The App Lab provides an interface in which young coders can work using tiles or text; see Figure 3-12. App Lab organizes command codes by type (similar to Scratch), and provides "hover help" for each command, with extensive examples, to support coders new to JavaScript. The interface also visually tracks the execution of a program, and even provides the ability to slow down program execution so that coders can see how commands and the execution of those commands transpires. Error tracking and debugging suggestions help your coder figure out and fix problems in her code. Program execution occurs in a smartphone emulator onscreen, giving coders the "feel" of building authentic programs and seeing them in action. Extensive help support and instruction in JavaScript are available through Code.org. One additional nifty feature of the App Lab is that coders can not only share their creations (or remix others' creations) online, they can also share them via Facebook and Twitter, or send them as texts for operation on their smartphones!

TECHNICAL STUFF

Technically, JavaScript is a *scripting* language (a specific type of programming language), which means it's a language used to mediate between programs to generate data. HTML and CSS are *markup* languages, which means they simply control the appearance and presentation of data. HTML and CSS aren't truly considered programming languages.

REMEMBER

Code.org features JavaScript as the programming language of choice for its AP Computer Science Principles course.

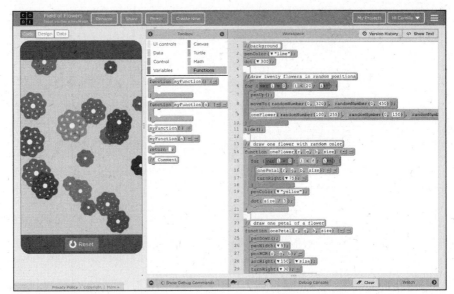

FIGURE 3-12:
The App Lab at
Code.org is a fun
and engaging tool
for learning
JavaScript.

Java

Java is a professional grade, general purpose programming language that is typically the highest level of programming taught in high school. Like Alice, it's what's known as an *object-oriented programming* (OOP) language, but unlike Alice, it's not a teaching language — it's the real deal. Java is considered a *strongly typed* language, meaning that your coder needs to declare every variable and identify its data type (and the type can't change within the program). This means your coder needs to do a bit more structuring of his program, and add a few more lines of code, than when using Python or JavaScript. Giant libraries of Java code, for every imaginable task, are available, and a key aspect of learning to program in Java is learning to access and use its libraries.

If your coder has reached this level of programming proficiency, it's not highly likely that he's asking for your assistance in learning to code. However, it's still important for you to know where your child is headed — and to have a bit of an idea of what Java code looks like when he reaches a course featuring Java.

For your coder to program in Java on his computer, he needs to install a no-cost Java Development Kit (JDK) and an Integrated Development Environment (IDE) to type, edit, and run code. An excellent, free IDE that is beginner-friendly is BlueJ (https://www.bluej.org); see Figure 3-13. BlueJ provides an easy-to-understand interface that presents a window for program classes and their relationships, along with a window for the Java code of each class. Color-coding, error-tracking, and other helpful tools assist the new coder in getting started with Java.

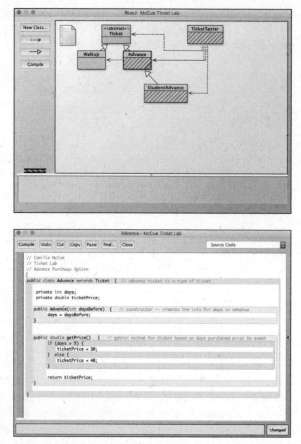

FIGURE 3-13:
BlueJ is a
beginner-friendly
IDE for creating
Java programs.

Another good way for your coder to begin working in Java is to use an online code-and-test playground with companion guidance. CodeHS provides a wide variety of free, online courses, featuring these associated playgrounds (which are called sandboxes). The Java offering is especially excellent! Every topic your coder needs to practice is addressed in the CodeHS Java course: Basic Java, Methods, Classes and Object-Oriented Programming, Data Structures, and Algorithms and Recursion. See Figure 3-14. Each topic is presented via a series of short "how-to" videos, examples, practice problems, and the sandbox programming area.

REMEMBER

Java is the programming language in which the College Board expects students to program in the AP Computer Science A course.

TECHNICAL
STUFF

For some electronics projects, other easy-to-use, free programming languages — specific to the components of the project — may be used. One example is the Arduino "language," which is really just a subset of the C++ programming language. When working with Arduino boards of all types, including Lily boards for e-textiles, your coder uses a special (free) Arduino IDE. Check out the Microsoft

Make Code site (https://makecode.com) for easy-to-access IDEs that allow young coders to write code for execution on a wide range of hardware products; see Figure 3-15. (The site also provides an area for coding Minecraft mods!) Getting used to programming in a variety of languages, and for a wide range of applications, is a desirable skill you should cultivate in your young coder. See Chapter 16 for a simple, complete project using Make Code and a micro:bit electronics board.

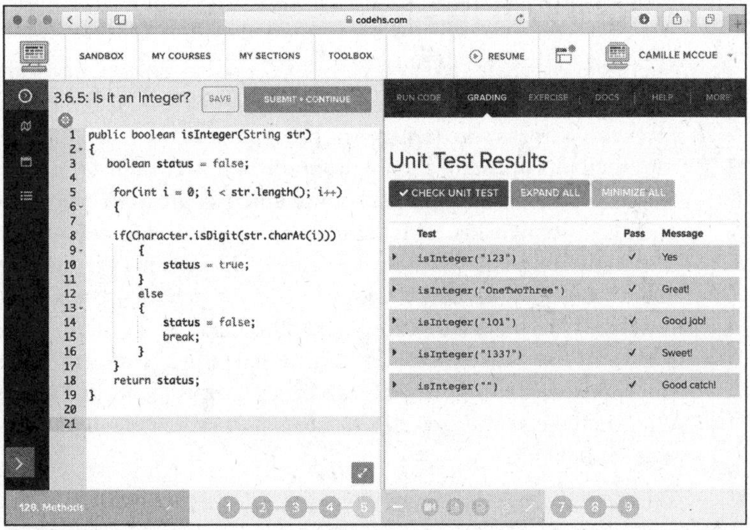

FIGURE 3-14: CodeHS provides a comprehensive online course in Java, along with a super online sandbox for writing and testing code!

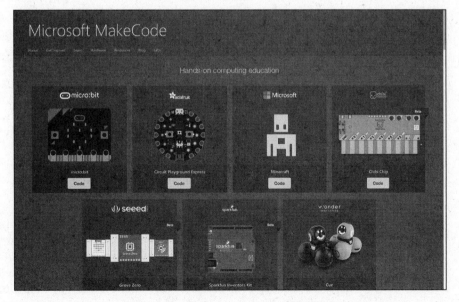

FIGURE 3-15: The Microsoft Make Code site provides IDEs for programming robots, Minecraft, and wearable electronics.

Other Awesome (Not-So-Free) Languages

In addition to the free languages listed in this chapter, you should be aware that several other awesome languages are excellent for young coders — and only require a small investment to acquire them.

MicroWorlds EX

MicroWorlds EX (http://www.microworlds.com) is a updated of version of the Logo programming language, suited to grades K-8. It provides an intuitive interface with a workspace (where the program executes), a command center (for testing small bits of code), a main programming area, and a toolbar and menu through which coders can access assets including characters objects, backgrounds, and sounds. MicroWorlds EX is unique in that it's the only youth-targeted programming environment that features line coding! However, as a teaching language, some professionals view working in this language as something that doesn't build towards "the bigger picture." (Camille disagrees!) MicroWorlds EX comes as a program you must install, but after installed, your computer doesn't require Internet access to run it. This can be a plus in schools or homes with inconsistent Wi-Fi connects. MicroWorlds EX costs $99 or $29 when purchased with *Coding for Kids For Dummies*.

Tynker

Tynker (https://www.tynker.com) is an online, Scratch-like programming environment that ramps up from simple tile-based coding to authentic languages including JavaScript. Tynker is beautifully organized by grade levels (best for grades K-8) and topics, including Minecraft modding. The creations your coder can build are stunning graphically. Further, Tynker provides outstanding curriculum materials and its own Content Management Systems (CMS) for tracking student performance. Tynker provides a few free modules, but to stick with it, coders have to incur a cost of a few tens of dollars, while schools may pay upwards of several hundred dollars for one or more classrooms.

GameSalad

GameSalad (https://gamesalad.com) is an extremely cool programming environment that allows coders to create real, publishable apps for distribution on Android and iOS devices. Coders as young as fifth grade can work in GameSalad, and there's really no age limit to when it times out — even professional programmers work in GameSalad! It features a unique drag-and-drop interface, and — as the name implies — it's mostly suited for the creation of games. Using

GameSalad, coders can take advantage of mobile sensors, such as the touch sensor and the accelerometer, to produce fun, modern games. Coders can also incorporate physics (gravity, density) and side-scrolling elements in their games. Game-Salad doesn't come with assets, so coders need to import their own images, music, and sounds, or else purchase asset packs to get started. The environment costs a few tens of dollars, but the ability to publish — and potentially sell — completed apps makes the investment worth it!

REMEMBER

Great "non-programming-language," away-from-the-computer resources for teaching and learning computational thinking, and computer science concepts are available at CS Unplugged (`http://csunplugged.org`).

2

Getting Your Hands on Code

IN THIS PART . . .

Explore text manipulation in different programming languages and make a Mad-Lib generator.

Discover how to place and move objects on a digital canvas and create an asteroid destroyer game.

Find out how to use graphics and sounds in programs you write and code a simple sound board.

Meet Admiral Grace Hopper.

Chapter **4**

Working with Words

This chapter guides you through a simple but fundamental task in coding — placing text-based information onscreen. Whether you and your coder are building an app, constructing a webpage, or coding some other type of computer program, you need to show information, instructions, or messages onscreen to your user. This information may be text, symbols, or numbers presented in human language, to allow communication between people and computers.

The first program that almost every new coder writes is one that displays the words, "Hello world!" It's a good way to get started as it takes little time to write such a program — a program that provides immediate gratification with its welcoming message. So say "Hello world!" (and a few other things) as you begin coding communications to display text.

Communicating with Text

On or off the computer, information and conversations use alphanumeric text and symbols to communicate. Before the days of ubiquitous laptops and smartphones, parents and teachers employed paper and pencils to write. The writings created (by hand!) took many forms: song lyrics, essays, and computations, even recipes! And each of these forms required a variety of characters, assembled in specific patterns, to make meaning. While all these characters can now be transmitted digitally via a keyboard and screen, you still use old-school methods of "working with words" — and doing so can help shape your understanding of how to code such text in your programs.

TIP

Play a quick game of "Pass the Note" with your coder. Without speaking, write a simple phrase on a piece of paper, then pass it to your kid. Statements such as, "Today is Tuesday," or "Sloppy Joes are my favorite meal!" are easy prompts to get the game underway. Your coder should write a new statement on a new line that continues the conversation. Take turns exchanging statements on paper, but resist the temptation to ask a question. Wrap up the game by looking at the paper and discussing the phrases together. What is the purpose of starting phrases on a new line? Are you limited in what information can be exchanged by not asking questions? What is different about making statements versus asking questions?

Showing Text Onscreen

Try showing a little bit of text onscreen in a few different programming languages. Most programming languages provide some way to display text so that you can convey information or directions to the user. Each language has its own unique way of issuing this command, which is generically called a *print* command. The text isn't printed on a printer, but is instead displayed on a computer screen or mobile device screen.

Using pseudocode

Every programming language is different, but a typical pseudocode expression for a print command looks something like this:

```
print ("words to be printed")
```

Some languages use single quotes, others use double quotes, and still others use no quotes surrounding the words to be printed, but this is the general structure.

Using Scratch

Scratch's version of print is the say command — it's used whenever you want to make a sprite speak or think text phrases. Figure 4-1 shows an example of a command block using say, and the resulting output.

FIGURE 4-1:
Use the Scratch
say command to
convey a simple
message
onscreen.

When the sprite is clicked, anything your kid types into the say field is displayed in the speech bubble by its sprite object. The think command performs the same task using a thought bubble instead of the speech bubble.

TECHNICAL
STUFF

In Scratch, you can type titles or other text directly onto the background in much the same way a theatrical scene designer would paint a backdrop for a stage production. In Bitmap mode, the text cannot later be edited, while in Vector mode, the text retains its editability. In this regard, text appears more as a graphic object than printed text. For additional information on working in bitmap and vector graphics modes in Scratch, see *Scratch for Kids For Dummies* by Derek Breen.

Using Python

In Python, you can show some text onscreen by using a print() command, followed by the phrase in single or double quotes inside the parentheses. Figure 4-2 shows an example of a command block using print(), and the resulting output.

```
Python 3.6
→ 1  print ("Hello world!")

Print output
Hello world!
```

FIGURE 4-2:
Python's print()
command
outputs text
onscreen.

Python requires you to use quotes (single or double) around the phrase you want to print. The phrase and quotes are enclosed inside a set of parentheses.

TECHNICAL STUFF

Your ability to use the print command in Python might allow you to do more than send this happy greeting! Among the many uses of Python, you and your coder may discover, the print command may be instrumental in conveying the status of a robotic arm you might build, or some data in a GIS (Geographic Information System) — both common applications of Python.

Using HTML

When building a simple webpage, a great deal of what you show onscreen is text. Webpages use HTML (Hypertext Markup Language) to display that text. HTML is more of a formatting language than an actual coding language. But because you and your kid likely want to tinker a bit with HTML, take a look at a simple example of how you can display Hello world! in a web browser:

```
<html>

<body>
<h1> Hello world! </h1>
<p>I live a fascinating life, how about you?</p>
</body>

</html>
```

Use Notepad (Windows) or TextEdit (Mac) to type the short text file — or "program" — shown here. Don't focus too specifically on the details at this point; just note a couple of key ways in which you can place text on a webpage. Any text you type between the <h1></h1> tags, called Level 1 heading tags, appears as a large heading. Any text you type between the <p></p> tags, called paragraph tags, appears as standard text. Save the file with an .html extension.

Double-click a .html file; it opens in a browser similar to the one shown in Figure 4-3. Now you can see your words on a webpage! For step-by-step instructions on building a simple webpage in HTML, see Chapter 14.

Using JavaScript in an app

In JavaScript, there are a few different ways to show text. One way is to place text into a text label for display in an app. The App Lab at Code.org provides a fun and easy way for your kid to tinker with using JavaScript to display a bit of text on a mobile device emulator. As shown in Figure 4-4, the JavaScript command tells the textLabel named greeting to display the text phrase Hello world!

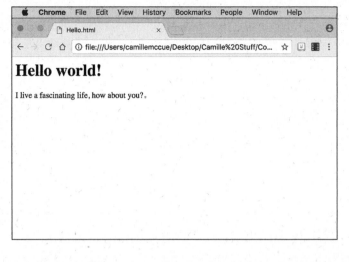

FIGURE 4-3:
HTML code
viewed in a web
browser.

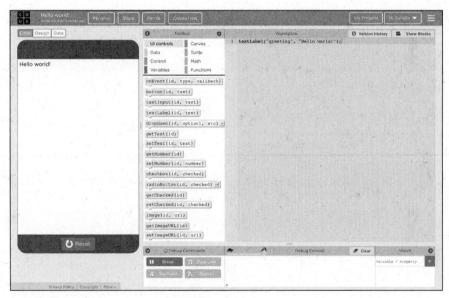

FIGURE 4-4:
JavaScript code
showing text
in a smartphone
emulator.

**TECHNICAL
STUFF**

An *emulator* is a *GUI* (Graphical User Interface) that shows, on your computer screen, how the computer program will run on the actual device. The Code.org App Lab allows you to test your app in its onscreen emulator, and then send your app to your smartphone for operation on your mobile device!

**TECHNICAL
STUFF**

Another way that JavaScript is used for displaying text is in webpage programming. You and coder kid have already seen that you can put text on a webpage using HTML, but JavaScript can do so as well. Which do you choose? The choice depends on the purpose of the text information on the webpage. Is the text literal, used for information such as headings, labels, and general textual content? If so, then HTML formatting commands are the better choice for displaying text. Or is the text dynamic, used for interaction (as in a button), or used in a way that changes depending on user input (as in messages)? In this case, you can write *scripts* — blocks of code — in JavaScript to show the desired text.

Using Java

Someday, your coder might take AP Computer Science A, perhaps as a high school student in the near future. What that day comes, he or she will likely use Java as the programming language in the course. The first programming command taught will most likely be a print command:

```
System.out.println ("Hello world!")
```

THE BIRTH OF THE GUI

Computers didn't always present information formats that are easy for humans to understand. Some of you parents, teachers, and coaches may recall a time when interacting with a computer meant typing commands on a line called command prompt: `C:/>`. During the disco era of the 1970s, researchers at Xerox PARC (Palo Alto Research Center) worked on developing new tools to make human-computer interactions easier and more natural.

They created new GUI — Graphical User Interface — formats, making communication easier and more understandable for human operators. The Xerox Star workstation shown here premiered one of the first GUI operating systems, paving the way for the Macintosh and Windows systems that later followed suit. Aren't you glad to have a GUI?

To test this, you need to install an *IDE (Integrated Development Environment)* for the Java programming language. That is a mouthful, and not something you have to worry about just yet, but it's good to know that the introductory skills you're helping your child build now are leading up to some real-world programming skills she can use in the future!

TECHNICAL STUFF

BlueJ is a free and fabulous IDE for beginners just getting started with learning Java. BlueJ provide tools for editing in both graphical and text-based modes, a debugger, compiler, and a virtual machine (so you can test your programs), along with user documentation. See Chapter 3 for more information on using the BlueJ IDE to program in Java.

Words In, Words Out

So far, you've only seen how to display text onscreen to communicate information to the users of your program. Text you "put out" from your program is called *output*. But how do you create interaction using text? Accepting text into a program is an important way to create interactivity in your code. The term *input* is used to describe "putting in" text (as well as other content, such as numbers). Your coder can write a program that asks for a person's name, saves that name, and then displays the name later in another part of the program.

TIP

Play an "Interview" game with your kid. Ask an easy question, such as, "What is your name?" and have your kid reply. Discuss with your kid the difference between a statement and a question (see Figure 4-5). After your child gives an answer to the question, discuss what you could do with that answer. Could you use that answer in a new phrase? Could you create a greeting with that answer? Could you transform the name input into a printed output?

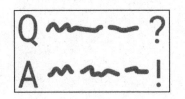

FIGURE 4-5: Play a question-and-answer interview game on paper.

You'll need a *variable* to store any piece of information the user inputs to your program. A *variable* is something that can change its value. For example, the variable name could store the value "George" at one time, and "Maria" at another time. Think of this storage process in the same way that your brain stores a snippet of information that is input through your eyes or your ears. We cover variables in much greater depth in Chapter 7. At this introductory stage, just know that your coder needs to include in his program the code for a variable to store a piece of information input by a user.

Using Scratch

In Scratch, you can accept user input using a simple built-in variable called answer. Scratch pairs the answer code tile with an ask code tile because the two commands form a natural pair. For example, the code block shown in Figure 4-6 asks the user, "What's your name?" and then waits for a response. The user types her name into the input field at the bottom of the GUI, and this input is stored in the variable answer. The answer variable is a *temporary* variable — it contains the user's name until the user inputs something else in another ask and answer code pair. Then, this value of this new input replaces the value previously stored in answer.

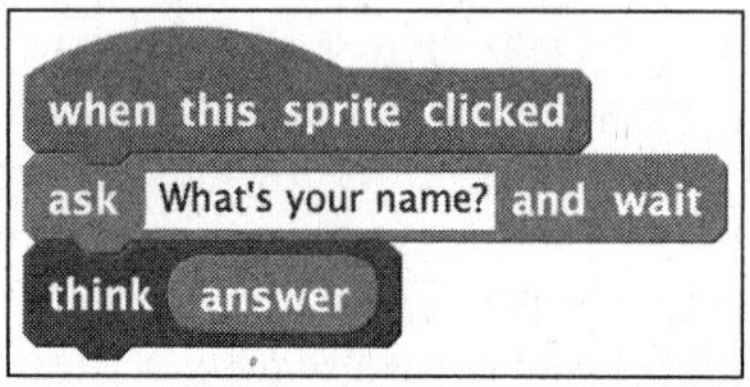

FIGURE 4-6:
Scratch code block using ask and answer to get user input.

After you get an answer, you can use the value stored in answer. For example, you can now show the stored name or words onscreen: Figure 4-7 shows how Scratch Cat can think the answer as though he's pondering your name deeply.

FIGURE 4-7:
Scratch output showing Scratch Cat think the value of the answer variable.

One neat aspect of the answer temporary variable, is that it comes "built-in" to Scratch — you don't have to *declare*, or create, this variable. Later on, you create and use other variables — but you need to create those variables yourself. This process is covered in Chapter 7.

Using Python

In Python, you accept user input by creating your own variable to store the input. You can investigate additional details about Python variables in Chapter 7. But for now, just open a Python editor, such as the one available at pythontutor.com (see Chapter 3). Then type the simple code shown in Figure 4-8 to accept a word in and print a word in Python.

```
Python 3.6

1  name = input("What is your name? ")
2  print (name)
```

Print output
```
What is your name? Buttercup
Buttercup
```

In this code, you create a variable called name and ask for the user to input a value to name by asking, 'What is your name?' Then, you print the value of name as output.

REMEMBER

When naming Python variables, start with an alphanumeric letter or underscore symbol. Do not use any spaces in the variable name. Python variables are case sensitive, so name is a different variable than Name.

When you execute this code, you obtain the results shown in Figure 4-8: a console asking you to submit the name, followed by a printout of the name.

Using HTML and JavaScript

To create an interactive webpage that accepts user input, use HTML and JavaScript together. The following code shows how you can ask a user for their name, submit the name with a button, then show the name onscreen:

```
<!DOCTYPE html>
<html>
<body>
```

```
<p>What is your name?</p>
<input id="userInput"> </input>
<button onclick="submitname()"> Submit </button>
<p id="demo"></p>

<script>
function submitname()
{
  var name=document.getElementById("userInput").value;
  document.getElementById("demo").innerHTML = name;
}
</script>

</body>
</html>
```

Use Notepad (Windows) or TextEdit (Mac) to type the code shown here. The Java-Script code is located inside the <script></script> tags, as shown in Figure 4-9. The code outside these tags is mostly responsible for formatting the information on the page and for calling the JavaScript code. Save the file with an .html extension. For additional details on coding webpages, see Chapter 14.

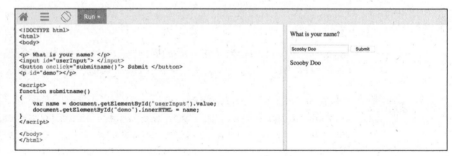

<image name="FIGURE 4-9">
FIGURE 4-9:
Execution of the "word in, word out" program in HTML and JavaScript.
</image>

REMEMBER

At first glance, you and your coder may feel the little program looks somewhat scary. That's because this program requires code covered in other sections of the book. Don't panic! Learning to program is like learning any other foreign language. Sometimes a vocabulary word or symbol is used that you don't yet know. Don't let this trouble you; just keep working with the new commands and in time, you'll be coding like a pro!

Using JavaScript in an app

Using JavaScript in the App Lab at Code.org, you and your coder can write a simple program that asks a user to type his name and then press a button to submit.

The program then shows the name onscreen in a smartphone emulator. Figure 4-10 shows the code.

FIGURE 4-10:
JavaScript code for a "word in, word out" program in the Code.org App Lab.

The code consists of two parts: "set up display" and "set up button event to produce name."

The "set up display" part is comprised of two text labels, a text input field, and a button. Line 2 shows a text label called intro that displays the text "What is your name?" This label is positioned by default in the top-left corner of the screen. Line 3 shows a text input field called nameField that displays " " (blank space); this the where the user types his name. The Line 4 code creates a text label called greeting that displays " " (blank space). This label is positioned in the location where the greeting is placed later. In Line 5, the command setPosition ("greeting", 10, 150, 100, 100) places the greeting label 10 pixels to the right and 150 pixels down from the top-left corner of the screen; it also makes the size of the label 100 pixels wide and 100 pixels high. Lastly, the code in Line 6 creates a button called submitBtn that shows the word Submit. This code is followed by a setPosition command in Line 7 that positions and sizes the button.

The "set up button event to produce name" part begins on Line 9 with an onEvent *event handler,* which causes the function makeName to execute when clicked. The function makeName creates (in Line 10) a variable name and sets it to the value of the text entered into nameField. In Line 11, nameField is hidden so that the user's entry is removed from the screen. Finally, in Line 12, the textLabel greeting field displayed the value of the name variable.

Figure 4-11 shows the operation of the word in, word out program in the smart-phone emulator.

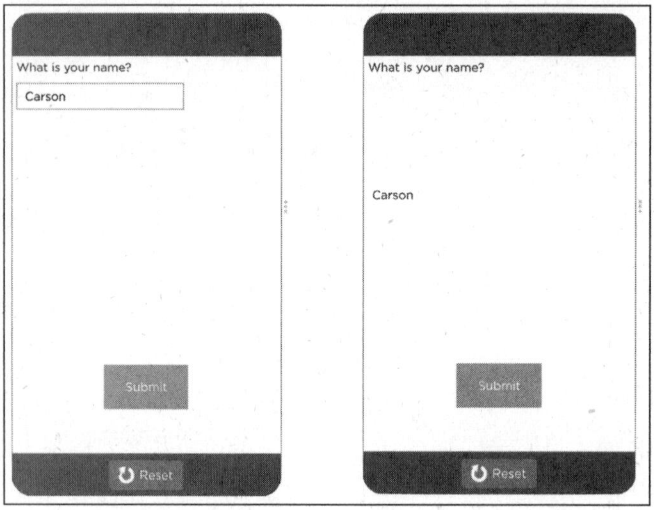

FIGURE 4-11: Operation of the JavaScript code for a "word in, word out" app.

A *default* setting is a setting that is automatically used when the user doesn't take any action, or write any code, to change or override that setting.

TIP

An *event handler* is a coding command that, when triggered, accepts inputs and runs a block of code. The event handler is triggered when it is clicked, swiped, shaken, or otherwise activated.

TIP

Combining Text Onscreen

Your kid likely wants to write code that combines the processes of accepting text input and printing text onscreen. Now that you know how to perform each of these tasks separately, you can put them together!

Using pseudocode

One common example of combining text from different sources is to ask a user for his name, store it in a variable, and then print a greeting that includes the name in the text, along with some other words. A pseudocode expression for this combined print command looks something like this:

```
print ("Congratulations " + name + ", you won a million
    dollars!")
```

Connecting text together, whether it's individual characters or complete words, is called *concatenation*.

TIP

To understand how concatenation works, play an "Idiom Charades" game with your coder using familiar idioms. For example, "Bark up the wrong tree," "Don't cry over spilt milk," "Kill two birds with one stone," "Rain cats and dogs," and "Elvis has left the building." The rules of this charade game are that you inform your partner of how many words in the phrase, then act out each word one at a time. Many kids won't know the idioms, so they have to work one word at a time to complete the phrase. After you finish playing, help your coder to understand that the phrase is comprised of four or five separate words, concatenated together, to create a new, complete phrase.

Using Scratch

In Scratch, you can concatenate text using the `join` command tile as shown in Figure 4-12. The `join` command is located in the Operators category. Note that you can concatenate both variable names and literal text, adding as many `join` tiles as you want! The output shows how `join` allows you to make your program say complete sentences, customized for the user!

WARNING

It can be frustrating to join extensive sections of text using the `join` command in Scratch. Every new chunk of text you concatenate requires an additional `join` command. Think carefully before you attempt to create a giant text paragraph using concatenation in Scratch — it's better to create several small paragraphs to keep the joining manageable.

Using Python and other languages

In Python, you can concatenate text using the + command shown in Figure 4-13. Variable names and literal text can be put together, adding as many + commands as needed. Literal text requires quotation marks around the text, while variables do not.

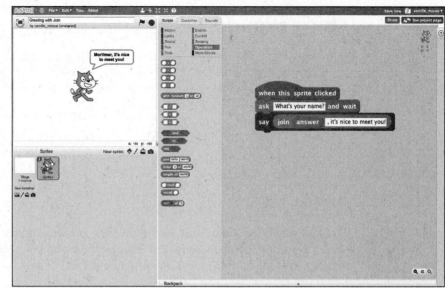

FIGURE 4-12:
Code using `join` to concatenate variables and literal text in Scratch.

Python 3.6

```
1 name = input("What is your name? ")
2 print (name + ", it's nice to meet you!")
```

Print output

```
What is your name? Mortimer
Mortimer, it's nice to meet you!
```

FIGURE 4-13:
Code using + to put together variable values and literal text in Python.

Most other languages your kid encounters use the + code to concatenate text for print output. Follow this format shown here!

WARNING

When concatenating words and numbers, most programming languages require that you convert a number to a type of word, called a string. This removes the property of working with the number mathematically, such as ordering it with other numbers, or doubling its value. For example, the following Python code converts an integer variable, age, to a string as it's concatenated with literals and other string variables (such as a person's name) for printing:

```
age = input("How old are you? ")
print(name + " is " + str(age) + " years old")
```

Formatting Text Onscreen

Your coder may be expressing an interest in formatting text onscreen to give it a more organized appearance, or even some flashy and fun flair! Some programming languages, such as Scratch, don't provide this option. But most programming languages, such as Python, provide codes for special characters and for creating line breaks. For example, this Python command uses a \n code to indicate where a line break occurs:

```
print("To be\nor not to be,\nthat is the question.")
```

This line of code prints like this:

```
To be
or not to be,
that is the question.
```

When formatting text for display in web pages, HTML — the "language of the web" — provides a wide ranges of options. Here is an example of HTML code demonstrating some of these formatting options:

```
<!DOCTYPE html>
<html>
<head>
<title>Greetings from the Web</title>
</head>
<body>
<h1>Formatting Text on the Web</h1>
<br>
<h2>You can use simple HTML tags to format your text.</h2>
<i>Are we having fun yet?</i>
<b>I'm glad you are!</b>
</body>
</html>
```

Figure 4-14 shows how the HTML appears when viewed in a web browser.

Table 4-1 presents several text formatting codes, or tags, your coder can use when creating her HTML code.

TECHNICAL STUFF

When placing text on a webpage, you set font, text color, and text size — as well as many other attributes — using CSS (Cascading Style Sheets). CSS is a language that works with HTML, but is independent of HTML. CSS adapts the display of the webpage for viewing on a wide range of devices small and large. See Chapter 14 for additional information on building webpages.

FIGURE 4-14:
Viewing the
HTML code,
featuring a
variety of text
formats, in a
webpage.

TABLE 4-1   ## Some HTML Text Formatting Codes

Code	Example	What It Means
<b> Howdy! </b>	**Howdy!**	Bold text
<i> Howdy! </i>	*Howdy!*	Italicize text
H ₂ O	H_2O	Subscript text
E = mc ²	$E=mc^2$	Superscript text
<h1> Big Idea </h1>	**Big Idea**	Heading Level 1 (there are 6 levels)
They lived happily ever after. The End.	They lived happily ever after. The End.	Insert line break

A Mad Libs Example

Now that your coder has learned the basics of writing code to input, format, and output text in a computer program, he undoubtedly wants to do something fun with his new skills. Creating a Mad Lib story is the perfect culmination of the skills acquired in this chapter. A Mad Lib is a short, silly story that is missing a few words. Two players play Mad Libs together, with one player asking the other player for words that are used to fill in the missing words. However, the player supplying the words doesn't know "the rest of the story" or how those words will be put together.

TIP

Get the hang of playing Mad Libs! Using a Mad Lib you find online or in a Mad Libs booklet, complete a story with your coder. Bonus: Because Mad Lib stories usually ask for missing words as parts of speech, working on this project reinforces grammatical concepts such as nouns, verbs, adjectives, and more!

First, as outlined in Chapter 2, invite your kid to "think aloud" with you about the big picture of creating a Mad Lib. Here are some steps you and she might brainstorm:

1. Find or create a short paragraph from which you'll remove a few words.

2. Note the part of speech or a description of each word type removed, for example, proper noun, small animal, adverb, or other.

3. Write code that presents simple text instructions for the user to follow.

4. Write code that invites the user to input a word for the first word type, stored as a variable.

5. Repeat Step 4 until the list of missing words is exhausted.

6. Write code to concatenate the input words with literal text to create the complete Mad Lib.

7. Print the complete Mad Lib onscreen for the user to view.

After you and your coder have brainstormed the process for designing and creating the Mad Lib program, your coder might choose to devise a flowchart for the program code. Chapter 2 provides guidance in creating such a flowchart.

Finally, your coder may choose to translate the flowchart into pseudocode (see Chapter 2), or else jump right into writing code for the Mad Lib program. You and your coder can write the Mad Lib program in any language. Figure 4-15 shows an example of the code written in Python.

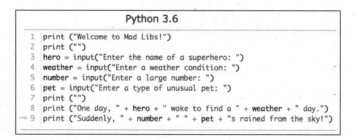

```
                    Python 3.6
1  print ("Welcome to Mad Libs!")
2  print ("")
3  hero = input("Enter the name of a superhero: ")
4  weather = input("Enter a weather condition: ")
5  number = input("Enter a large number: ")
6  pet = input("Enter a type of unusual pet: ")
7  print ("")
8  print ("One day, " + hero + " woke to find a " + weather + " day.")
9  print ("Suddenly, " + number + " " + pet + "s rained from the sky!")
```

FIGURE 4-15: Mad Lib code in Python.

Figure 4-16 shows the output and result of the Mad Lab program in operation. Invite your coder to get creative by adding new variables and literals to her program. The program can be as short and silly, or as long and laughable, as she wants it to be!

```
Print output

Welcome to Mad Libs!

Enter the name of a superhero: Aquaman
Enter a weather condition: sweltering
Enter a large number: 37 trillion
Enter a type of unusual pet: sloth

One day, Aquaman woke to find a sweltering day.
Suddenly, 37 trillion sloths rained from the sky!
```

FIGURE 4-16:
Mad Lib program
in operation.

TIP

It's a good idea to write and test incrementally. As you program, test code often to make sure that each line (or each block, consisting of several lines) does what you want it to be doing before writing additional lines.

REMEMBER

When writing code, it make take a little time, and several attempts, for your coder to get the program operating just as she intends. This process is called *debugging*, or removing the errors from, the code. Encourage your coder to stick with it and use logical strategies for getting her code fully functional. Chapter 13 offers a variety of troubleshooting techniques to debug code.

Chapter **5**

Knowing Where You Are... and Where You're Going

This chapter helps you acquire the skills you need to perform geometry tasks when programming. Specifically, you find out how to position an object and set it in motion onscreen. If your kid is writing code to create an animated game or build a model, then placing objects in different positions and moving them around is a key skill.

Here, you and your coder discover the basics of working with x and y coordinates, as well as how to point an object in any direction. We also show you how to make objects move, set the speed of objects, code some practical programs that include using randomness to scatter many objects into different positions, and determine whether two objects collide.

Acting Out Position, Unplugged

Finding out "where you are" is fundamental to creating any kind of program that involves objects onscreen. In the real world, you use a wide range of descriptions to indicate where you're located (see Figure 5-1).

FIGURE 5-1:
Everyday signs
indicate your
position.

Coding uses systems and rules similar to mathematics to determine position. These rules identify where you are in two directions: the x-direction and the y-direction.

>> x-direction identifies position left to right, horizontally across the screen

>> y-direction identifies position top to bottom, vertically across the screen

The x-direction and the y-direction are each specified by a number. The two numbers are written together to form an (x, y) coordinate pair, or *coordinates*, such as (4, 20) or (100, 200).

TIP

Some programming languages and certain applications, such as electronics projects, also include the z-direction. When three dimensions are involved, the z-direction is the vertical direction — the direction in which gravity acts in the real world.

The coordinate (0, 0) may identify a different position from one programming language to another (see Figure 5-2). When your coder is working in Scratch, (0, 0) the location is the center of the stage. This means that there are coordinates with negative values for x positions to the left of (0, 0), and coordinates with negative values for y positions lower than (0, 0). In JavaScript, (0, 0) is the location at the top-left corner of the screen. As you move down the screen in Scratch, y values decrease, but as you move down the screen in JavaScript, y values increase.

FIGURE 5-2:
Scratch places the
(0, 0) coordinate
in the center of
the screen (left)
while JavaScript
places (0, 0) in the
top-left corner
(right).

(0, 0)

(0, 0)

One way you can understand the big picture of a computer program is to act it out, unplugged. Try playing a classic game of Battleship! (See Figure 5-3). The game, played by you and your young coder, involves each player hiding plastic ships of various sizes on a game board. Alternatively, you can draw a game board on a piece of paper, as a 10 by 10 grid, and then draw ships on the board. Create a variety of ship sizes from two to five grid blocks in size. Label each ship location by its horizontal coordinate, a letter of the alphabet (A through J); and its vertical coordinate, a number (1 through 10). Take turns attempting to "hit" an opponent ship by calling out a location on the game board. The goal is to hit and sink all enemy ships. Again, a key understanding of Battleship is that you can represent position on the two-dimensional game board by a coordinate pair, such a A-5, or H-10.

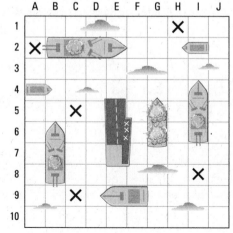

FIGURE 5-3:
Designating
position using a
coordinate pair in
Battleship.

Another fun way to explore coordinates is to play a city scavenger hunt by providing your kid with a number pair that represents the *geolocation* — the latitude and longitude in degrees — of a famous city. (See Figure 5-4.) You can find these geolocations on the Internet in advance. Then provide the list of coordinate pairs to students and invite them to use a traditional map, a globe, or Google Maps to locate the cities. For example, type 36.17° N, 115.14° W into Google Maps to reveal Las Vegas!

REMEMBER

The key takeaway is that you can locate any place in two dimensions using a coordinate pair.

USING COORDINATES TO SCRATCH THAT ITCH

Finding position can be especially important for everyday tasks such as locating a store by its address or "finding the coordinates of Point Z" in geometry class. And it can be extra important when scratching an itch! More, specifically, it can help guide the frustrating process of locating the exact position of an itch in order to guide the nails of the designated stretcher.

Fortunately, there's a Chindogu Back Scratcher's T-Shirt to help guide the process. Chindogu (Chindogu.com) is a Japanese curiosity that takes the form of a nearly useless invention. As Chindogu.com suggests, "It is expected that people with perpetually itchy backs will take to wearing shirts like these at all times and soon be instinctively aware of all coordinates with the grid committed to memory. Meanwhile, for the occasional itcher, the T-Shirt comes with a handy cheat sheet."

Setting and Finding Position

Setting the position of an object means assigning it coordinates to put it in a specific place onscreen. *Finding* the position of an object means identifying its coordinates to know where it's located.

Using pseudocode

While each programming language uses its own structure for setting and finding coordinates, a typical pseudocode expression you may write to set the position of an object looks like this:

```
setx x-coordinate
sety y-coordinate
```

Or

```
setposition (x-coordinate, y-coordinate)
```

To find the current position of an object, you can write pseudocode for each separate coordinate: x-position for the x-coordinate of the object, and y-position for the y-coordinate of the object. You can also write position to describe the object position as a coordinate pair.

Using Scratch to set position

To set the x-coordinate of an object in Scratch, use the set x to *number* command in the Motion category (see Figure 5-5). The minimum value of the x-coordinate ranges is –240, and the maximum value is 240.

FIGURE 5-5:
Use *set x to number* command to set the x-coordinate of an object in Scratch.

To set the y-coordinate of an object in Scratch, use the set y to *number* command in the Motion category (see Figure 5-6). The minimum value of the y-coordinate ranges is –180, and the maximum value is 180.

FIGURE 5-6:
Use *set y to number* command to set the y-coordinate of an object in Scratch.

To set both the x-coordinate and y-coordinate of an object in Scratch, use the go to x: *number* y: *number* command in the Motion category (see Figure 5-7). The range of the x-coordinate value is –240 to 240, and the range of the y-coordinate value is –180 to 180.

TECHNICAL STUFF

In Scratch, you can set the size of an object using the set size to number % command in the Looks category as shown in Figure 5-8. This sets the size of the object as a percentage of its original size. Percentages smaller than 100 shrink the object. Percentages larger than 100 grow the object.

Using Scratch to find position

To find the x-coordinate of an object in Scratch, use the x position command in the Motion category. To find the y-coordinate of an object in Scratch, use the y position command in the Motion category. You and your coder can use these commands in your programs when you need to write commands that require information about an object's position.

As you code, sometimes you want to position an object (sprite) onscreen and then get its coordinates. You can do this for any sprite using either of these methods (see Figure 5-9):

>> Select the checkbox next to the x position command and the y position command in the Motion category to show these values onscreen.

>> On the thumbnail of the sprite, click the "i" icon to expand its information center and then view the x: and y: values displayed there.

In both methods, the coordinates of Scratch Cat are (60, -18).

Using JavaScript

To set both the x-coordinate and y-coordinate of an object in JavaScript, identify the object you want to position, and then use the setPosition command.

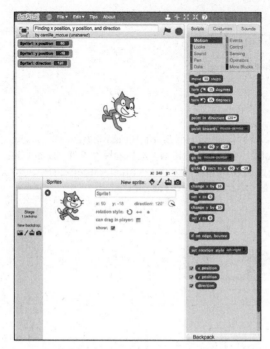

FIGURE 5-9:
Two ways to
view the
current x- and
y-coordinates
of a sprite.

Here are the steps for how to position an image of a mouse onscreen in the Code.
org App Lab, using JavaScript.

1. In App Lab, click the Design button above the emulator of the mobile device.

2. In the Workspace, select Image ⇨ Choose.

   The Choose Assets dialog box opens.

3. Click the Upload button.

4. Select the file you want, and then click the Choose button.

   The uploaded file appears in the dialog box as shown in Figure 5-10. The name
   of the uploaded image file shown here is mouse.png.

5. In the App Lab program workspace, type these commands:

```
image("character", "mouse.png");
setPosition("character", 160, 225, 100, 100);
```

Here is what these commands do: The first command creates an image reference
identification, character, and links the file, mouse.png, to this identification. The
second command displays the image in character according to four quantities:
the x-coordinate of the object, the y-coordinate of the object, the width of the
object in pixels, and the height of the object in pixels.

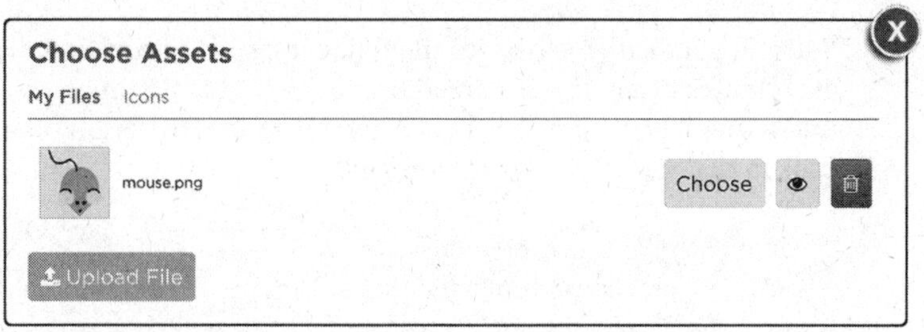

Choose Assets

My Files   Icons

mouse.png   Choose 👁 🗑

⬆ Upload File

FIGURE 5-10:
The Choose
Assets dialog box
for uploading an
image for display
in App Lab.

**TECHNICAL
STUFF**

In App Lab, the range of the x-coordinate value is 0 to 320, and the range of the y-coordinate value is 0 to 450. When using JavaScript to program images displayed on a webpage, these values have larger maximum values, representing the larger size of a computer screen.

Figure 5-11 shows the mouse positioned at the coordinates (160, 225), which is the exact center of the screen. You can see that the mouse is positioned by its upper-left corner where the tip of its tail is located. The mouse has a width of 100 pixels and a height of 100 pixels.

Reset

FIGURE 5-11:
Use the
setPosition
command to set
the position
of an object in
JavaScript.

To find the x-coordinate of an object in JavaScript, use the `getXPosition` (`"character"`); command where `character` is the identification reference of the object. To find the y-coordinate of an object in JavaScript, use the `getY Position("character");` command where `character` is the identification reference of the object.

You and your coder can write the following code to find and display onscreen the coordinates of an object named character. This assumes you have uploaded an image file and assigned it to the reference identification, character. Type this code in the App Lab program workspace.

```
var x = getXPosition("character");
var y = getYPosition("character");
textLabel("xcor");
textLabel("ycor");
setText("xcor", "x-coordinate is " + x);
setText("ycor", "y-coordinate is " + y);
```

Here is how this code works:

>> The var x variable gets the x position and the var y variable gets the y position of the object.

>> The two textLabel commands create locations onscreen, called xcor and ycor, to display information.

>> Each setText command displays a value in a text label. The value of x displays in the xcor label and the value of y displays in the ycor label.

Figure 5-12 shows the output of this code.

FIGURE 5-12:
Use the get XPosition and getYPosition commands to get the position of an object in JavaScript.

ADMIRAL GRACE HOPPER: WRITING NATURAL PROGRAMMING LANGUAGES

Born in 1906, Grace Hopper showed analytical abilities early in life, always wanting to know what made things tick — which explains why, as a child, she disassembled every clock in her house! Encouraged throughout her youth by her parents, Grace pursued the study of math and physics during her university years, earning her PhD in mathematics from Yale.

Grace was serving as a professor at Vassar during World War II when she decided she could do more for her country by joining the United States armed services. In 1942, Grace enlisted in an all-women division of the Navy called WAVES. She was assigned immediately to work on a Bureau of Ships computation project, programming a Mark I computer at Harvard. Grace authored multiple papers on coding and was so impassioned by working in computer science, she continued working at the lab on a Navy contract many years after the war. During this time, she coined one of the most well-known terms in the practice of computer programming: bug. The story was that, while working on the Harvard Mark II computer, a glitch repeated, disrupting program processing. When Grace and her colleagues tracked down the problem, it turned out to be a live moth caught in an electrical switch inside the computer. By removing the moth, the first "debugging" took place! Grace recorded the event in the computer log book — and included the "bug" in her entry.

Photo credit: https://upload.wikimedia.org/wikipedia/commons/8/8a/H96566k.jpg

(continued)

(continued)

After the war, Grace was asked to consult on developing the UNIVAC computer, an early computer brought to market in 1950. There, she worked on crafting a high-level programming language, called COBOL, which uses natural "human" words to make it easier for humans to write code. She also developed what is known as a *compiler* — a tool that translated high-level programming code into machine code that the computer could process. Grace pointed out that, with her creations, "I could say 'Subtract income tax from pay' instead of trying to write that in octal code or using all kinds of symbols."

Because of her extraordinary skill set and work ethic. Grace continued rising through the ranks of the Navy, eventually reaching the rank of Admiral. She also kept consulting with many of the early, giant, computer companies. During these years, she encouraged the migration from big, centralized systems to networked desktop computers, and she contributed to the development of yet another programming language, FORTRAN. Grace Hopper recognized the need to stay nimble, and continue evolving when working in the world of computer science. As she once said, "Humans are allergic to change. I try to fight that. That's why I have a clock on my wall that runs counter-clockwise."

Photo credit: https://techcrunch.com/2016/11/17/grace-hopper-and-margaret-hamilton-awarded-presidential-medal-of-freedom-for-computing-advances/

Positioning Objects Randomly

Your coder can position an object at a random position onscreen. She can use a random position for the x-coordinate, the y-coordinate, or both.

Using Scratch

To set a random x-coordinate for an object in Scratch, use two commands: the set x to *number* command in the Motion category and the pick random *number* to *number* command in the Operators category. Assemble the commands as shown in Figure 5-13. The minimum value for the random command is -240, and the maximum value is 240.

FIGURE 5-13:
Set a random
x-position of an
object in Scratch.

TIP

Set a random x-coordinate and a constant y-coordinate when you want to create a game in which objects fall from changing locations at the top of the screen. For example, your coder can create a game in which "it's raining cats and dogs" such that the cats and dogs appear to fall from all over the sky, dropping down from the top of the screen at random x positions.

To set a random y-coordinate for an object in Scratch, use two commands: the set y to *number* command in the Motion category and the pick random *number* to *number* command in the Operators category. Assemble the commands as shown in Figure 5-14. The minimum value for the random command is -180, and the maximum value is 180.

FIGURE 5-14:
Set a random
y-position of an
object in Scratch.

TIP

Set a constant x-coordinate and a random y-coordinate when you want to create a game in which an objects launches from a random position at the side of the screen. For example, your coder can create a Paddle Bounce game in which the ball enters the playfield from the left side, and the paddle moves vertically along the right side. Your coder wants the ball to enter from different positions up and down the screen to create variety for the player during the game.

To set a random position, including both x-coordinate and y-coordinate, for an object in Scratch, use the go to random position command in the Motion category (see Figure 5-15). Note that the go to command tile can toggle between mouse-pointer and random position.

TIP

Your coder can position many objects into random positions at one time to create a scattering effect. This is a common technique for creating a game app that scatters things for a player to collect. This technique also works for creating real-world models when you want to scatter people in random positions in a location, such as shoppers in a mall. See the Asteroid Blaster project at the end of this chapter for a simple game that uses this technique.

Using JavaScript

To set a random x-coordinate of an object in JavaScript, identify the object you want to position, and then use the setPosition command along with a randomNumber command to identify the range of x-values that you want. The minimum of the x-coordinate value is 0 and the maximum is 320.

To set a random y-coordinate of an object in JavaScript, identify the object you want to position, and then use the setPosition command along with a randomNumber command to identify the range of y-values that you want. The minimum of the y-coordinate value is 0 and the maximum is 450.

Here are the steps for setting a random position of an image of a mouse onscreen in the Code.org App Lab, using JavaScript. (See the JavaScript example in the previous section, "Setting and Finding Position" for details on adding an image to the screen.) This code sets both a random x-coordinate and a random y-coordinate for the image:

```
image("character", "mouse.png");
setPosition("character", randomNumber(0, 320),
    randomNumber(0, 450), 100, 100);
```

Figure 5-16 shows the mouse positioned at randomly selected coordinates. The Run button is pressed three times, with the result of each press shown.

FIGURE 5-16:
Randomly
selected position
of a mouse on
three execution
cycles of code in
JavaScript.

Setting and Finding Direction

Setting the direction of an object means pointing it at any angle around a circle. *Finding* the direction of an object means determining the angle at which it is pointed.

The starting angle for direction is measured as 0 degrees, and there are 360 degrees of measurement as you rotate around the circle. The 360 degree direction represents a full rotation, and identifies the same direction as 0 degrees. The headings of a compass are each separated by 90 degrees. If you start at North and rotate 90 degrees clockwise, you are facing East; if you rotate another 90 degrees clockwise, you are facing South.

TECHNICAL
STUFF

The 0 degree position for direction may identify a different compass heading from one programming language to another.

Using pseudocode

A typical pseudocode expression you can write to set the direction of an object is:

```
setHeading angle
```

Here, angle can be any value from 0 degrees to 360 degrees.

In some programming languages, angle is measured in a unit called *radians.* Two pi radians equals 360 degrees — an entire circle.

Using Scratch

When your coder is working in Scratch, use the `point in direction` *angle* command to set the angular direction of an object. A direction of 0 degrees is North; measurement around the circle is clockwise so that 90 degrees is East, 180 degrees is South, and 270 degrees (also called -90 degrees) is West. Figure 5-17 shows a command that sets the heading to 120 degrees (which is southeast).

You and your coder can find `setdirection` commands in programming languages that are geared towards video game creation. This includes GameSalad and Swift. LOGO-based languages and Python, through the Tkinter module, also include directional commands. JavaScript and Java are not especially well-suited to exploring `setdirection` commands at an introductory level as this type of content is the not the main programming focus of these languages.

To find the direction of an object in Scratch, use the `direction` command in the Motion category (see Figure 5-18). Your coder can use this command in her programs when she needs to write commands that require information about an object's direction.

direction

As you code, sometimes you want to find an object's current direction. You can do this for any sprite using either of these methods (refer to Figure 5-9):

>> Select the checkbox next to the `direction` command in the Motion category to show this value onscreen.

>> On the thumbnail of the sprite, click the "i" icon to expand its information center and then view the direction value displayed there.

TECHNICAL STUFF

Setting values and finding values of variables is a common activity in programming. In languages such as Java, coders often perform "set" and "get" tasks through small subprograms called *methods* (see Chapter 15). For example, a programmer writing code for a veterinary office may create an object that represents a pet. The program includes a `setter` method that allows the vet to create a record for a new client by setting the name, breed, and age of the pet. The program also includes code allowing the vet to get the name, breed, and age of the pet (from the saved information) using a `getter` method.

Setting Object Direction Randomly

Your coder can point an object at a random angle onscreen. He can rotate an object any degree angle to create variation in the heading at which the object points.

Using Scratch

When your coder is working in Scratch, use two commands to point an object in a random direction: the `point in direction` *angle* command in the Motion category and the `pick random` *number* to *number* command in the Operators category. The random number range is 0 to 360 degrees (see Figure 5-19).

FIGURE 5-19:
Set a random direction of an object in Scratch.

point in direction (pick random 0 to 359)

TIP

Because 0 degrees and 360 degrees are the same position, angle measure is often set as 0 to 359, or as 1 to 360. The random number picker only produces whole numbers, so limiting the range this way prevents duplication of the 0 angle position.

TIP

You and your coder can set object direction randomly for each object when you want to create multiple objects onscreen that can move in different directions.

Turning

Turning means changing the direction that an object is pointing it. You can turn an object left or right. You can also code repeated turning to create rotation, like a spinning top.

Using pseudocode

A typical pseudocode expression you can write to turn an object is:

```
turn angle
```

Here, a clockwise turn angle can be any value from 0 degrees to 360 degrees. Similarly, a counterclockwise turn can be any value from 0 to −360 degrees.

A typical pseudocode expression you can write to make an object rotate continuously is:

```
forever [turn angle]
```

This command causes the object to keep turning forever. Use a small turn angle to make the object rotate slowly. Increase the turn angle to make the object turn faster. For example, turn 10 creates a faster turn rate than turn 5. You can also add a wait, or delay command inside the forever command to give additional control over the turn speed.

Using Scratch

When you and your coder are working in Scratch, use a turn angle degrees command to turn an object. There are two command tiles for the turn: a turn right command (clockwise) and a turn left command (counterclockwise). Use any number of degrees, including decimal values if needed, from 0 to 360 (see Figure 5-20).

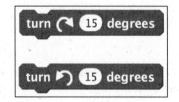

FIGURE 5-20: Use turn angle degrees commands to turn an object in Scratch.

REMEMBER

When combining the random command with turns, set the range of whole numbers from 0 to 359 to avoid duplication of the 0 angle position.

See Figure 5-21 to see how you can combine the turn command with forever (in the Control category of commands) to make the object spin without stopping.

FIGURE 5-21:
Use forever
with turn angle
degrees to
make an object
spin without
stopping in
Scratch.

```
forever
    turn ↻ 5 degrees
```

Acting Out Motion, Unplugged

Moving an object means changing its position onscreen. You and your young coder can move an object whenever you want to code a car to drive or a ball to bounce.

Get up out of your seat, gather some friends, and play a little game of Traffic Light (see Figure 5-22) to set the stage for working with motion! Traffic Light is an updated version of the game Red Light, Green Light that includes a Yellow Light and turn signals. It requires players to move at different speeds, change directions, start and stop, and occasionally move backwards.

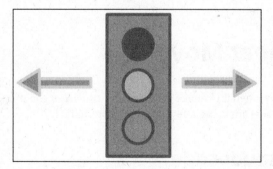

FIGURE 5-22:
Play Traffic Light
to set the stage
for working with
motion.

Here are the rules:

>> The person who is the commander stands at one end of a gym or field. All the players stand at the opposite end of the field.

>> Players are motionless until the commander calls out a command.

>> At any time, and in any time interval, the commander calls out a command indicating the color of the light.

>> When the commander calls out "Green Light" players run towards the commander. When the commander calls out "Yellow Light" players walk towards the commander. When the commander calls out "Red Light" players stop.

>> When the commander calls out "Right Turn" players must make one square turn (a 90-degree turn) to the right, relative to their current position. When the commander calls out "Left Turn" the players must make one square turn (a 90-degree turn) to the left, relative to their current position.

>> When the commander calls out "Reverse" players must continue facing their current direction, but move backwards on the commands that follow.

>> Any player who doesn't follow the direction issued by the commander is out and must return to the starting line to re-enter the game.

The goal is to be the first player to reach the commander — the person calling the commands.

TIP

Ask your coders to discuss the role of sequence with regard to the commands issued by the commander. Encourage her to draw parallels between the execution of this game and the execution of a computer program!

WARNING

Remind Traffic Light players to move carefully and watch out for other players, especially when they are moving backwards, to avoid collisions.

Making an Object Move

An object moves when it changes position over time. You can program an object to move in your program using a few different commands.

Using pseudocode

Each programming language uses its own special command to move an object, and you can write different pseudocode expressions to represent the process of moving an object onscreen. The move *number* (measured in number of pixels) pseudocode command represents moving an object some distance in the direction in which the object is pointing. An example is move 5 or move 15, with the larger number representing a larger distance moved.

Another way to make an object move is to change its x-coordinate or its y-coordinate.

```
changex number
changey number
```

Changing the x-coordinate forever creates horizontal motion. Changing the y-coordinate forever creates vertical motion.

To make an object move constantly, place a motion command inside a `forever` command:

```
forever [move number]
forever [changex number]
forever [changey number]
```

TIP

Move forever commands are useful for making games and models. For example, coding several cars to move forever in the horizontal direction allows your coder to create traffic for a Crossy Road–style game.

Using Scratch

To make an object move in Scratch, set the direction of the object using two commands: the `point in direction` *angle* command in the Motion category, and the `move` *number* `steps` in the Operators category (see Figure 5-23). The range of `point in direction` is 0 to 360 degrees. For the `move` command, use any number; negative numbers move the object backwards. The larger the number, the bigger the move. Note that `move` makes the sprite object move in a straight line, not spin in place.

FIGURE 5-23: Use the `point in direction` *angle* command and the `move` *number* `steps` number command to move an object in Scratch.

To create horizontal motion, use `change x by` *number* using any number; negative numbers move the object to the left and positive numbers move the object to the right. See Figure 5-24.

FIGURE 5-24:
Use the change
x by *number*
command to
move an object
horizontally in
Scratch.

To create vertical motion, use change y by *number* using any number; positive numbers move the object up and negative numbers move the object down. See Figure 5-25.

FIGURE 5-25:
Use the change
y by *number*
command to
move an object
vertically in
Scratch.

To make an object move constantly, place any motion command inside a forever command. Figure 5-26 shows the shows the move *number* steps inside forever.

FIGURE 5-26:
Place any move
command inside
the forever
command to
create constant
motion in
Scratch.

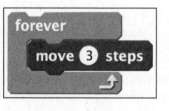

**TECHNICAL
STUFF**

Scratch doesn't have a wrapping feature on its stage. When a moving object reaches the edge of the screen, it stops. You can counteract this by making an object bounce off the side of the screen. To do so, add an if on edge, bounce command as shown in Figure 5-27.

FIGURE 5-27:
Add a if on
edge, bounce
command to
make an object
bounce off the
edge of the stage.

Another way you can keep an object moving at the edge of the stage in Scratch is to create your own code for wrapping. You can make an object leave one edge of the stage, and then appear at the opposite edge of the stage. Figure 5-28 shows code for an object that moves right and when it reaches the right side of the stage instantly repositions itself on the left side of the stage. You can find the inequality operators in the Operators category. See Chapter 10 for additional information on forever and repeat until loops.

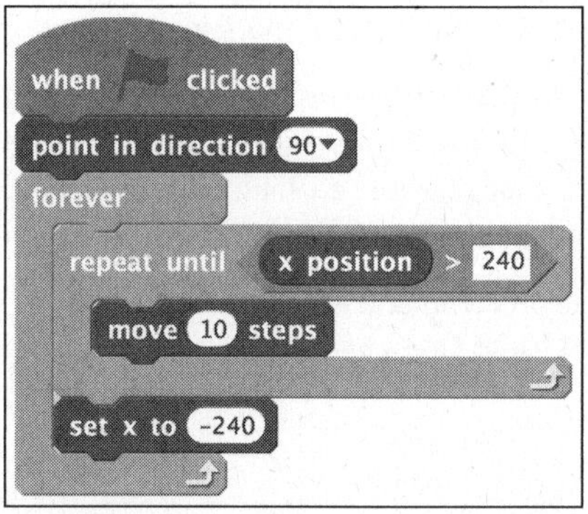

FIGURE 5-28:
Create stage wrapping so that an object appears to continue moving when it reaches the edge of the stage.

```
when       clicked
point in direction 90▼
forever
    repeat until   x position  > 240
        move 10 steps

    set x to -240
```

Using JavaScript

To make an object move in JavaScript, you code the starting position of the object and then make the position change a small quantity during a time interval.

The following code moves a mouse object left to right, across the screen in the Code.org App Lab, using JavaScript. (See the JavaScript example in the previous section, "Setting and Finding Position" for details on adding an image to the screen.) The mouse x-coordinate begins at 0. Its y-coordinate stays constant at 150.

```
image("character", "mouse.png");
var xpos = 0;
timedLoop(250, function () {
 xpos = xpos + 1;
            setPosition("character", xpos, 150, 100, 100);
            });
```

Here's what each line of code does in this program:

» Line 1 identifies the object you want to move. For example,
   image("character", "mouse.png");

>> Line 2 creates a variable for x-position of the object (xpos) if you want to make the object move horizontally. Alternatively, create a variable for the y-position of the object (ypos) if you want the object to move vertically. (For more information on working with variables, see Chapter 7.) Initialize the variable by setting it equal to the starting value for the object. For example, `var xpos = 0;`.

>> Line 3 creates a timed loop to indicate how often the object will move. In a timed loop, 1000 equals 1 second. A time loop set at 250 executes one time every quarter-second. (See Chapter 10 for more information on loops.)

>> Line 4 increments the position variable inside the timed loop. (For more information on working with variables, see Chapter 7). This causes the position of the object to change a little each time the loop executes. For example, `xpos = xpos + 1;`.

>> Line 5 uses a `setPosition` command inside the timed loop to set the object x-coordinate to `xpos`.

Asteroid Blaster

You can combine scattering, motion, and direction code to create a simple scene of objects flying and bouncing around onscreen. Adding an event such as clicking an object to make it disappear can help your coder turn the scene into a game!

Figure 5-29 shows an example of code, in Scratch, for a simple Asteroid Blaster game you can code using the commands and concepts in this chapter. All commands are on the Rocks sprite (which looks a lot like an asteroid!).

Here are some tips for writing this code:

>> Use the scissors tool to cut Scratch Cat from the stage.

>> At the Stage thumbnail, choose New Backdrop ⇨ Choose Backdrop from Library icon and select Stars from the library

>> In the Sprites area, choose New Sprite ⇨ Choose Sprite from Library icon and select Rocks from the library. The Rocks sprite serves as one asteroid.

>> On the Rocks sprite, assemble the code tiles in Figure 5-29. Note that the `clone` command creates copies of the Rocks sprite to make it appear that many asteroids are located on the stage. Adjust the number of asteroid rocks you want to create in the `repeat` code. For more information on repeats and other loops, see Chapter 10.

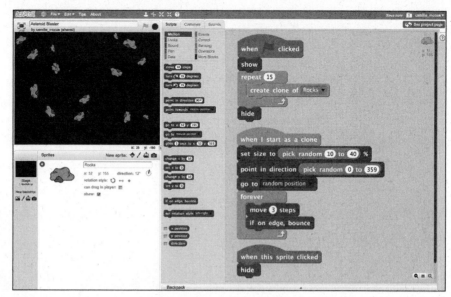

FIGURE 5-29:
Scattering,
motion, and
direction codes
are combined to
build an Asteroid
Blaster game.

**TECHNICAL
STUFF**

REMEMBER

The Asteroid Blaster program uses a clone command to create clones of the Rocks sprite. Each clone possesses the same attributes and behaviors of the original Rocks sprite. When the program is not executing, the clones do not exist and are not visible.

The `when green flag clicked` and `when this sprite clicked` commands are *event handlers.* Event handlers react to an action by the user, such as a click, by executing some code.

The finished game looks like Figure 5-29. The user starts the game by clicking the green flag. She then tries to blast all the asteroids by clicking each one with her mouse. Try creating your own version of the game, modifying commands and the sprite object to create your own custom version!

Chapter 6

Getting Fancy with Graphics and Sound

Using graphics (images, animations, and videos) and sound in your programs can make them more exciting, personal, and bring them to life. This chapter helps your young coder find the graphics and sounds you're looking for, and gives you tips on knowing which file types and sizes are best for the program you're trying to write. A lot of graphics and sounds are available online for free, but finding ones that are safe, legal, and appropriate is important.

Aside from image or sound sizes, this chapter also shows how to combine images and sounds in your programs to make them come to life. For example, in video games when the player clicks a chicken, they might hear a "squawk-A!". And when the player walks through mud they might hear "squish-squish."

You and your coder can use graphics and images to go beyond the built-in assets that some programming environments provide, and make each program you write unique. This is a great way to lead a group of young coders in a similar activity, while enabling them to each be creative and create something different!

Sizes of Images and Sounds, Unplugged

Images and sounds are both represented in digital forms. Images, for example, are represented by pixels, which are tiny dots that can display light. Each pixel can have one color, and an entire image can have any number of pixels. For example, a simple black-and-white image of a smiley face could be 10 pixels by 10 pixels and each pixel is either black or white, similar to the left image in Figure 6-1.

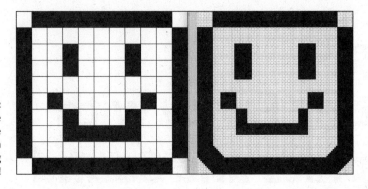

FIGURE 6-1:
More pixels in the same space create a smoother looking smiley face!

But you could also make an image a black-and-white smiley that was 100 pixels by 100 pixels in the same amount of physical space. Imagine if each of the large squares, either black or white, were really 100 squares each. You could make your image more precise because each pixel, still restricted to only one color, is smaller. The right image in Figure 6-1 shows how the bottom of the face could be more rounded if you had more pixels. You can imagine spending the time to make each of the 10,000 pixels either black or white to create an overall image which appears to have rounded edges and circular eyes.

Sound files are stored similarly, using small chunks of information. Instead of pixels, each sound has a certain number of samples per second. Each sample can represent a tone. So a low sample rate sound doesn't have a lot of details in the music compared to a high sample rate sound. You can hear an example of this on YouTube (`https://www.youtube.com/watch?v=96jFvdteqWI`).

Activities surrounding images and sounds

A fun activity to do with young coders to introduce them to digital media is a pixel art challenge. Give them two different pieces of grid paper; one where there are 10x10 squares and one where there are 100x100 squares. Then give them an image and ask them to re-create the image on each sheet of paper, but each square can only be ONE color. This shows them how, with more pixels, you can have more detail in your image.

Another activity you can do with your coder is to set up the room with simple, drawn images of different things that would make different noises: animals, different terrains, even objects like cars. Place the images around the room and when you touch one, have your coder make a noise that would make sense for that image. Then switch who is walking around touching images, and who is making the noises. This activity can help your young coder understand that images can be associated with noises. This is a fun project to do when you transition from an unplugged activity to a coding activity, a sound board of sorts!

Knowing your sizes

Knowing the right sizes of images and sounds to use for your programs is going to be important for making your programs run quickly, smoothly, and look and sound good. It's also useful to learn for other applications as well, such as social media profile images and storing songs on your iPhone. For example, if you want to upload an image to Twitter for your profile picture, the image must be at least 400 pixels by 400 pixels. If the image has fewer pixels, then Twitter stretches your profile picture to fill the space and it looks pixelated and blurry. The image also must be less than 2MB.

Although the number of pixels or sample rate of an image or sound is important for looks, the size of the actual file (in K or MB) is important as well. Most images you work with should be under 500K and most sounds you work with should be around 1MB — these are short sounds like a knock at the door. A typical song that is about 3.5 minutes long is around 3.5MB.

REMEMBER

The smaller the files, the easier downloading and uploading your media is, and the faster your programs can load your media. Anyone using your programs will appreciate how fast they run!

Using Graphics in Your Programs

Finding, downloading, and using graphics in your program is fast and easy, as long as you know how to find ones that are the right size, legal to use, and in the right format for the application you are using. The next few sections guide you through what you need to know to successfully make your programs more unique with pictures!

Image file types

There are two main types of image file types: raster and vector.

Raster file types essentially define each pixel in the image, specifically the placement of pixels to form the image, and the percentage of red, green, and blue that the pixel displays. You're most likely to encounter raster file types in your everyday interactions with digital images. Raster file types don't re-size as well as vector file types. To double the size of a raster file type image, the computer essentially creates new pixels, giving it the color of the average color of the pixels surrounding the location of the new pixel. This is why if you download a raster file type image, and make it bigger, it becomes blurry.

The three types of images that you mostly likely work with are JPEG, PNG, and GIF. JPEG images use a compression algorithm to store the information about each pixel that typically makes the file size smaller, but can cause the quality of the image to deteriorate after saving and re-saving the image many times. JPEG images are saved as .jpg or .jpeg, interchangeably. PNG and GIF images use a lossless compression algorithm to store the information about each pixel, making the file sizes larger, but keeping the quality of the image. Both have transparency, meaning that if you find a PNG or GIF online that you want to use, you can remove a solid background from the image for use in your programs. The animation capabilities of GIF files have made them popular in sharing simple animations with few colors. PNG images are saved as .png and GIF images are stored as .gif. You can easily convert an image from one file type to another, as shown in Figure 6-2.

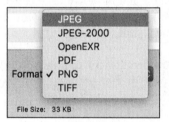

FIGURE 6-2: Exporting images to another type.

Vector file types contain more information than raster files, such as geometric shapes found within the image. Vector file types your coder is likely to encounter are SVG and CGB, and are often used with complex image applications (for example, Photoshop). Some programming languages, such as Scratch, contain assets that include vector images. The geometric shapes in these images can be selected and altered individually to create new composite images.

Creating images

Using images in your programs makes the programs you write more unique and personalized. So creating your own images to use in your programs can be rewarding. One easy way your young coder can create his own images is to take a picture with a digital camera or mobile phone, and save the image onto your computer. Images from digital cameras and mobile phones often are JPEG or PNG, and most programming applications allow you to use both formats.

Other than taking real photos with a camera, you can also create digital images on your computer. You can use high-end image applications such as Photoshop or Illustrator, but you can also use free apps like Microsoft Paint (Windows) or Google AutoDraw. Recently, a lot of online applications make it relatively easy to make images that you might often use on social media. Your coder may also want to check out Canva.com — a great, free option, especially for making background images for the programs he writes.

Another great way to get young coders involved in creating their own characters and images for their programs is to have them draw on paper, and either scan the image or take a picture with your digital camera or mobile phone. This can make a program even more unique and creative! After an image is on your hard drive, you can often remove any white space to make the character more realistic. Figure 6-3 shows how to get rid of unwanted white space in a PNG image using the Preview application on a Mac: Use the magic wand to select the background, delete it, and re-save the image. The same process can be used to remove a background when working in Paint.

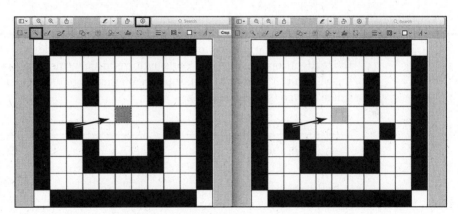

FIGURE 6-3:
Removing unwanted white space using Preview on a Mac.

Finding images on the web

Finding images on the Internet can be fairly easy, but finding the right images that are legal to use, and the right format and size, can be tricky. One of the first places to search is Google Images; go to google.com in your web browser, and enter a search term, and in the list of results click Images at the top.

TIP

Searching through Google Images can yield great results; however, if your coder is young, you might want to consider turning on the Safe Search feature, just in case a search query displays something inappropriate. It's also always advisable to conduct searches *with* your coder, to make sure you know what he's looking at and what he's downloading. To turn Safe Search on, choose Settings ⇨ Search Settings and check the box next to the Safe Search option. Figure 6-4 shows these steps.

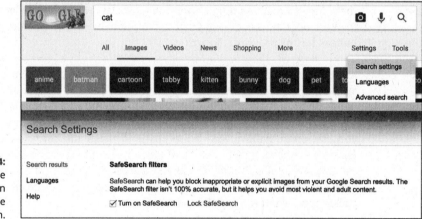

FIGURE 6-4:
How to enable
Safe Search on
Google Image
search.

The next, most important thing to do is to make sure you're downloading images that you're legally allowed to use. Google Images has made this a lot easier with a Usage Rights option. Click the Tools button and a new menu bar appears above the image results. Choose one of the options on the Usage Rights menu that is appropriate for you (see Figure 6-5):

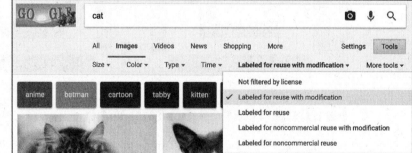

FIGURE 6-5:
Choosing the
right usage rights
on Google Image
search.

- » **Labeled for Reuse with Modification:** Choose this one if you plan to publish the image elsewhere where you expect to make money.

- » **With Modification:** Choose this option if you think you might want to make any changes to it; for example, remove white space, crop the image, or add annotations to it.

- » **Labeled for Noncommercial Reuse with Modification:** This option is probably the one that suits you best. You can edit the image if you'd like and use it in your programs.

REMEMBER

It's important to make sure that your young coder understands why it's important to find and use images that she's legally allowed to use. Many people make careers on creating digital media for others to use. Some of these people have opened their creations for free, public use, while others rely on the income they receive from selling these creations. Just like your coder wouldn't want someone taking the program that she writes and using it for free, without any credit to her, these artists have made specific decisions regarding how they want to share what they have made.

After you find an image that you like, click it to get more information about it, such as the size of the image in pixels, the website where you can get the image, and the link directly to the image. Google also provides you with other images that are similar to the image you have chosen. See Figure 6-6.

FIGURE 6-6:
Google Images provides helpful information including image size, image source, and related images.

If you click View Image, a new tab opens with a URL directly to the image. This is useful if you want to import images into App Lab, for example. If you click Visit, a new tab opens to the website where this image originates. You can typically find other images on the same site and might end up finding a good source of images for future projects, too. Some of the most popular are pexels.com and pixelbay. com. From the website, you can often download different sizes of the same image, and sometimes even different file types.

Sometimes you find a free image on a website like pexels.com that is legal to use within your programs. However, a lot of these websites also *sell* images. So if you decide to find images on a website, make sure that each image you download and use is either free and legal to use, or that you pay for them.

Importing a JPEG or PNG in Scratch

Using custom images in Scratch is very easy and can be rewarding for your young coder. This section shows how to get your own image into Scratch instead of using a sprite or costume that Scratch provides. After you find and download the image you want to add into Scratch as a new sprite, follow these instructions for getting it into your program. Open Scratch and follow these steps:

1. **Click Create in the upper-left corner.**

   The Scratch editor now opens.

2. **In the Sprites area in the bottom-left corner of the editor, click the File Upload button (see Figure 6-7), and choose your image.**

   You now see an "Uploading Image" message in the stage area.

FIGURE 6-7:
File upload on Scratch for new sprites.

3. **(Optional) When your image is uploaded, make any alterations you want to it.**

   - *Remove the background:* Click the magic wand and outline the part of the image you want to keep, as shown in Figure 6-8.

   - *Resize the image:* Click the Selector, and then click and drag around the entire sprite. Let go of your mouse, and you can use the squares on the corners of the blue selection square to re-size the image.

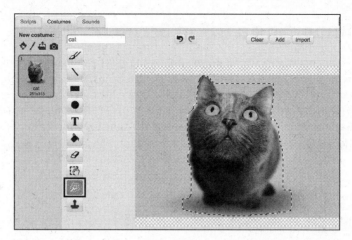

FIGURE 6-8:
Remove the background of a sprite in Scratch.

Now your sprite is on your stage, and you can select it and add code to it, just like you do with the sprites that Scratch provides!

WARNING

When you resize any sprite in Scratch, always make sure that you center the sprite. Though it can be hard to see, a small crosshairs is at the center of the Costume editor, as shown in Figure 6-9. If your sprite is not centered on this crosshair, then when you write code for your sprite to turn right 90 degrees, for example, the sprite turns about the crosshair, *not* the center of the sprite, making it look like the sprite isn't turning correctly.

TIP

In Scratch, your coder can also import an image as a costume to be worn by a sprite.

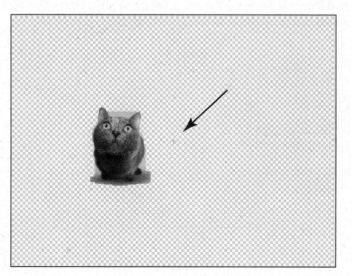

FIGURE 6-9:
Ensure your sprites are centered on the crosshairs in Scratch's Costume editor.

Importing a GIF in Scratch

To import a GIF in Scratch, you follow the exact same instructions as the previous section for importing a JPEG or PNG. The neat thing about using a GIF is that if you find an animated one (like the GIF found at https://upload.wikimedia.org/ wikipedia/commons/7/72/Sleeping-cat.gif) Scratch automatically imports each frame of the animation as a new costume for your sprite! Figure 6-10 shows the sleeping cat GIF imported into Scratch.

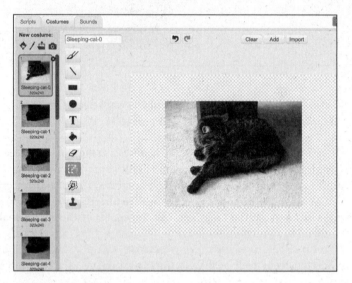

FIGURE 6-10:
Costumes created for each frame in an animated GIF when in Scratch.

And then you can write a small program to make the animation play! Figure 6-11 shows this program.

FIGURE 6-11:
A simple program to animated a GIF in Scratch.

Importing a JPEG, PNG, or GIF in JavaScript

Importing images into Code.org's App Lab using JavaScript is very easy. All you need to know is the URL of the image to load it into the program. You should make sure you find an image that is about 200 pixels by 200 pixels. If you're using Google Images to find your images, click the View Image button on the image that you choose, and copy the URL of the image. After you have the URL of the image you want to use, follow these steps to put the image in your app:

1. **Click the App Lab button under the Start a New Project heading.**

Under the UI Controls category of blocks is an `image` block.

```
image("ID", "URL");
```

If you don't see this placeholder code, simply type it yourself.

2. **Replace** `ID` **with the name you want to use to reference this image and** `URL` **with the URL of the image you want to use.**

Your URL might be really long, which is okay!

```
image("cat", "https://upload.wikimedia.org/wikipedia/commons/thumb/c/c5/
    PEO-smiling_cat_face_with_heart_shaped_eyes-7.svg/200px-PEO-smiling_
    cat_face_with_heart_shaped_eyes-7.svg.png");
```

3. **Click Run on the phone emulator on the left of your App Lab environment to see your picture!**

If you decide to use an animated GIF in App Lab, the animation automatically plays when you click Run. Try it out! Just replace the URL with one like `https://upload.wikimedia.org/wikipedia/commons/7/72/Sleeping-cat.gif` and click Run.

TIP

If you want to upload an image that you've saved on your computer into App Lab, you can do that too! Just make sure you're in Blocks View by clicking Show Blocks in the top right of your App Lab coding environment. Then, click the down arrow that is directly to the left of the URL string, and select Choose. A dialog box opens where you can choose the image file you already have on your computer, and it uploads directly to Code.org!

Adding Sound to Your Programs

Using images to make your programs more interesting is fun, but adding sound to your programs really brings them to life. Just a fair warning, after you teach your young coder how to add sounds, he may never want to stop playing the silly fart noise that he found! It might be helpful to have headphones for this next section, especially if you're leading a group of young coders.

Sound file types

Just like with images, sound files are broken into three categories; uncompressed, lossless compression, and compressed (lossy compressed).

>> Uncompressed audio file types such as WAV (the audio file type most used on Windows computers) have no compression at all. These files are therefore larger, but have a high quality of playback, because every tone is represented within the file as it was originally recorded. Sound effects including creaky doors and howling wolves are usually WAV files.

>> Lossless compression audio file types do some compression, which allows the file to be a bit smaller, but the data is still 100 percent represented within the file.

>> Compressed audio files such as MP3 (the audio file type most used on devices universally) are the smallest of the audio files because information is removed from the file such as parts of sound that have the least effect on what humans can hear. This can cause MP3 audio files to have a reduction in quality compared to WAV audio files. This is how most music files are stored.

You most likely encounter WAV and MP3 file types in the digital sounds your coder works with, and in this chapter we focus on using MP3 files.

Creating original sounds

Creating original sounds can be a lot of fun for you and your coder. You can create song clips that you sing yourself, or make silly noises that only you know how to make. Capturing those sounds digitally isn't too difficult either.

One of the easiest ways is to use a mobile phone. Most mobile phones have a recorder app available in the app store. For example, on the iPhone you can use the free Voice Recorder and Audio Editor app to easily record something you say, and then share the MP3 that gets created either through AirDrop, email, or some other app that you use to get data from your phone to your computer.

If you're writing a program in Scratch and want to create an original sound, you can choose the sprite that the sound is available to, then click the Sound tab, and click the microphone at the top center of the programming environment. A recorder opens, and as long as you have speakers on your computer, you can record an audio sound.

The first time you try creating a sound on Scratch, you have to give your web browser and Flash access to your microphone. You most likely see two popup windows asking for permission to use the microphone. Make sure that you do this with your young coder.

Finding sounds on the web

When you want to find high quality MP3 audio files on the Internet to use in your programs, it's important that you only use audio files that you're legally allowed to use. One of the best places to find sounds is on soundbible.com. soundbible.com has thousands of audio clips available completely for free, as well as some that you can pay for. If you go directly to `http://soundbible.com/royalty-free-sounds-1.html` you find audio clips that you can download that either have Attribution 3.0 or Public Domain licenses.

Attribution 3.0 simply means that you're allowed to use the file (non-commercially), but you have to give credit to the original creator of the sound. So, if you use one of these sounds in a Scratch project, for example, include an attribution to the original sound creator in the description of your program when you publish it, as shown in Figure 6-12.

FIGURE 6-12: An example of giving credit to an audio file creator in Scratch.

Public domain audio files means that the audio file is free to use and you don't have to give credit to the original creator of the sound.

WARNING

It's important to be careful what your young coder does regarding audio files. We have had many students who have wanted to use a popular song, so they record the song on a mobile phone and then upload the recording to their programs. Though this may be innocent, it's important to teach your young coders about licenses and why they're important. Encourage them to sing the song themselves or try playing the music on an instrument they're learning.

Importing sounds into Scratch

Importing sounds into Scratch is very simple and can make the programs you write so much more exciting! After you have an MP3 file that you have legally downloaded onto your computer, open an existing project or start a new one in Scratch. Then, follow these steps to get your sound into your program:

1. **Choose a sprite that you want the sound to be associated with.**

For example, you can have a GIF of a sleeping cat and a sound of sawing wood. You can make the cat sound like it was snoring with the sound of sawing wood.

2. **Click the sprite that you chose, and then click the Sound tab in the center of the programming environment.**

You should already see a "pop" sound, which is the default sound that gets added to any sprite you upload. (If you want, you can delete this sound by clicking the x on the pop sound icon.)

3. **Click the folder with the up arrow (see Figure 6-13) and choose the MP3 file that you had previously downloaded.**

FIGURE 6-13:
The upload button for adding a sound to a sprite in Scratch.

4. **(Optional) Add a snippet of code to play the sound until it's done, and then insert the sound command into a forever loop.**

Figure 6-14 shows the code to do that.

Importing audio into JavaScript

Importing sounds into App Lab can be done in just three easy steps:

1. **Click the App Lab button under the Start a New Project heading or open an existing project.**

Under the UI Controls category of blocks is a playSound block.

```
playSound("URL", true);
```

If you don't see the placeholder code, you can write it yourself.

2. **Replace** URL **with the URL of the sound you want to use and then either leave the** true **as true, if you want your sound to keep repeating, or change it to** false, **if you want your sound to play once and then stop.**

If you're getting your sounds from soundbible.com, then you have your sound downloaded on your computer. Just click the Show Blocks button at the top right of your programming environment, click the down arrow to the left of the URL in the playSound block, select Choose, and upload the sound file to Code.org. After you've done that, the URL is replaced with the file's name:

```
playSound("sawing-wood-daniel_simon.mp3", true);
```

3. **Click Run on the emulator on the left of your App Lab environment to hear your sound play.**

Creating a Sound Board

The first few sections in this chapter guided you through getting images and sounds into your programs in Scratch and in JavaScript via App Lab. In this section, you combine all that work into one program: a simple sound board! This is a great project for young coders, because each one can be completely unique, while the code and process is the same. This makes leading a group of coders in this activity easy for you as a coding mentor, but still fun for the coders because they have creative control!

This section walks you through creating the simple sound board in Scratch, though with the guidance in the earlier chapters, you can adapt these instructions to work in App Lab as well. Your coder can even do a similar project in other programming environments such as GameSalad (see Chapter 3) if he'd like.

Remember, before starting to code, you and your coder should have a plan for what you want to make. Because this project requires a lot of Internet searching and/or image and sound creating, it's best to know what you want to do first.

1. **Start with five images and five sounds that you want to have in your sound board. List them on a piece of paper.**

2. **Sketch where you want each image to go on your screen.**

   It doesn't have to be in a grid-like pattern. For example, you could have an entire scene of animals in a forest.

3. **Find all the images (JPEG, PNG, or GIF) and sounds (WAV or MP3) and download them onto your computer.**

TIP

   Put all the files you need into one folder to make them easier to find and upload later.

4. **In Scratch, create a new project called "Simple Sound Board."**

5. **Upload each image as a sprite into Scratch. Edit the images in the Costume tab if you need to get rid of backgrounds or you want to resize them.**

6. **Arrange the sprites how you want them onscreen.**

7. **For each sprite, upload one sound using the Sounds tab for that sprite.**

8. **Write the code for each sprite to wiggle and play the sound when they're clicked.**

   Each sprite has the same code, shown in Figure 6-15, but the sound filenames are different.

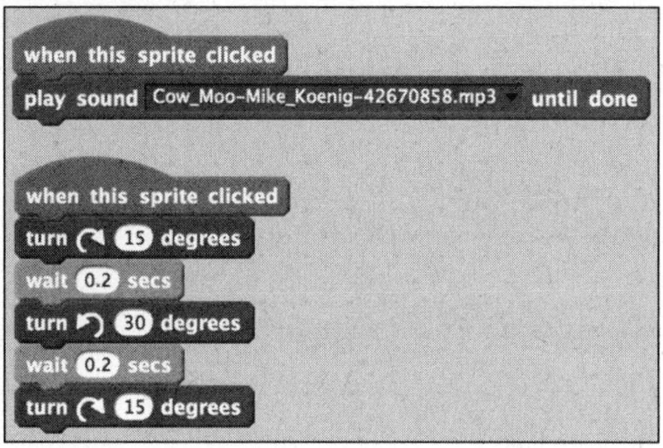

FIGURE 6-15:
The code needed
for each sprite in
your simple
sound board.

Congratulations! You have used images and sounds to create an interactive sound board! An example of a sound board is shown in Figure 6-16. You can check out the one we built for this book at `https://scratch.mit.edu/projects/195810761/`.

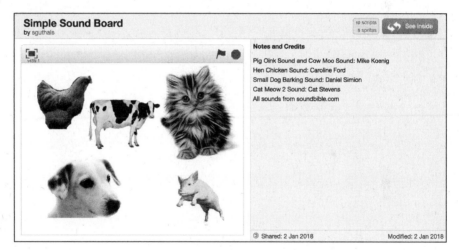

FIGURE 6-16:
A sound board
you can
build, too!

3

There IS Math on This Test!

Learn how computers track data and values with the use of variables and create a tiny stock clicker.

Use math in your programs and create a crypto code breaker.

Explore how you can use logic in your programs to create programs like rock, paper, scissors.

Discover two aspects of programming that highlight what computers do best: dealing with data and repeating mundane operations over and over.

Meet Seymour Papert.

Chapter **7**

Tackling These Ever-Changing Variables

This chapter helps you gain proficiency in working with *variables*, an algebraic entity that is ubiquitous in coding. Variables allow your coder to build in change and variation to her code. For example, if she writes a program that presents birthday greetings to its users, she can use a variable for the name of the celebrant. That way, instead of printing onscreen, "Happy Birthday to You," your program can show a more personalized greeting such as "Happy Birthday to Camille," or "Happy Birthday to Sarah."

You can use variables to give the programs that you and your coder write greater flexibility, so that the programs can be used over and over again. In this chapter, you find out how to create and use variables for a wide variety of purposes, from storing the names of people to scoring points in a game.

Acting Out Variables, Unplugged

Creating and using variables are processes your coder performs in most computer programs she writes. In the physical world, you use variables all the time, whether you know it or not! (See Figure 7-1.)

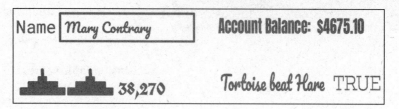

FIGURE 7-1:
Variables and
their values
appear in
everyday life.

As in daily life, computer code involves variables of many different types. Here are some examples of variables:

>> Login and password fields on a form are words, of the String variable type.

>> Game scores and lives are numbers, measured as non-negative integers.

>> Bank account balances, measured as currency, are numbers measured specifically to two decimal places.

>> A quiz question, written as a True or False statement, is a variable of the Boolean type.

Variable parts

Each variable consists of three parts: a type, a name, and a value.

Variable types

Variable type indicates the nature of the quantity that is stored in the variable. Like a restaurant genre — Italian, Asian Fusion, All-American — the type indicates "what's inside." Variable types consist of number, text, and Boolean:

>> **Numbers, such as integers or decimals:** Integers are negative numbers, zero, or positive numbers without a decimal. They're used for a variety of purposes including counting objects or scoring a game. The code for an integer is typically int. Decimals are numbers that include a decimal point and digits after the decimal. They're used for quantities that require precision, such as temperature or grade point average. The code for a decimal number is typically double.

>> **Text, such as strings or characters:** Strings can be individual characters, but are usually words and phrases. In some programming languages, such as Java, strings have unique code they can use. The code for a string variable is typically String. Characters are individual letters, numbers, or symbols. The code for a character variable is usually char.

>> **Boolean:** Boolean variables have only two states: true or false. The code for a Boolean variable is usually `Boolean`.

Many languages, such as Java, require that you declare variable types. Other languages, such as Scratch, allow you to use all these variable types, but don't require that you declare the type. Python infers the type from the assignment of the first value to the variable name.

Variable names

The name of a variable is how the program refers to the variable. Just like naming a newborn baby, you name variables in your computer programs to make clear the quantities you're referencing. A variable name doesn't change; only its value. For example, the variable `age` consists of an integer that increases over time.

Variable names typically follow a specific formatting that depends on the programming language. Creating good variable names is just as important as giving humans good names. Share these guidelines with your young coder regarding how to name variables:

>> Variable names should be meaningful, and should avoid default names such as `variable1` or `newvariable` (or, "Hey you!" if you're talking about humans).

>> As a general rule, use letters and numbers for variable names, but be sure to begin with a letter.

>> Most programming languages distinguish between upper- and lowercase versions of a variable. For example, Scratch views `Age` and `age` as different variables.

>> Do not include spaces in variable names. (The exception is Scratch, but your coder should avoid this practice.)

>> Underscore symbols can be used to create visual spacing between words in a variable name. You can also use underscores to start a variable name.

>> Avoid trying to name a variable a reserved word. Reserved words are codes that already exist within a programming language. For example, avoid naming a variable `byte` or `switch` when working in JavaScript as these are reserved words and cannot be used.

>> Consider using camelCase format to name variables. This format mimics the low and high positions on a camel's back, as shown in Figure 7-2. A variable name such as `myTotalCalories` or `myMondayCalories` starts with a lowercase letter and then has an uppercase letter at the start of each new word.

FIGURE 7-2:
Use camelCase
format to name
variables: like a
camel's hump,
start low (with a
lowercase letter)
and then go high
(with an
uppercase letter)
at the start of a
new word.

numCars   dailyGrowthRate
submitStatus   breedDogAvailable

**TECHNICAL
STUFF**

Some evidence shows that coders are better able to read code (their code and code written by others) when using snake_case, not camelCase naming. In snake_case, multiple words (for instance, in a variable name) are separated by underscore symbols. So a camelCase variable name could be `daysSince2000`, while a snake_case of the same variable would be `days_since_2000`.

Variable values

The value of a variable is the current quantity contained by the variable. The value that is stored in a variable is dependent upon its variable type (if the variable has a type). Here are some examples:

» Integer values, such as –4, 0, or 27 are stored in `int` variable types.

» Decimal values, such as –11.56, 0.0, or 27.2964 are stored in `double` variable types.

» String values, such as "Party on!" or "123 Eatery" or "85" or "Numb3r$" are stored in `String` variable types.

» Character values, such as 'Z' or '5' or '%' (with single quotes) are stored in `character` variable types.

» Boolean values, such as true or false, are stored in `Boolean` variable types.

REMEMBER

A variable name doesn't change; only its value. For example, the variable `age` consists of an integer that increases over time. At one time during program execution, `age` may contain the value 16, and at another time, `age` may contain the value 18.

Dramatizing variables

To understand variables and each of the three parts of a variable, act it out, unplugged! Try playing a Categories game (see Figure 7-3) as an analogy for setting up variables. Two or more players can participate, and each player needs a small whiteboard or paper and pencils. A stopwatch or timer is also required.

FIGURE 7-3:
Play a categories
game as an
analogy for
setting up
variables.

VERY, VERY, VARIABLES

Many grownups recall their experience with variables as having something to do with sitting in a math class, eyeing an equation on the chalkboard, and being asked to respond to the request, "Find x." Your coder may soon be (or may already be) reliving that same scene at his or her school. Unfortunately, this first introduction to variables can be confounding for youth, who often wonder, "How did math suddenly shift from using numbers to using letters?" The challenges pile up even further when the letters look like numbers (ever notice how lower case "b" is confoundingly similar to the number "6"?). And the frustration mounts further when youth are asked to work with multiple variables that look annoying like one another (case in point: the letter "u" and the letter "v"). Camille's mother, Beverly, a math teacher by trade, has a great method of reducing the confusion when teaching variables: Use an everyday object or cartoon doodle to stand for the variable. Instead of writing, 3x+12x, write 3☎+12☎ or similar. Your young coder may catch on more quickly to the concept of "three telephones with twelve telephones equals how many telephones" than diving in immediately to the use of "x" as a variable name. Then you can gently transition him to the idea of using "t" to represent telephone, or "x" to represent xylophone!

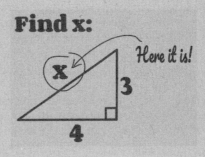

During each round, one player proposes a category, and the other players have 30 seconds to create as many names as possible for the category. Each name must also be accompanied by a value. Here is how each part of the Categories game relates to working with variables:

>> **Category stands for variable type:** For example, a category could be animals.

>> **Name stands for variable name:** An example name could be dogs or cats.

>> **Value stands for variable name:** An example value could be Marmaduke or Garfield.

Think of as many categories, names, and values as you can, writing down answers before the time expires on each round. Play a total of three rounds for each person in the game. The winner is the person who creates the greatest number of valid names and values!

I Do Declare (And Initialize)

With a few exceptions, variables don't exist in your program until you create them. The process of specifying a variable type and establishing a variable name is called *declaring* the variable. The process of giving the new variable a value is called *initializing* the variable.

Using pseudocode

Each programming language uses a specific structure for declaring and initializing variables. Here is the general pseudocode for these processes:

Action	Pseudocode	Examples
Declare a variable	`variable type` `variable name`	`string dogName` `int personAge`
Initialize an existing variable	`variable name =` `variable value`	`dogName = "Pepper"` `personAge = 17`

Declare and initialize a variable in one step	`variable type`
	`variable name =`
	`variable value`
		`string dogName = "Pepper"`
		`int personAge = 17`

Using Scratch

When creating variables in Scratch, your coder doesn't need to declare a variable type. Scratch variable types are inferred from the context of the code. You need only to create a variable by naming it. Variables in Scratch can be created on the stage and on any sprite.

To create a variable in Scratch, follow these steps:

1. **Go to the Data blocks and choose Make a Variable.**

   The New Variable dialog box appears.

2. **Type a variable name in the Variable name field, as shown in Figure 7-4.**

3. **Decide whether this variable is for one sprite or all sprites:**

   - *For All Sprites:* Select this option if the variable applies to all the sprites or if the variable is located on the stage. For example, if you're creating a scoring variable or a timer that applies to the entire program.

   - *For This Sprite Only:* Select this option if the variable applies only to a specific variable. For example, you may choose to create a health variable for every sprite in a game. The health variable for each sprite changes according to interactions of that sprite only.

TECHNICAL STUFF

Variable *scope* describes "the reach" of a variable and its value. A global variable can be referenced and updated from everywhere in the program. A local variable is known only within certain confines. For example, it's local to a sprite in Scratch, a function in JavaScript, or a private method in Java.

New Variable
Variable name: gameScore
● For all sprites   ○ For this sprite only
▨ Cloud variable (stored on server)
OK   Cancel

FIGURE 7-4:
Create a new variable in Scratch.

TIP

Scratch has a few built-in variables and sensors that you don't have to create to use them in your programs. One key variable your coder can use is the answer variable, which is part of the ask and answer pair. You can find the answer variable in the Sensing category of Scratch (see Figure 7-5). The ask and answer pair is used for data input: ask requests input from the user and the answer variable stores that input.

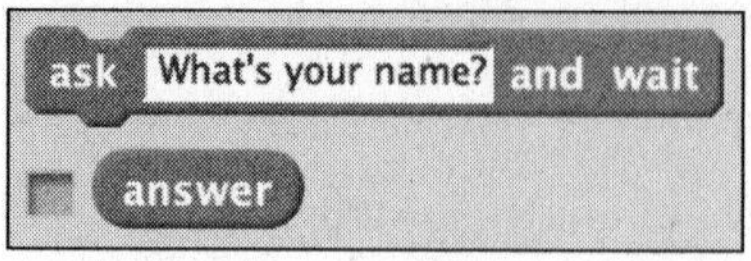

REMEMBER

For string variables, Scratch doesn't require that you place the variable value in quotes.

WARNING

While most programming languages don't allow spaces in variable names, Scratch does! Similarly, most programming languages disallow starting a variable name with a number, although this is also permitted in Scratch. However, while Scratch allows variable names such as Favorite Songs and 8ballPrediction, because most other languages don't allow these practices, it's best to avoid them.

To initialize a variable that's been created in Scratch, follow these steps:

1. **Go to the Data blocks and drag the** set variable name to value **code tile to the workspace, as shown in Figure 7-6.**

2. **Select the variable you want to set by pressing the drop-down tab and select the variable you've created.**

3. **Type the value into the field to set the value you want.**

   A value can be a number, text, or Boolean.

FIGURE 7-6:
The set variable code tile is used to initialize a variable value.

set gameScore to 0

Using Python

When creating variables in Python, your coder doesn't need to declare a variable type. Python variable types are inferred from the context of the code. Create a Python variable by naming it and initializing it.

To create a variable in Python, anywhere in your code, type a variable name, followed by an equals sign, followed by a value.

For numerical values, type the value. For strings (text), type the value surrounded by quotes. For example,

```
myShoeSize = 9
parcelWeight = 4.25
animal = "Rabbit"
courseGrade = 'A'
status = false
```

WARNING

Be careful when naming variables in Python. Don't start Python variable names with a number, and don't include spaces in variable names, or you receive an error message. If you want to add a bit of space between two words in a Python variable name, use an underscore symbol. You can also start a variable name with an underscore; for example, `_myVariable` is a valid variable name.

Using JavaScript

When creating variables in JavaScript, your coder doesn't need to declare a variable type. JavaScript variable types are inferred from the context of the code.

Create a JavaScript variable by declaring and naming it: anywhere in your code, type `var` followed by the variable name:

```
var catName;
```

JavaScript: I'M EVERYONE'S TYPE

Sometimes your coder wants to change the variable type of a variable already created in JavaScript. Unlike Python, JavaScript is somewhat of a chameleon: it is A-OK with a variable change type during the execution of a program. For example, your coder can shift between using a variable named item as an integer and as a string, and he doesn't have to do anything special to make the shift. JavaScript automatically takes care of the change of type. In its disregard for typing, JavaScript behaves more like Scratch than Python.

To initialize a variable that has been created in JavaScript, type the variable name, followed by =, followed by the value:

```
catName = "Mr. Boots";
```

To declare and initialize a variable in a single step in JavaScript, type var followed by the variable name, followed by =, followed by the value:

```
var catName = "Mr. Boots";
```

With regard to variable scope — and generally speaking — JavaScript variables inside of functions are local (known only inside their respective functions), while variables outside all functions are global (known across the entire program).

TIP

Use the var declaration command only once for each variable in a program. You can change the value of a variable at any time, but you should declare the existence of the variable ("bring it into being") only once.

WARNING

JavaScript doesn't allow spaces in variable names. To add space between words in a variable name, use an underscore symbol. You can also start a variable name with an underscore, for example, _myVariable. You should also avoid starting a JavaScript variable name with a number.

Using Java

When creating variables in Java, your coder needs to declare a variable type. Create a Java variable by declaring its type and naming it. Create variables near the start of your program so that they're located in one easy-to-find place location. Type the variable type followed by the variable name:

```
int myAge;
double mySalary;
String myLastName;
char myBuilding;
boolean hasClearance;
```

To initialize a variable that has been created in Java, type the variable name, followed by =, followed by the value:

```
myAge = 29;
mySalary = 820.25;
myLastName = "Smith";
myBuilding = 'C';
hasClearance = true;
```

To declare and initialize a variable in a single step in Java, type the variable type, followed by the variable name, followed by =, followed by the value:

```
int myAge = 29;
double mySalary = 820.25;
String myLastName = "Smith";
char myBuilding = 'C';
boolean hasClearance = true;
```

WARNING

Avoid using spaces in variable names in Java (use underscores if desired), and avoid starting a Java variable names with a number.

Checking on Variable Values

Your coder may want to see the value of a variable onscreen. Seeing the value onscreen may provide the user valuable information. For example, a score variable or a timer shows their values to inform the user of important information as the program executes. Additionally, seeing the value onscreen may be helpful when testing a program to make sure it's executing as you intend. For example, if a character is supposed to disappear when it reaches a specific x-coordinate — but it doesn't disappear — showing the value of the character's coordinate onscreen may help you troubleshoot errors in your program.

Using Scratch

To show a variable value onscreen in Scratch, follow these steps:

1. **Go to the Data blocks code tile category.**

2. **Select the check box next to the name of the variable you want to see.**

   The variable indicator appears onscreen, as shown in Figure 7-7. The current value of the variable is constantly updated in the indicator.

FIGURE 7-7:
See the value of a variable onscreen.

Using Python

To show a variable value onscreen in Python, type the code print (*variable Name*) at any location in your code. The current value of the variable appears onscreen.

Using JavaScript

To check a variable value in JavaScript, your coder has a few options:

>> **To view a value in the console, type the code** console.log(*variable Name*) **in your HTML code.** This method is useful when your coder wants to track a variable value for program development purposes. See Figure 7-8 for

an example of this process. The HTML program is typed in TextEdit, saved as an `.html` file, and then opened in a web browser using File ➪ Open File. In the web browser, the console log is opened by choosing Develop ➪ Show Console. Note that the value of the variable age, which is 7, displays in the console.

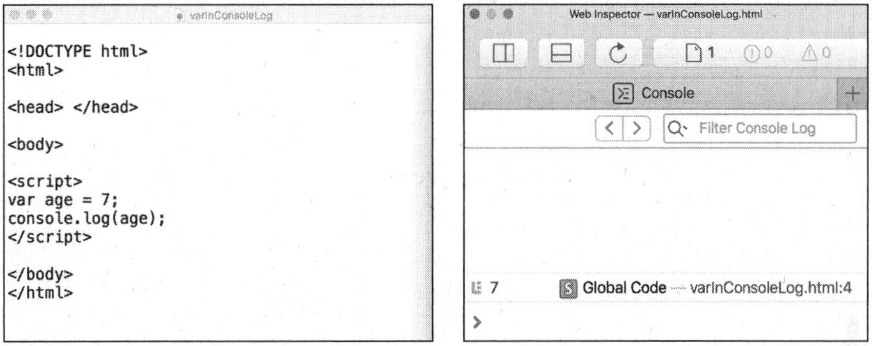

FIGURE 7-8:
Using the console log in JavaScript to see a variable value.

>> **To view a value onscreen in the user interface, type the code `write` (`variableName`) in your HTML code.** This process is similar to that shown in Figure 7-8, but instead of logging the output in the console, this writes the output onscreen in the user interface. For example, the following code displays the value 7 onscreen:

```
var age = 7;
write(age);
```

>> **When writing JavaScript in the Code.org App Lab, you can type the code `textLabel("valueLabel", variableName;)` at any location in your code.** This code also displays the value 7 in onscreen, in the location designated by the text label named `valueLabel`:

```
var age = 7;
textLabel("valueLabel", age);
```

These last two methods are useful when your coder wants to show a variable value onscreen for the user to see.

See Chapter 14 for details on using JavaScript with HTML in the construction of a webpage.

Using Java

To track a variable value in Java, type the code `System.out.print (variable Name)` at any location in your code. The current value of the variable appears onscreen. Figure 7-9 shows an example in the BlueJ IDE (discussed in Chapter 3).

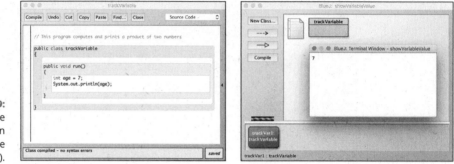

FIGURE 7-9: Seeing a variable value onscreen in Java (using the BlueJ IDE).

Incrementing and Decrementing Variables

Your coder can write code that changes the value of a variable under certain conditions as the program executes. A common way to change a variable value is to increment it. To *increment* a variable means to increase it by the same amount at each change. For example, your coder may increment a scoring variable by +2 each time a basketball goal is made. Decreasing a variable in this way is known as *decrementing* the variable value. Your coder may decrement a timer by −1 each time one second on the clock elapses.

Using pseudocode

The general format for incrementing or decrementing a variable value is as follows:

Action	Pseudocode	Examples
Increment a variable	variable = variable + change	score = score + 1 numTwins = numTwins + 2
Decrement a variable	variable = variable − change	timeRemaining = timeRemaining − 1 cost = cost − 5

TIP

Boolean variables aren't incremented nor decremented. A Boolean variable exists only in one of two states: true or false.

Using Scratch

To increment or decrement a variable in Scratch, follow these steps (see Figure 7-10):

1. Go to the Data blocks code tile category.

2. Select the change *variable name* by *value* code tile and drag it into your program.

3. Press the tab beside the variable name and select the variable whose value you want to change.

4. Type a number for the increment or decrement in the value field. Use a positive number to increment the value. Use a negative number to decrement the value.

FIGURE 7-10:
Changing a variable value in Scratch.

Using Python

To increment a variable value in Python, type the code

```
variableName = variableName + value
```

at the location in your code where you want to change the value.

To decrement a variable value Python, type the code

```
variableName = variableName - value
```

at the location in your code where you want to change the value.

Using JavaScript

To increment a variable value in JavaScript, type the code

```
variableName = variableName + value;
```

at the location in your code where you want to change the value.

To decrement a variable value in JavaScript, type the code

```
variableName = variableName - value;
```

Using Java

To increment a variable value in a Java program, type the code

```
variableName = variableName + value;
```

at the location in your code where you want to change the value.

To decrement a variable value in a Java program, type the code

```
variableName = variableName - value;
```

Creating a Stock Ticker

A stock ticker is a large LED sign that shows how stocks are performing in the stock market, as shown in Figure 7-11. They're usually displayed at financial institutions to keep investors apprised of trade volumes (numbers of stocks bought and sold) and share prices (the cost of any one share) for various companies. Even Times Square has a giant stock ticker!

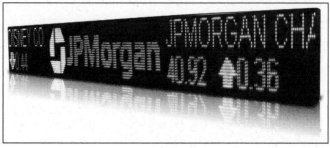

FIGURE 7-11:
A stock ticker
tracks stock
performance in
the stock market.

Figure credit: http://www.tickerplay.com/wp-content/uploads/ 2017/01/LED-Stock-Ticker-Tape.png

Your coder can explore variables by creating a tiny stock ticker using a micro:bit electronics board. The micro:bit consists of an LED screen, several sensors, and a small microprocessor for executing code. By coding a simple program and transferring it to the micro:bit, your coder can simulate a real LED display! A stock ticker that Camille created is shown in Figure 7-12.

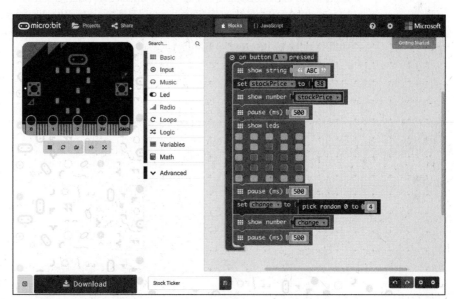

FIGURE 7-12:
Code a simulated
stock ticker using
variables.

Chapter 16 provides in-depth coverage of the micro:bit, and offers your coder details about its features and operation, how to write code for the micro:bit, and how to transfer code to the board.

Here are some tips for writing this code:

 Write your code in the IDE located at the Microsoft Make Code site at https://makecode.microbit.org.

>> Drag out the code tiles and snap them together as shown.

>> The first item shown in the ticker is the name of the company, in this case ABC.

>> In the Variables category, create two variables: stockPrice and change.

>> The up arrow indicates that the change in the stock value is an increase; alternatively, you can use a down arrow to indicate a decrease. You could also choose to make the LEDs randomly select either an up arrow *or* a down arrow.

>> The value of the change is computed as a random number. You can change the range of the random number produced. (See Chapter 2 for additional information on working with random numbers.)

>> Note that, using the processes outlined in this chapter, a variable value is computed, assigned to the variable, and then displayed.

The ticker can be operated onscreen in the emulator, or uploaded to an actual micro:bit. The user starts the action by pressing button A to see the ticket display the company name, the stock value, and the change. Encourage your coder to code and wire up the ticker, and then modify his creation to include additional stocks that may be of interest to him!

Chapter **8**

Computing Using Math

M ath operations consist of everything from adding and multiplying to using exponents. This chapter helps you gain proficiency in working with math operations, coaching you in how you can use these computational tools in your computer programs. For example, your coder can write code that uses math to find the average of a group of test scores, or figure out whether a number is even or odd, or pick random numbers for a dice roll.

Acting Out Math, Unplugged

Math is something you use every day. You figure out how many quarts of paint you need to cover all four walls of your room. You divide dog bones to make sure each beagle and corgi gets his fair share. You compute a tip to reward the pizza delivery person for getting that large pepperoni to you fast and hot (see Figure 8-1). Speaking of fast and hot, fast is determined by a number — a relative quantity of time; and hot is determined by a temperature.

Here are some other numerical quantities and computations that is performed with math:

>> Weighing a baby at the pediatrician's office to determine her rate of growth

>> Paying for movie tickets and snacks at the theater

» Measuring the time it takes for a student athlete to run a sprint or a marathon

» Carefully scooping out the right quantity of each ingredient for a recipe.

» Determining how many cells exist after a single cell divides several times

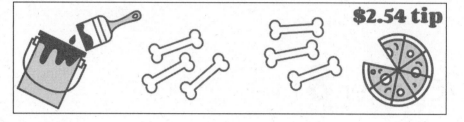

Number types

When working with math operations in your code, your coders need to know about the different types of numbers they can use. Each number type is suited to a different purpose:

» **Integers are negative numbers, zero, or positive numbers.** They don't have decimal place digits. Integers can be used for a variety of purposes. They can indicate position on a number line or a coordinate grid. They can be used to count things. They can be used to count the number of likes on a YouTube video! In programming languages that require a number type to be declared, the code for an integer is typically int.

» **Decimals are numbers that have a decimal point and digits after the decimal.** They can be negative, zero, or positive in value. Decimals are used for number quantities that require precision. Weight, salaries, land acreage, and clocks measuring elapsed times at sporting events. In programming languages that require a number type to be declared, the code for a decimal number is typically double.

See Chapter 7 for more information on number typing.

Dramatizing math

To understand mathematics and math operations in coding, try some math activities, unplugged. Play a board game with your coder. (See Figure 8-2.) Almost all board games involve rolling dice, summing their values, and moving a marker around the board to build counting skills. Playing dominoes does as well. Games such as Monopoly also involve buying and selling and can help your coder in working with currency. Card games such as twenty-one and Old Maid help players build skills in probability as they try to determine the chances on drawing the cards they want, or don't want. In this age of apps and video games, you may also find that you and your coder enjoy a little game time that doesn't involve screen time!

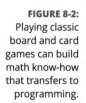

FIGURE 8-2: Playing classic board and card games can build math know-how that transfers to programming.

Figure credit Monopoly: https://www.amazon.com/Winning-Moves-Games-1126-Monopoly/dp/B002JSM3KQ/ref=sr_1_5?s=toys-and-games&ie=UTF8&qid=1517968792&sr=1-5&keywords=monopoly

Figure credit playing cards: https://www.amazon.com/Bicycle-Playing-Card-Deck-2-Pack/dp/B010F6BAES/ref=sr_1_5?s=toys-and-games&ie=UTF8&qid=1517968919&sr=1-5&keywords=standard+playing+cards

SEYMOUR PAPERT: PROGRAMMING, BOTH CHALLENGING AND FUN

Seymour Papert once said, "I prefer software where kids build something and run into problems they have to solve." A founding member of both the MIT Artificial Intelligence Laboratory and the MIT Media Lab, the professor was famous for his progressive thinking about teaching and learning, even characterizing the Rs (reading, writing, and arithmetic) as an "obsolete skill set." He possessed a deep belief in the abilities of children to think in complex, innovative ways, championing the notion that they should be given tools of technology to capitalize on those abilities.

Born in South Africa in 1928, Seymour lived his childhood long before the development of the first computers. He was well into his computing career before the introduction of the first personal computers, including the Apple II in the late 1970s. (Some of you parents remember having one of those!) But Seymour predicted that computers would eventually be ubiquitous, and was an early proponent of computers in the classroom — with unique views about what students should actually do with those computers.

(continued)

(continued)

Seymour promoted a type of educational philosophy called *constructivism*, in which learners are coached in mentally constructing their own knowledge through experiential learning and reflection. He went a step further, calling his extended concept, *constructionism*, a philosophy that espoused physically constructing objects in the real world. He viewed the process of children constructing their own programs — not using pre-made software — as an empowering learning endeavor in its own right, and one that built the foundation for future innovative work.

Seymour worked extensively with children, observing them program, and watching them grapple with the messy challenges coding presents. He marveled at their thinking processes: their creative prowess, their ability to "concretize" ideas as functional programs, and their persistence in troubleshooting and debugging code.

Two of the "coolest tools" Seymour developed were the Logo programming language and the Logo turtle. Logo invited young coders to use natural commands to draw geometric figures, exploring distance, turn angles, and repeat commands. The Logo turtle was a physical turtle, equipped with a pen, which — when given the programming code — actually drew the geometric figures on paper. It literally brought code into the real world.

As a programming coach, you're continuing the legacy of Seymour Papert and his belief in children as authentic programmers!

Figure credit: Cynthia Solomon/MIT Media Lab

Doing Simple Math

In most programming languages, math operations are already built-in so that your coder can simply use them when needed. However, in other languages, some math operations may needed to be activated at the start of the program before you can use them.

Using pseudocode

Programming languages follow the same general rules with regard to performing math operations. Table 8-1 shows general pseudocode for these operations with an example of integers and decimals.

TABLE 8-1 **Pseudocode for Basic Math Operations**

Operation	Pseudocode	Examples
Add two numbers	number1 + number2	23 + 5 2.78 + 1.2
Subtract two numbers	number1 - number2	13 - 28 4.22 - 9.00
Multiply two numbers	number1 * number2	33 * 12 5.34 * 6.7
Divide two numbers	number1 / number2	12 / 4 5.5 / 2.0
Combining simple operations	number1 * number2 * number3	5 * 6 * 10 6.5 * 3.25 * 0.75

Using Scratch

Scratch, similar to other block-based coding languages, has simple blocks that support basic math operations, as shown in Figure 8-3. Scratch supports adding integers and decimals.

Scratch also supports combining simple math operations. Figure 8-4 shows a set of blocks that adds four numbers together.

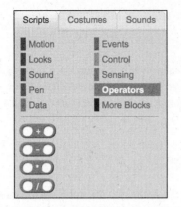

FIGURE 8-3:
Scratch provides blocks for basic math operations.

FIGURE 8-4:
Scratch allows you to combine basic math operations.

TIP

One thing to point out to young coders when they're writing in a block-based language such as Scratch is that to add four numbers, you only need three add blocks.

Using Python

Basic math operations in Python look very similar to pseudocode. This makes sense, considering Python aimed to be a language that was approachable and familiar for humans (see the sidebar about Guido van Rossum in Chapter 3). Python supports math operations for integers and decimals, although in Python a decimal is called a *float*. For adding, subtracting, multiplying, and dividing, you would follow the pseudocode (refer to Table 8-1). For example, addition in Python for integers and floats is like this:

```
3 + 5
2.78 + 1.2 + 5.6
```

REMEMBER

This is actually true for most text-based languages. For example, that's exactly how you would add two numbers in Java and JavaScript as well!

Doing Advanced Math Operations

Although you can do a lot with adding, subtracting, multiplying, and dividing, sometimes you need more advanced mathematical operations. Additional operations that might come in handy are changing the sign of a number, finding the exponent, computing absolute value, and calculating the square root, as well as combining math operations with variables.

Using pseudocode

Just like the basic math operations in the previous section, more advanced math operations can support integers and decimals in almost all programming languages. Table 8-2 shows examples of how you might write code for changing the sign of a number, and for other advanced math operations. It also shows how to write pseudocode when using variables in advanced math operations.

TABLE 8-2   **Pseudocode for Advanced Math Operations**

Operation	Pseudocode	Examples
Change the sign of a number	`-1* number1`	`-1 * (-13)` `-1 * 4.22`
Using exponents	`number1 ^ number2`	`3 ^ 5` `2.78 ^ 1.2`
Getting the absolute value	`|number1|`	`|13|` `|-4.22|`
Getting the square root	`√number1`	`√16` `√9.4`
Assigning values to variables	`int number1 = value1 int number2= value2`	`int number1 = 5` `int number2 = 9`
Using variables in math operations	`int product = number1 * number2`	`int product = 45`
Assigning values to variables	`double height = value3 double width = value4`	`height = 2.4` `width = 6.0`
Using variables in math operations	`double perimeter = 2*height + 2*width`	`perimeter = 16.8`

Turn to Chapter 7 to find out how to declare a variable and how to give a variable a new name.

Using Scratch

Scratch provides users with a number of math operations beyond the basic four. Figure 8-5 shows how to change the sign of a number: multiply the number by negative one (-1). In this way, a positive number becomes negative, and a negative number becomes positive.

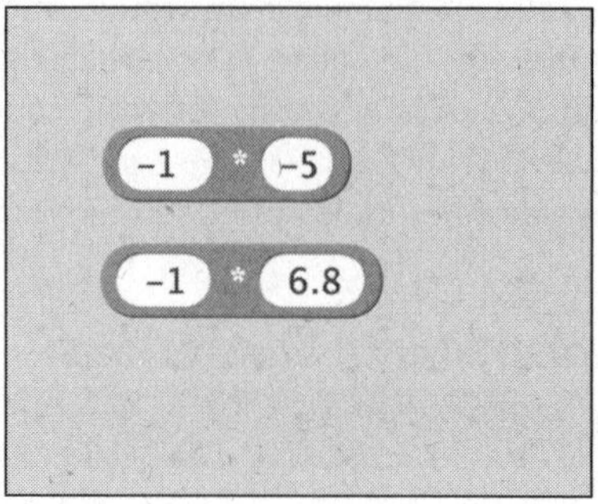

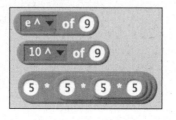

FIGURE 8-5:
How to negate a value in Scratch.

Finding an exponent in Scratch can also be a bit tricky. There isn't a simple block for $number1^{number2}$. There are two blocks for exponent functions, shown in Figure 8-6, but are specific to $e^{number1}$ and $10^{number1}$. These blocks can be found under Operations (see Figure 8-7). To write the function for $number1^{number2}$, you basically have to write all the multiplications, also shown in Figure 8-6.

FIGURE 8-6:
Three ways of finding the exponent in Scratch.

Scratch makes a lot of the other advanced math operations very easy! Finding the absolute value and square root of a value uses one block, which can be found under the Operations category. Figure 8-7 shows the block and all the choices you have for it. Absolute value is represented as abs and square root is represented as sqrt. The block starts as sqrt.

Combining variables with math operations in Scratch is really easy. Basically, anywhere there is a circular opening you can either type a number or drag in a variable. For example, Figure 8-8 shows some of the math operations throughout this chapter using variables.

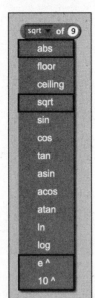

FIGURE 8-7:
Exponent,
absolute value,
and square root
in Scratch.

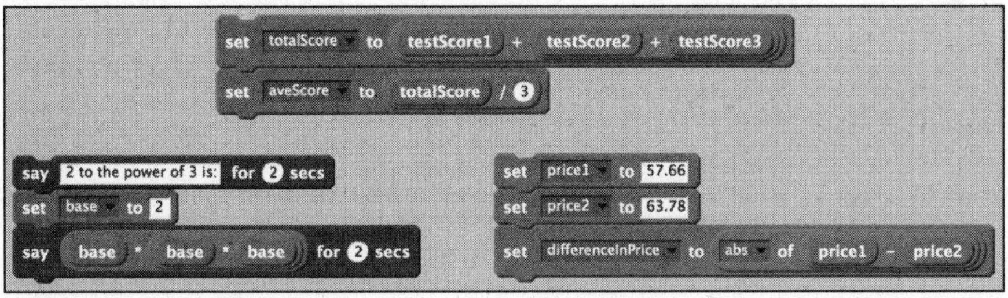

FIGURE 8-8:
Examples of
variables being
used to solve
advanced math
operations in
Scratch.

Using Python

Negating a number, finding the exponent, absolute value, and square root in Python are all straightforward. You can perform all three operations on integer or decimal (float) numbers.

Negating a number in Python pretty much only makes sense if you're trying to negate the value of a variable; otherwise you would just use the positive or negative number. Although, you can still negate a number directly, just add parenthesis for clarity:

```
-(number1)
```

Examples

```
-(5)
-(-8.99)
```

Exponents are pretty much the same as the basic math operations (like adding) and use a special symbol:

```
number1 ** number2
```

Examples:

```
3 ** 5
2.78 ** 1.2
```

Getting the absolute value of a number in Python requires you to use a function. Functions in Python (and other text-based languages) are special commands or subprograms that you call in your code. Typically, you pass the function a parameter (a value for the function to use in a computation) and the function returns an output value to you. You might have already encountered some functions if you worked through earlier chapters in this book. For example, a function in JavaScript from Chapter 5 is:

```
getXPosition("character");
```

Here's the Python code for absolute value:

```
abs(number1)
```

Examples are

```
abs(-7)
abs(8.9)
```

Finding the square root of a number is even a little more complicated than finding the absolute value when coding in Python. First, you have to import a Math library so that Python knows how to evaluate this method (which is another type of subprogram you can call in Python).

```
import math
math.sqrt(number1)
```

Examples are

```
import math
math.sqrt(16)
math.sqrt(99.89)
```

For additional information on subprograms your coder can write in his code, see Chapter 12.

Finally, using variables in more advanced Python math operations is very similar to using them in Scratch — basically you replace numbers with variables! A couple examples are here:

Finding the absolute value with variables:

```
costOfTable1 = 66.89
costOfTable2 = 90.54
differenceInCost = abs(66.89 - 90.54)
```

LIBRARIES IN CODE

As you write more and more code, you'll start to realize that others have written a lot of pieces of code that might be useful to you. One of the reasons we love being coders is that you can optimize what a computer does best and what a human does best. Figuring out a solution to a common problem might be something that humans are really good at. But having each human figure out that exact same solution over and over seems pointless, when a computer could easily use the solution that was first created for everyone! Sharing solutions to common problems is often done through *libraries*. The name *library* is very fitting; think of the last time you wrote a paper where you had to reference other people's work. When we were younger, that meant going to a physical library, finding the right book, page, and passage, and then referencing that passage in a quote in our paper. When coding, it's essentially the same thing! You first tell your program where to find the library. Within that library there might be a number of functions and methods that you want to reference within your code. But after you identify the right function or method, the computer does what it does best — it searches in the library you referenced for the function or method you're trying to call and it executes the code within that function or method for you. You don't have to re-write that function or method in *your* code, because it's already written in the library!

Finding the square root with variables:

```
areaOfSquareRoom = 196
lengthOfOneWall = math.sqrt(areaOfSquareRoom)
```

Oh So Mod — Using the Mod Operation

Another useful operator that can be tricky for young coders at first is *modulo*, also referred to as *modulus* and *mod*. The mod of two numbers is the remainder after a division of two numbers.

This operator can be useful for writing applications based on real-world scenarios. For example, say you have $20.00. You want to pass out exactly $3.50 to as many friends as possible, and you want to know how much money you will have leftover. So you would want to solve the questions "What is the quotient of 20.00/3.50?" and "What is the remainder of 20.00/3.50?" The answer to this word question would be "You can give 5 friends $3.50 and you will be left with $2.50."

TIP

What is really great is that Google provides a mod function on its online calculator! So if you and your coder are ever debugging (see Chapter 12), you can check your mod equation on Google fairly easily. Just go to google.com and type "number1 % number2" and the calculator appears with your answer. For example, Figure 8-9 shows checking 63 % 19. There is even a button for mod on the calculator; it's the % symbol.

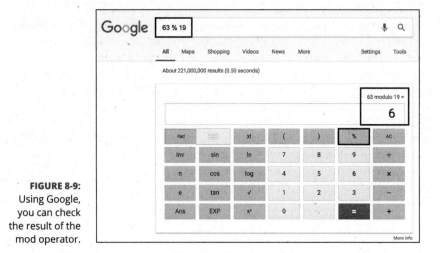

FIGURE 8-9:
Using Google, you can check the result of the mod operator.

Using pseudocode

Mod in pseudocode is often represented with the % symbol, because that is most commonly used in text-based languages like Python and Java.

```
number1 % number2
```

Examples are

```
30 % 7
6.89 % 5.9
```

Using Scratch

In Scratch, you can find a mod block under the Operators category. For example, Figure 8-10 shows the mod block evaluating 9 mod 8, which equals 1.

FIGURE 8-10: The mod block found in the Scratch Operators category.

Using Python

In Python, the mod operator is very similar to the basic math operations such as adding, subtracting, multiplying, and dividing. You simply use the % symbol between the numbers. It's exactly like the pseudocode examples for both integers and decimals.

Ordering Those Operations (PEMDAS)

Most programming languages follow the standard math order of operations, often referred to as PEMDAS: Parenthesis, Exponent, Multiplication, Division, Addition, Subtraction, from left to right. However, it's common practice in coding to use additional parentheses to help ensure the correct order is being followed.

Using Scratch

Because Scratch doesn't have a parenthesis symbol, it behaves differently when it comes to the order of operations. Basically, each individual block is evaluated first because each block is basically representing an operation within parentheses. For example, Figure 8-11 shows a compound math operation using addition and division. The order of operations for Figure 8-11 written in pseudocode is:

```
8 + 6
10 + 14
24 / 3
aveScore = 8
```

It can also be viewed all in one line like this:

```
aveScore = (10 + (8 + 6)) / 3
```

Using Python

Python follows the PEMDAS rule, although two operations aren't accounted for in PEMDAS; negation and mod. Negation (N) comes after parenthesis, but before exponents: PNEMDAS. Mod (m) is at the same level as multiplication and division: PNEMDmAS. Some examples of how Python would evaluate compounded math operations are here:

Compound math operation without parenthesis:

```
print( 5 * 9 % 8 + 9 / 3 )
8
```

The steps that Python takes are:

```
5 * 9 = 45
45 % 8 = 5
9 / 3 = 3
5 + 3 = 8
```

Compound math operation with parentheses result in a different computation:

```
print( 5 * ((9 % 8) + 9) / 3 )
16
```

The steps that Python takes are:

```
9 % 8 = 1
1 + 9 = 10
5 * 10 = 50
50 / 3 = 16
```

Rounding

Rounding in coding can get a little tricky because of the two types of numbers that are often used: integers and decimals. If you're using math operations on integers only, then the resulting answer will also be computed as an integer.

The only time when integers round is during division, and programming languages tend to round down, regardless of what the remainder is. For example:

```
14 / 3 = 4
15 / 3 = 5
16 / 3 = 5
```

When working with decimals only in math operations, programming languages typically evaluate the operation and might vary between languages and machines for how precise the result is. For example:

```
14.00 / 3.0 = 4.666667
15.0 / 3.00 = 5.0
16.77 / 3.99009 = 4.20291271625
```

When combining integers and decimals is where it can get interesting. Typically programming languages default to the most precise result. So if you add an integer and a decimal, the result typically is a decimal. For example:

```
60.8 + 7 = 67.8
```

Rounding via casting in Java

In a typed programming language, where you specify what type the values are that you're using, you can explicitly cast either the number in the operator, or the result to an integer or a decimal. *Casting* means to tell the computer explicitly what type you want a value to be, instead of letting the computer determine what type a value is based on its properties. Notice in the following examples that programming languages typically round down, regardless of how close to the next integer the decimal is. For example, in Java you might have the following:

```
(int)60.8 + 7;
67

int sum = (int)(89.333 + 1.555);
sum = 90

int sum = (int)(89.3 + 1.7);
sum = 91

double quotient = (double)8 / 3;
quotient = 2.6666666666666665

double quotient = (int)8.4 / 3;
quotient = 2.0
```

When adding precision, you can perform explicit or implicit casting. *Implicit casting* is when the programming language adds precision to numbers based on all the numbers being used in the operation. *Explicit casting* is described in the section coming up.

```
double quotient = 8 / 3;
quotient = 2.0

double quotient = 8.0 / 3;
quotient = 2.6666666666666665
```

Rounding decimals to integers via methods

Although rounding occurs often between integers and decimals during math operations, most programming languages also have a rounding method that can be used to explicitly round decimals to the nearest integer. This is the same in standard math operations:

```
5.5 = 6
5.4999 = 5
```

Figure 8-12 shows a few examples of rounding in Scratch.

FIGURE 8-12:
Example of using the round math operator block in Scratch.

The following table shows a couple rounding examples in both Python and Java:

Language	Example	Result
Python	`round(5.5)`	6
Python	`round(5.4999)`	5
Java	`Math.round(5.5);`	6
Java	`Math.round(5.4999);`	5

Some programming languages even have functions that let you round to a certain decimal! For example, Python's round function can be extended to include a second parameter where you specify how many digits after the decimal you want the number rounded to:

```
round(5.5985, 2)
5.60

round(5.46732, 4)
5.4673
```

Generating and Using Random Numbers

Being able to use random numbers can be a lot of fun when writing interactive programs. Random numbers can help you and your young coder create a dice rolling simulation, or make a game where each gem that is collected gives you a random number of points, or even create scattering where many sprites are positioned in random locations onscreen!

Using pseudocode

When trying to find a random number between two numbers, it's important to know whether you're including the two numbers that are your boundaries, or not including them. For example, a random number between 1 and 5 *inclusive* could be 1, 2, 3, 4, or 5. While a random number between 1 and 5 *exclusive* could only be 2, 3, or 4. You might also want to decide to include the first number, but not the last. For example, a random number between 1 and 5 including 1 but excluding 5 could be 1, 2, 3, or 4. To specify this with pseudocode, you would typically use the symbol [to denote inclusivity of the number and (to denote exclusivity.

The functions (with examples) needed to choose a random number are:

Pseudocode	Examples
random(number1, number2)	random(1, 100) -> 2...99
random[number1, number2]	random[1, 100] -> 1...100
random(number1, number2]	random(1, 100] -> 2...100
random[number1, number2)	random[1.5, 100) -> 1.5, 1.6, 1.7 ... 99.7, 99.8, 99.9

Using Scratch

Scratch provides an easy to use the random block under the Operators category, as shown in Figure 8-13. Scratch's random block is *inclusive*. The random block returns an integer if both values given are integers, and returns a decimal even if one of the numbers is a decimal. The precision of the decimal matches that of the most precise parameter given.

FIGURE 8-13:
Example of using
the random
operator block in
Scratch.

Using Python

To use the random function in Python, you have to first import the random library. You can then call the `randint` function to find a random integer or the `uniform` function to find a random float (decimal). Both the `randint` and `uniform` functions are inclusive.

Functions (with examples) to choose a random number are:

Python	Examples
randint(number1, number2)	randint(1, 100)
uniform(number1, number2)	uniform(5.5, 6.8)

Coding a Crypto Code Maker

After you and your young coder have a handle on the different math operations that are available to you in coding, it can be really fun to find ways to create fun programs that use those operations! One that doesn't always come to mind is making a cipher! Ciphers are a lot of fun to build because they can offer additional play outside of building the program — you and your coder can write letters to each other using the secret code that only the cipher you built can solve!

Building a simple crypto code maker in Scratch is actually pretty quick! The cipher built in this section is also known as a Caesar Cipher. Basically you give a shift amount and a letter and the program moves through the alphabet by the shift amount, looping around to A if it gets to Z, and gives you the secret letter. For example, if you wanted to tell your young coder the plaintext word "hi," you could use a shift to move each letter to a new position in the alphabet, obscuring the original message. With a shift of 6, the plaintext, "hi" becomes the ciphertext word "NO."

It might be a good idea to play this game with a paper and pencil with your young coder before you start coding, because then you have an idea of what needs to be built! You can even have your young coder write the steps that they use to figure it out as they play with the unplugged version!

To build the crypto code maker in Scratch, follow these steps:

1. Create a list called "letters" in Scratch that contains all 26 letters.

You can check out Chapter 11 for more explanations on lists.

2. Create four variables that will keep track of the ciphertext (output), plaintext (input), shift, and position of the counter used during the algorithm.

Your list and these four variables are visible under the Data category, as shown in Figure 8-14. You can find out more about variables in Chapter 7 if you need a refresher.

FIGURE 8-14:
The four variables and one list you need in your crypto code maker code.

TIP

Make sure your ciphertext, plaintext, and shift amount variables and your letters list are visible on the stage by selecting the check box next to them. Because the position variable is keeping track of the position as you iterate through the alphabet, it doesn't have to be visible on the stage, so make sure you uncheck the box next to it. Your stage should look something like Figure 8-15.

FIGURE 8-15:
The stage of
your crypto
code maker
should be
similar.

3. **Ask the user for the plaintext letter and the shift amount. Be sure to save the answers from the user in the appropriate variables.**

   Figure 8-16 shows how to ask and save the responses.

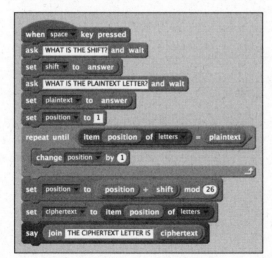

FIGURE 8-16:
The completed
code for the
Scratch crypto
code maker.

4. **Starting at position 1 in the list (A), iterate through the list of letters until you reach the letter that the user submitted.**

   When this loop ends, the variable position holds the number that corresponds with the plaintext letter given by the user (for example, 1 is A, 2 is B, and so on).

5. **Add the shift amount to the position, then mod by 26.**

You have to mod by 26 to allow the cipher to start back at A if it reaches Z. For example, if the plaintext letter the user submits is X and the shift is 6, the ciphertext is D. You can evaluate this mathematically as well: X is at position 24. 24 + 6 is 30. 30 % 26 is 4. 4 is the position of letter D.

6. **Get the ciphertext letter from the list, and display it to the user.**

All the code for this entire code maker is shown in Figure 8-16.

TIP

As a bonus challenge, can you have your young coder figure out how to make a reverse version of this program? See if he can build a version to convert ciphertext into plaintext!

Chapter **9**

Helping with Logic Operations

ogic is the heart of programming. A computer program is essentially a giant set of logic statements, or rules, that execute in order. Similar to any decision-based field — law, forensic science, football, driving — programming enumerates rules that are put together logically. As the program executes, different subsets of rules are accessed, testing *conditions* and producing *decisions*, or *outcomes*. Outcomes then lead to the execution of other subsets of rules within the program, and so on.

This chapter guides you in helping your young coder master the application of logic in coding. Specifically, it helps you coach him in writing *conditionals*, also called *if-then* commands, beginning with easy ones. You also use *and, not,* and *or* commands to construct intended meaning in a conditional. Combining several logic operations together allows your coder to build up to increasingly more complex commands. By the end of the chapter, you and your coder will be logic pros!

Simple Logic, Unplugged

When you ask your kid to, "think logically," what do you mean? You probably want him to look at a fact, or perhaps multiple facts, and then based on some set of conditions, make a decision. For instance, you tell your teen that, "If your room is clean, then you can go to the movies." The two of you survey his room only to find a smelly T-shirt hanging from the fan, an empty salt-and-vinegar chips bag stuffed in the corner, and fluffs of Corgi fur wafting through the air. Because his room is not clean, he didn't fulfill the condition you established. Therefore, his consequence is that he doesn't go to the movies. When he later summons you to re-evaluate his room and you find it spotlessly clean (ta-da!), he has now fulfilled the condition of cleanness, resulting in the consequence that he can now attend the movie.

Whether you previously realized it or not, life is full of if-then statements! "If you save your money, then you can afford a vacation." "If you reduce your calorie consumption, then you lose weight." This type of decision-making is part of the selection process in programming. Selecting a path directs your program to move to a different place as lines of code execute in sequence. (See Chapter 2.) Even songs feature conditional statements. Remember Paul Simon's lyric, "If you'll be my bodyguard, I can be your long lost pal." Or, one of Camille's personal favorites from Men Without Hats, the Safety Dance (see Figure 9-1), "If your friends don't dance, then they're no friends of mine!" Our editor, Rebecca, loves hearing another great song featuring a conditional, "If I Had a Million Dollars," by the Barenaked Ladies. Work together with your young coder to assemble and share a list of everyday if-then statements. If you do it. . . then it will be fun!

FIGURE 9-1:
Conditionals in the Safety Dance: If your friends don't dance, then they're no friends of mine!

Figure credit: https://upload.wikimedia.org/wiki
pedia/en/7/7a/The_Safety_Dance_single.jpg

Challenge your coder to brainstorm other types of selection processes he might use in his daily life. For example, he might perform an if-then-else each afternoon as he tackles his homework: "If I have homework, then I'll complete the assignment, else I'll play video games." Another, more advanced type of selection process he might use involves making a decision among several choices. In programming, this type of programming structure is called a *switch:* the program switches to select the consequence that meets the identified condition. For example, when playing basketball, a `switch` statement might involve every current option for advancing the ball to the basket: shooting, driving in for a layup, passing to a teammate, and so on. Another example is, when watching television, your coder may endlessly press the remote button, switching from channel to channel in an entertainment selection process.

Programming Simple Conditionals

Logical operations in a computer program are implemented as *conditional statements*, also called, `if-then` control commands. `If-then` commands allow your coder to, given certain conditions, make a consequence occur. The `if` portion of the statement is followed by the *condition*, and the `then` portion of the statement is followed by the *consequence*.

In pseudocode

Here is the general, pseudocode format of a conditional:

```
if condition then consequence
```

The `if` portion of a conditional can only return two possible values: true or false. For this reason, it's considered a Boolean operation (see Chapter 7 for more information on working with Booleans). When the `if` portion of a conditional is true, the `then` portion is executed. When the `if` portion of a condition is false, the `then` portion is not executed.

Your coder can use a wide variety of conditions in a simple conditional statement. Similarly, he can use a wide range of consequences as well. Here are some pseudocode examples:

```
if (revenue > $100000) then (add $5000 bonus to salary)
```

```
if (switch is on) then (sound the alarm)
```

In Scratch

Your coder can create a simple conditional with a Boolean condition. Figure 9-2 shows an `if-then` command that is part of a Rock, Paper, Scissors game. This command determines whether two players, Ann and Bob, show the same hand. Here, if Ann hand = Bob hand, then the game announces a tie!

Your coder can expand this if-then command into an if-then-else structure to make other comparisons in the Rock, Paper, Scissors game, as outlined in the last section of this chapter.

In Python

Your young coder can use Boolean values and conditionals to control the execution of his Python programs. Here is a simple example:

```python
dogBreed = "Corgi"

if dogBreed == "Corgi":
    print("That is the best type of dog, ever!")
```

Be sure to use the == symbol to measure equivalence. The = symbol is used to assign values. Here is another example of using logic operations and conditionals in Python, this time using an if-then-else structure:

```python
gameScore = 5000
highScore = 10000
if gameScore > highScore:
    print("You earned the new high score!")
    highScore = gameScore
else:
    print("Game over, better luck next time.")
```

In JavaScript

Your coder can also use Boolean values and conditionals to control the execution of programs he writes in JavaScript programs. The following is an example of a simple if-then conditional:

```
var time = 22;
var message;

if (time > 20) {
    message = "Good evening";
}
```

Here is another example of using logic operations and conditionals in JavaScript, this time using an if-then-else structure. This structure is useful when your coder wants to program a small number of paths, or choices, as consequences of the conditional (or conditionals).

```
var time = 15;
var message;

if (time > 20) {
    message = "Good evening";
} else if (time > 12) {
    message = "Good afternoon";
} else {
    message = "Good morning";
}
```

When assigning a value, use the = symbol. When measuring equivalence, use the == symbol (or, in Java, use the .equals() method to compare.

When writing conditionals, remind your coder that the conditional "breaks out" of the if-then, or if-then-else, structure after it finds a true condition (and executes it). If it never finds a true statement, the program executes the else consequence; if there is no else, then the program simply continues to the next sequential line of code following the conditional.

These JavaScript programs only set the value of the message variable. They don't print the message. To do so, you need to use output commands such as window. alert() or console.log() within script tags (see Chapter 14).

Another way your coder may need to use logic operations and conditionals in JavaScript is by writing a switch structure. This structure is used when your coder wants the program to execute one of many possible code blocks. Here, the switch is triggered by the first case (the expression) that evaluates to true. It then "breaks out" of the switch structure. If no expression triggers the switch, the last block — the default block — is executed.

```
var exam = 72;
var letter;
switch (true) {
    case grade >= 90:
        letter = "A";
        break;
    case grade >= 80:
        letter = "B";
        break;
    case grade >= 70:
        letter = "C";
        break;
    case grade >= 60:
        letter = "D";
        break;
    default:
        letter = "F";
}
```

Notice that each case of the switch is evaluated in the order written, from top to bottom. For example, a grade of 88 doesn't trigger the first case (the "A" case), but it does trigger the second case (the "B" case). Thus, a letter is set to "B" and the program breaks out of the switch structure.

It's important to note that order matters in a switch. For instance, placing the "D" case at the top causes a grade of 88 (which is >= 60) to evaluate to true, thereby producing the wrong result. Place the most restrictive case at the top, and work down to the least restrictive case, ending with a default value that serves as a catchall.

In Java

Coders working in Java can control the code selection process using a wide variety of logical operations, conditionals, and switch statements. Here are some examples of the previous programs, now written in Java using the BlueJ IDE (see Chapter 3 for details on BlueJ and other development platforms). The programs also include output statements.

Figure 9-3 shows an if-then-else conditional written in Java, and the result of the program execution.

Figure 9-4 shows a switch statement written in Java along with the result of the program execution.

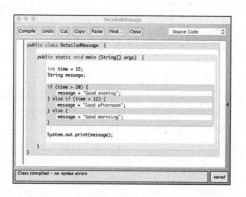

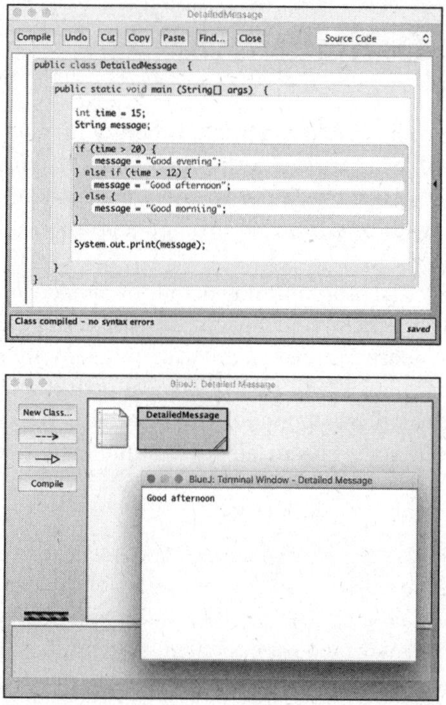

FIGURE 9-3: Java code, written in BlueJ, showing an if–then–else conditional that prints messages based on time of day (top), and its output (bottom).

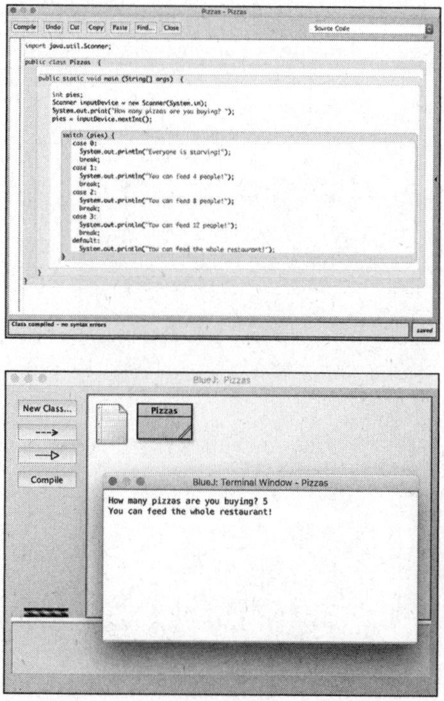

FIGURE 9-4: Java code, written in BlueJ, demonstrating use of a switch statement for selecting pizza serving quantities (top), and its output (bottom).

Advanced Logic, Unplugged

Young coders typically code simple conditionals before moving on to more complex logic. Your coder will want to level up his logic skills by putting together more than one condition. Doing so allows him to create *compound conditionals*, facilitating the selection of many different routes through a program.

Prior to diving into the actual programming details of *compound conditionals* (many conditionals put together), help your coders cement the logic of working with multiple if-then statements in more familiar settings. Many beloved childhood board games and puzzles are predicated on logical operations, including Guess Who, Clue, and Mastermind. Playing and winning the game requires players to construct and use conditionals, specifically compound conditionals. Here is what each game addresses:

>> Guess Who (Figure 9-5) is a sort of whodoneit? two-player game that's perfect for the early elementary crowd. In Guess Who, each of two players possess a set of characters with different hair color, eye color, and clothing accessories. Each player selects a "mark" and her opponent attempts to guess the identity of the mark by asking true/false questions to eliminate characters. Following the elimination of all characters who don't match, the character who remains is the mark. Ultimately, finding the mark is a process of executing a compound conditional statement. For example, "if the person (is a redhead and wears glasses and not male) then the person is the mark."

FIGURE 9-5: Guess Who is an away-from-computer game that requires the use of conditionals to identify a mark.

Figure credit: https://www.amazon.com/Winning-Moves-Games-1191-Guess/dp/B00S732WJE

» Clue (Figure 9-6) is another classic whodoneit? game, with multiple players working to solve a murder mystery. Players of all ages, from elementary schoolers through octogenarians enjoy Clue. Game action involves each player rolling dice to move game pieces around the board and make conjectures about who committed the crime, the type of murder weapon, and the room in which the crime occurred. Following each conjecture, other players report a part of the conjecture as true or false. Learning what is true and false provides clues that advance the player ever closer to solving the mystery. Best of all, your young coder will learn that, determining whether "Colonel Mustard did it and he did it in the Ballroom and he used the Candlestick," is great practice for writing complex conditionals!

FIGURE 9-6:
Conditionals help players figure out whodoneit in the classic board game, Clue.

Figure credit: https://www.amazon.com/Winning-Moves-Games-1137-Classic/dp/B00349MPQQ/ref=sr_1_4?s=toys-and-games&ie=UTF8&qid=1516039490&sr=1-4&keywords=clue

» Mastermind (Figure 9-7) is a code-making and code-breaking two-player game in which one player makes a code and her opponent works to break the code. Kids of middle school age and older find this game incredibly fun and addictive. Each code consists of four pegs, which can be arranged in any sequence using pegs of six different colors. The code breaker takes a shot in the dark on the first guess, for example guessing purple-purple-yellow-yellow.

The code maker then indicates, how many pegs are not correct; how many are the correct color and not correct position; and how many are the correct color and correct position. However, the code breaker doesn't know the status of any individual peg, so she has to test different possibilities on each new guess. (Interestingly, getting nothing right on a guess is extremely helpful because it eliminates all the colors in the guess!) The code breaker has ten tries to break the code. Your coder will find herself combining multiple conditionals in her head, to eventually crack the code — and building her logic skills for programming as an added benefit!

FIGURE 9-7:
Mastermind requires keeping track of many compound conditionals "in the head" to break a secret color code.

Figure credit: https://www.amazon.com/Mastermind-Game-Strategy-Codemaker-Codebreaker/dp/B00000DMBF/ref=sr_1_4?s=toys-and-games&ie=UTF8&qid=1516039649&sr=1-4&keywords=mastermind+game

Coding Compound Conditionals (aka, AND, NOT, and OR Will Get You Pretty Far!)

As your coder constructs his programs, he uses logic operations to make decisions about which code needs to execute, and under which conditions. The if-then statements he wants to construct may need to consist of more than one condition — they may need *compound* (multiple) conditions to execute the consequence. The main logic operations your coder uses to create compound conditional are and, not, and or. Here is what each one means:

» **and** means that every condition is true.

» **not** changes the Boolean value of a statement: true becomes false, and false becomes true.

» **or** means that at least one of the conditions is true.

In pseudocode

Here is the general pseudocode format of a compound conditional:

```
if homework is done and it's after 9pm then go to bed
```

The `if` portion of a compound conditional can only return a Boolean value: true or false (see Chapter 7 for more information on working with Booleans).

Here are some examples of compound conditionals in pseudocode:

```
if (weight >= 40 lbs and height >= 38 in) then (use booster
    seat)

if (not fuse tripped) then (electrical current flows)

if (SAT > 1500 or ACT > 33) then (earn scholarship)
```

Compound conditionals in Scratch

Your coder may want to construct a Frogger-style video game, and needs to control the game action based on conditions of the game at different times. Here's how your coder can write code for logic operations in his game.

And

Figure 9-8 shows a portion of the game using the **and** operation in Scratch. The frog object has three variables — `lives`, `timer`, and `y-position` (see Chapter 5 for details on working with position, and Chapter 7 for details on working with variables). When the green flag is pressed, the values of `lives`, `timer`, and `y-position` are set. The `say` command announces the Boolean value of the logic operation

```
lives > 0 and timer > 0
```

Because both statements are true, the frog announces `true`.

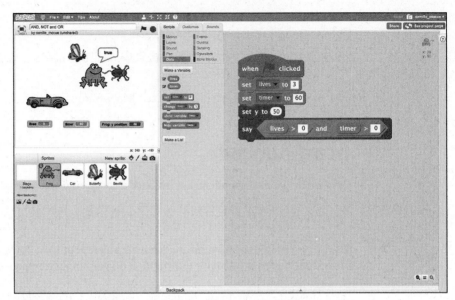

FIGURE 9-8:
The and
command
executes when
all conditions
are true.

Not

Figure 9-9 shows a new version of the game using the not operation in Scratch. When the green flag is pressed, the values of lives, timer, and y-position are set. The say command announces the Boolean value of the logic operation

```
not touching car
```

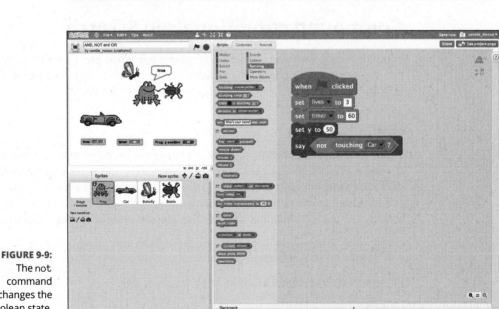

FIGURE 9-9:
The not
command
changes the
Boolean state.

The value of touching car is false, so the value of not touching car is true. The frog announces true!

Or

Figure 9-10 shows another version of the game demonstrating the or operation in Scratch. When the green flag is pressed, the values of lives, timer, and y-position are set. The say command announces the Boolean value of the logic operation

```
touching beetle or touching butterfly
```

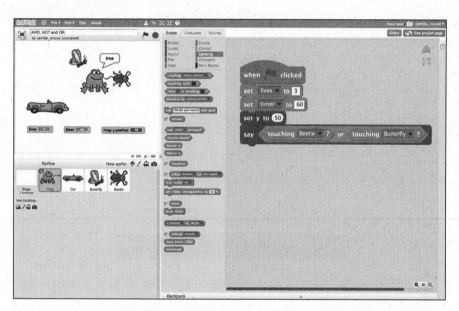

FIGURE 9-10:
The or command executes when at least one condition is true.

The value of touching beetle is true, and the value of touching butterfly is false. So the frog announces true!

Figure 9-11 shows a slightly altered version of the game conditions involving the or command. In this case, the beetle is no longer caught by the frog's tongue and they aren't touching. The value of touching beetle is now false, and the value of touching butterfly is also false. So the frog announces false.

In Python

For young coders working in Python, compounding logical operators allow for structuring more precise control in their programs. For example, a program may be structured to compute different paychecks for people with different salaries, bonuses, and other variables. Table 9-1 shows the logical operators your young coder uses in Python.

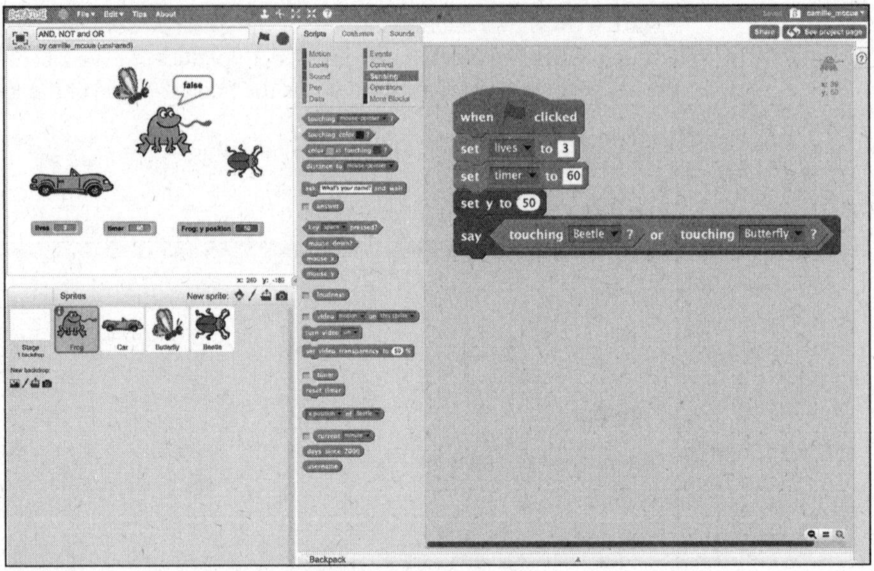

FIGURE 9-11:
The or command yields false when none of the conditions is true.

TABLE 9-1

Logical Operators in Python

Operator	What It Means
==	equivalent to
and	and
not	not
or	or

Figure 9-12 shows an example of code snippet that uses logical operators in Python. The example shows code that computes different paychecks for people with different salaries, bonuses, and other variables. The code references three variables: pay, salary, and bonus, where the current value of each is pay = 50000, salary = 40000, and bonus = 10000. The code and its execution are created in pythontutor.com.

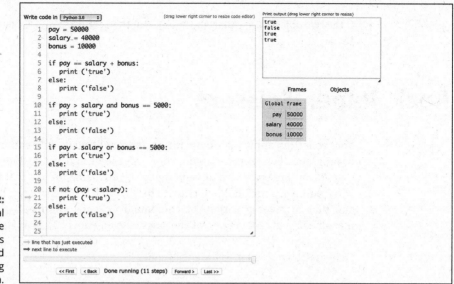

FIGURE 9-12:
Python logical operators are shown in this code snippet and execution, using pythontutor.com.

In JavaScript

Coders can also use logical operators in JavaScript to control the execution of their programs. Table 9-2 shows the logical operators your young coder uses.

TABLE 9-2

Logical Operators in JavaScript

Operator	What It Means
==	equivalent to
&&	and
!	not
|| (double pipes)	or

In Java

When programming in Java, young coders can — with a few exceptions — use the same logical operators shown for JavaScript in Table 9-2. A key exception your coder needs to know is how to compare objects. The equality of objects should not be tested using the == operator. Instead, when trying to determine equivalence between the object values, use the .equals() method. Here is an example:

```
name.equals("Speedy Gonzales")
```

If the two objects are equal, the `equals` method returns `true`. Otherwise, it returns `false`.

Rock, Paper, Scissors

Your coder can apply logical operators and conditionals by creating a wide variety of programs. For example, invite your coder to design and execute a Choose Your Own Adventure story — a fun and thought-provoking project that merges literacy with coding in a meaningful context (see Chapter 2). Or challenge him to create an app that includes a variety of compound `if-then` commands, such as a slot machine or a digital version of the classic Rock, Paper, Scissors game!

Here are some tips for writing this code:

>> Create a background with labels for the two players. You can use any names you want. (We use Ann and Bob here.)

>> Create two sprites, Ann hand and Bob hand, with three costumes for each sprite: rock, paper, and scissors. You can draw these costumes or import clip art from the web. (See Figure 9-13.)

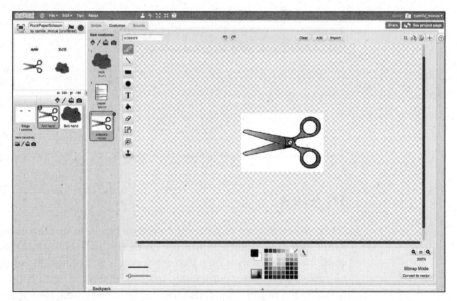

FIGURE 9-13: In a Rock, Paper, Scissors game, each sprite is a "hand" that possesses the same costumes — a rock, a piece of paper, and a pair of scissors.

>> In the Variables category, create two variables: ann and bob. The variables hold the names of the costumes worn by the sprites.

>> For the Ann hand, drag out the code tiles and snap them together as shown. The set ann to pick random 1 to 3 command assigns a random number for the variable ann. The switch costume to ann then places costume number ann on the Ann hand sprite. (See Figure 9-14.)

>> For the Bob hand:

- Drag the code tiles and snap them together as shown. The set bob to pick random 1 to 3 command assigns a random number for the variable bob. The switch costume to bob and then places costume number bob on the Bob hand sprite. (See Figure 9-15.)

- The code if ann = bob then say Tie! is an if–then–else conditional that checks whether the variables for the costumes are equal. If they are, then Ann and Bob created the same item (for example, they both created paper). This results in a tie.

- If the tie condition is not met, the else consequence is executed. This else statement selects and runs a new if–then–else statement. The if condition is a compound conditional consisting of three or statements: each of these or statements is an outcome in which Ann wins (for example, Ann has rock and Bob has scissors). The else condition is the catchall in which Bob wins (any outcome in which Ann did not win).

Encourage your coder to invent his own new games using selection to create varied paths for the players!

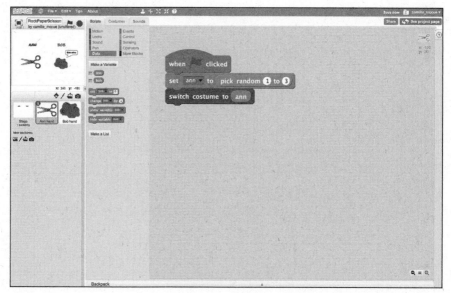

FIGURE 9-14:
Pressing the green flag causes a random costume to be applied to the ann sprite.

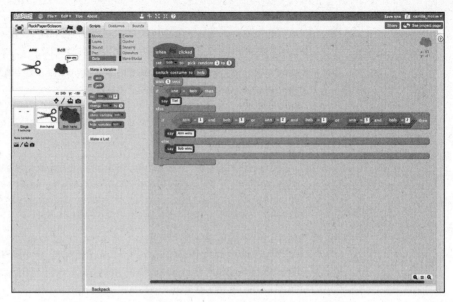

FIGURE 9-15:
Pressing the green flag causes a random costume to be applied to the bob sprite. It then checks for a tie or a winner!

Chapter **10**

Getting Loopy

L oops are a type of control command that are common to every programming language. Computers are really good at repeating the same action over and over again, which is great because as humans, that can get really boring!

Loops can be useful for a variety of purposes. You could animate a cloud in a video game to move from the left of the stage to the right and back to the left and repeat that throughout the entire game. Or you may want to compute how much money you would have after one year if you invest an initial quantity into a bank account that accrues compound interest. Consider placing $100 into that account, with a daily interest rate of 1%! Day 1 you would have $100, day two you would have the balance * 1.01, which would be $101.00, day three you would have the balance * 1.01, which would be $102.01, and so on. If you loop through the process of computing balance = balance * 1.01 for 365 iterations, you would have $3,778.34 at the end of the year! It would be a pretty long program if you had to write balance = balance * 1.01 over and over, 365 times, without using a loop!

Loops, Unplugged

You and your young coder can explore loops in many ways in the physical world. Loops repeat actions until a certain condition is met; for example "Take a bite of food until your plate is clean." A condition for a loop can also be very specific with how many times it repeats, for example "Take one step until you have taken ten steps" would be a loop that you know repeats exactly ten times. But with code, you can also get tricky and have a loop that says "Take two steps until you have taken ten steps," which would actually only repeat the action "take two steps" five times instead of ten! Either way, loops always have a condition and a set of actions that will repeat until the condition is met.

Repeat fun, unplugged

A really fun and easy way to introduce your young coder to loops and repeating actions is to throw a dance party! Identify five dance moves: clap, stomp, wiggle, jump, and squat. Then write a series of moves on one line on the white board (or even a piece of paper):

```
Repeat 2 times:
   Clap, clap, clap
   Repeat 3 times:
      Stomp, stomp, clap
   Wiggle, jump, squat, jump
Clap
```

The entire dance would consist of 33 actions in total, but you only have to write 11! You can even have your young coders write their own dances using the same actions!

Random loop conditions, unplugged

One fun way to get your coder understanding how the conditions and actions of loops work is to pass out a sheet with a number line on it from 1 to 18 and give each person a die. In teams of two, have each person roll the die five times. The first number that they roll is the starting position on the number line, the next three numbers they roll are added together and is the ending position on the number line, and the fifth number that they roll is the increment value that they use as their action. Code.org offers a really great worksheet for this activity as part of its For Loop Fun puzzle found at `https://studio.code.org/s/course4/stage/8/puzzle/1`.

Figure 10-1 shows an example of two players playing one round of the game. Player 1 rolled a 3, then rolled three numbers that added to 12 (maybe 5, 6, and 1), then rolled a 4. So she started at 3, ended at 12, and added each 4th number, totaling 21 points!

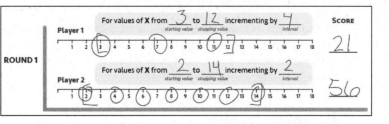

FIGURE 10-1:
A sample of the
number line
unplugged
activity from
Code.org.

Loop Types and Structures

Most programming languages have two main types of loops: *while* and *for*. While loops are also called *conditional loops* because they're based on a condition where you won't typically know how many times the actions repeat. For example, "Take a bite of food until your plate is empty" would most likely be written as a while loop because depending on how big the bites are, you might have to take 10 bites or 20! For loops are also called "counted loops" because they are based on an exact number of times you want something to repeat. For example, "Take one step until you have taken 10 steps" would most likely be written as a for loop because you take exactly 10 steps.

Programming languages also have another type of while loop: do-while. The difference between a while and do-while loop is simply when the condition gets checked. In a while loop, the computer checks the condition first, then performs the action if the condition is true. For example, "Take a bite of food until your plate is empty" in a while loop would first check to see whether the plate is empty; if it isn't empty then you take a bite. This can be a good idea, because if your plate is already empty then it doesn't make sense to take a bite. In a do-while loop, the computer checks the condition after the action has been performed at least once. For example, "Take a bite of food until your plate is empty" in a do-while loop you take a bite no matter what, and then check to see whether the plate is empty. This probably makes more sense in this context, because it isn't likely that you were given an empty plate.

For loops also have two types. A typical for loop has a starting point, a condition, and an increment amount (similar to the Random Loop Conditions unplugged activity shown earlier in this chapter). Oftentimes, for loops have a starting number, a condition which specifies when the loop should stop iterating, and a number by which you should increment for each iteration of the loop. For example, you have 10 baskets and want to put an egg in all of the even-numbered baskets. The starting number would be 2, the condition for when the loop should stop would be when you have reached 10 baskets, and the number by which you should increment is 2. Then you would put an egg in baskets 2, 4, 6, 8, and 10. Another type of for loop is called the for-each loop. A *for-each loop* simply iterates through all the items in a list. (Chapter 11 goes into more detail about lists.) This can be very useful if you want to perform the same action for every item. For example, "Give each of your classmates a high five" would best be represented as a for-each loop; for each classmate, give him a high five.

Infinite loops

Something that often trips up young coders is infinite loops. An *infinite* loop is any type of loop that never stops repeating. This can happen pretty easily if you set your conditions incorrectly. For example, if your young coder is 8 years old and you have a while loop that says "while you are older than 7 years old, do a jumping jack," then your young coder has to do jumping jacks FOREVER!

Infinite loops often make your program either look like it's not doing anything, or just crash. In Chapter 13 you can find out how to debug infinite loops.

REMEMBER

You can also create a specific form on an infinite loop on purpose, for instance, coding a forever loop in Scratch to play background music that loops the entire time a game is being played. To break an infinite loop, you might need to use an if-then statement such as "if the player loses all lives in frogger, then stop all." (See Chapter 2 for a description of these conditional statements.)

Actions repeated in loops

The last thing to know about all loop types is that you can have as many actions as you want in the loop. It could just be one action — "take a bite" — that you have to repeat, but it could also be eight actions — for example, if you're wrapping a lot of gifts, your actions to repeat might be "grab a gift from the unwrapped pile of gifts, take the price tag off the gift, measure the quantity of wrapping paper, cut the paper to the right measurements, fold the paper around the gift, tape the paper closed, write a message on the gift, place in the pile of wrapped gifts."

Conditions of loops

As you might have noticed already, the conditions of loops are always of Boolean type. Chapter 7 introduces you to Boolean types if you need a refresher, but simply speaking a Boolean gives two choices: true or false. The condition of a loop always evaluates to either true or false, to know if the action(s) inside the loop repeats again, or the loop ends and the rest of the program continues.

Using pseudocode

Most programming languages have the same general structure for while loops, do-while loops, and for loops. Loops are written with indentation to make it clear which actions are a part of the repetition, and which actions simply come after the loop.

While loops:

```
while(condition)
action1
action2
...
END_WHILE
```

Examples:

```
while(sunIsUp)
    playOutside
END_WHILE
```

```
while(rightArrowKeyIsPressed)
    moveRightOneStep
END_WHILE
```

Do-while loops:

```
do
    action1
    action2
    ...
while(condition)
```

Examples:

```
amount = 0
do
    amount = amount + 5
while(amount < 50)
```

```
do
    takeBiteOfFood
while(plateHasFood)
```

For loops:

```
for(starting_bound; condition; increment)
action1
action2
...
END_FOR
```

Examples:

```
balance = 0
for(days = 1; days <= 365; days++)
    balance = balance * 1.01
END_FOR
```

```
for(walls = 1; walls <= 4; walls++)
    walkForwardLengthOfWall
    turnRight(90degrees)
END_FOR
```

For-each loop:

```
for(item in list)
action1
action2
...
END_FOR_EACH
```

Examples:

```
for(classmate in class)
    highFive
END_FOR_EACH
```

```
totalScore = 0
for(score in testScores)
    totalScore = totalScore + score
END_FOR_EACH
```

Explicit infinite loop:

```
while(TRUE)
action1
action2
if(condition)
```

```
    BREAK_LOOP
...
END_WHILE
```

Examples:

```
while(TRUE)
    exploreCave
    if(flashlightDies)
        BREAK_LOOP
END_WHILE
```

```
while(TRUE)
    number = askUserForNumber
    if(number is 5)
        BREAK_LOOP
END_WHILE
```

An expression such as `points++` means `points = points + 1`. Similarly, `countdown--` means `countdown = countdown - 1`.

REMEMBER

Using Scratch

Scratch offers three different type of loops, all shown in Figure 10-2, found under the Control category. The repeat loop is just like a for loop; it repeats exactly the number of times specified by the coder. The forever loop is one that is unique to Scratch; it repeats until the user presses the red stop sign, or uses a Stop block. It's basically a deliberate infinite loop! The repeat-until loop is just like a while loop; it repeats until the condition that the coder specifies is reached.

WARNING

A typical while loop continues repeating the actions while the condition is true, and stops when the condition becomes false. In Scratch, the repeat-until loop continues repeating the actions while the condition is false, and stops when the condition becomes true. This can be really tricky for anyone, but especially young coders who're switching between Scratch and other programming languages. The best way to mitigate this problem is to read the code in English. For example, the code for a typical while loop might read as "While my plate has food, take a bite", whereas the code for a Scratch repeat-until loop might be read as "Repeat taking a bite until my plate is empty." When in doubt, write it out!

Here are some examples of simple Scratch programs you might want to write using each of the types of loops that Scratch offers.

FIGURE 10-2:
Scratch provides three different types of loops.

Repeat loop

The program shown in Figure 10-3 shows a repeat loop where you can have your sprite draw a shape on screen. You can change the number of times the loop repeats and the turn angle to create other shapes too. Give it a try!

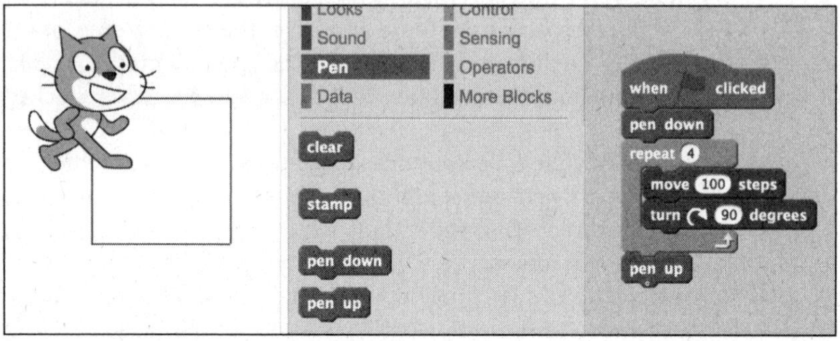

FIGURE 10-3:
A simple Scratch program that uses the repeat loop.

Forever loop

The program shown in Figure 10-4 shows a forever loop where the character follows the mouse pointer! So anywhere you move your mouse, the character points towards it and moves 10 steps. Try changing the number of steps that the sprite takes each time to see what happens when you press the green flag!

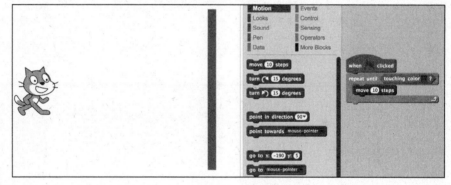

Repeat-until loop

The program shown in Figure 10-5 shows a repeat-until loop where the character moves forward until it touches the color red. This can be used with random numbers and more than one character to create a race game!

FIGURE 10-5:
A simple Scratch
program that
uses the
repeat-until loop.

Using Python

Python has two types of loops that it supports: while and for-each. A while loop can be written as a do-while loop however, and a for-each loop can be written to simulate a basic version of the for loop (where you start at one number and increment by one each iteration of the loop).

TECHNICAL
STUFF

When you want to use a Python for-each loop like a for loop, use the range function. In this case, range includes the first number and excludes the second number. So if you want to print all the numbers from 1 to 10, your range parameters is `range(1, 11)`.

In Python you *must* make sure that everything is indented properly. This means that any action that is repeated is indented once from the loop. If you have an action that you want to happen when the loop is done iterating, it should not be indented. For example:

```
while condition
    actionToBeRepeated1
    actionToBeRepeated2
actionToHappenAfterLoopCompletes
```

While loops:

```
while condition:
    action1
    action2
...
```

Examples:

```
count = 1
while count <= 10:
    print count
    count = count + 1
```

```
number = 0
while number != 5:
    number = input("Guess the number ")
print "You guessed the right number"
```

Do-while loops:

```
action1
while condition:
action1
```

Example:

```
number = input("Guess the number ")
while number != 5:
    number = input("Guess the number ")
print "You guessed the right number!"
```

For loops:

```
for variableName in range(number1, number2):
   action1
   action2
...
```

Example:

```
for count in range(1, 10):
   print count
```

For-each loops:

```
for item in list:
   action1
   action2
...
```

Example:

```
classList = ["Sarah", "Camille", "Steve", "Rebecca"]
for classmate in class:
   print "Hi " + classmate"
name = "Sarah"
for letter in name:
   print letter
```

Explicit infinite loop:

```
while True
   action1
   action2
   if condition:
break
...
```

Example:

```
while True:
   password = raw_input("what is the password? ")
   if password == "password":
     break
print "Congratulations, you now have access"
```

Nesting Loops

If you played the Repeat Fun unplugged activity at the beginning of this chapter, then you've already seen a nested loop! Nested loops are basically a loop within a loop. This can be useful for making drawings like fractals or fun shapes that repeat but slightly change each time, creating ASCII art, or even having complex repetitions. The examples in the following sections show how nesting loops can help create some fun programs. You can nest any kind of loop inside any other kind of loop. For example, you can nest a for loop inside a while loop!

TECHNICAL STUFF

A fractal is a geometric object that has self-similarity — it shows the same pattern whether you're looking at it far away or close up. Fractals can provide mathematically accurate models of coastlines, mountains, and other real objects from nature. Loops (specifically, *recursive* loops) are used to code fractals. One of the earliest uses of computer graphics in big-screen movies was the creation of fractal-based scenery for the transformation of the Genesis planet in Star Trek II: The Wrath of Khan. Khhannnnn!

Using pseudocode

Nesting loops can happen in any combination. Here are some examples of nesting loops, but this list is not exhaustive.

For-each loop nested inside a for-each loop:

```
for(item in list)
   action1
   for(item in list)
      action2
      action3
...
   END_FOR_EACH
   action4
END_FOR_EACH
```

Example:

```
jellyBeanCount = 0
for(jar in jars)
   for(jellybean in jar)
      jellyBeanCount = jellyBeanCount + 1
   END_FOR_EACH
END_FOR_EACH
```

While loop nested inside a for-each loop:

```
for(item in list)
    action1
    while(condition)
        action2
        action3
...
    END_WHILE
    action4
END_FOR_EACH
```

Example:

```
for(room in house)
    while(wallsWhite)
        paintWallsBlue
    END_WHILE
END_FOR_EACH
```

Using Scratch

Nesting loops in Scratch can be a lot of fun when you introduce the pen and start drawing fun shapes. Here are some basic examples of nesting loops in Scratch.

Repeat loop nested inside a repeat loop

Figure 10-6 shows an example of a Scratch program that draws 10 concentric squares. The outer repeat loop is responsible for repeating 10 times for each square. The inner repeat loop is responsible for repeating 4 times, for each line and turn in each square.

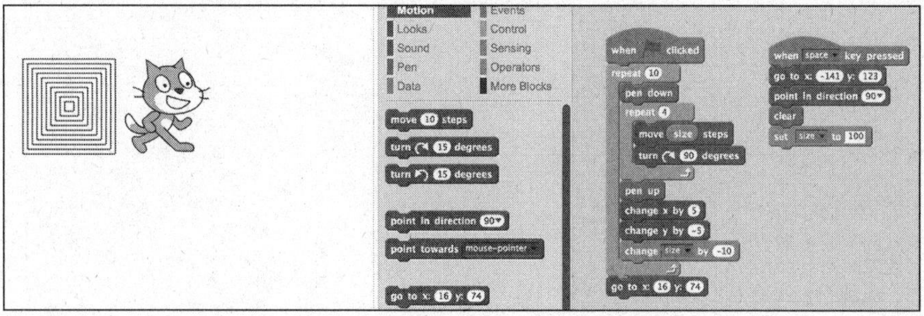

FIGURE 10-6:
A Scratch program that nests a repeat loop inside another repeat loop.

Repeat loop nested inside a repeat-until loop

Figure 10-7 shows an example of a Scratch program that draws squares in random places around the screen until the user presses the space key.

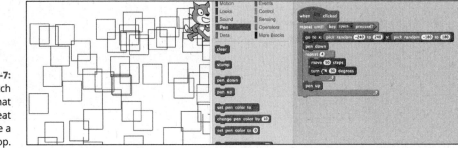

FIGURE 10-7:
A Scratch program that nests a repeat loop inside a repeat-until loop.

Using Python

One of the most fun programs to write in Python with nested loops is ASCII art. In coding, each character and symbol that you can type on a keyboard has a number representation called its ASCII number. Although in today's programming languages, you can type the character or symbol in your program, in the past you would have to use the ASCII number representation. ASCII art is basically when you create a picture using characters or symbols. There are some pretty amazing ASCII art examples, such as the one in Figure 10-8. As a kid, Camille used to have ASCII portraits of all the Star Trek: The Original Series cast members on her wall!

FIGURE 10-8:
An example of an ASCII art picture showing a lion from Wikipedia.

You can create a simple ASCII art program in Python using nested loops! For example, to create this pattern:

```
#
##
###
####
#####
######
#######
########
#########
```

The algorithm might be:

```
Print 1 # on Row 1
Print 2 # on Row 2
Print 3 # on Row 3
...
```

You could represent this using nested loops too!

```
for row in range(1, 11):
    rowText = ''
    for column in range(1, row):
        rowText = rowText + '#'
    print rowText
```

Coding the Classic Fibonacci Sequence

A fun program to write with your young coder that uses loops is to create the Fibonacci Sequence. The Fibonacci Sequence is a series of numbers that appears in art and nature, including the proportions of the Mona Lisa and the spirals of a nautilus shell. As a reminder, the Fibonacci Sequence is represented as:

```
Fₙ = Fₙ₋₁ + Fₙ₋₂
Where
F₀ = 0
F₁ = 1
```
$$F_n = F_{n-1} + F_{n-2}$$
$$\text{Where}$$
$$F_0 = 0$$
$$F_1 = 1$$

In other words, start with the first two numbers as 0 and 1. The next number is the sum of the two numbers preceding it. So the first ten numbers of the sequence would be:

0, 1, 1, 2, 3, 5, 8, 13, 21, 34

To write this in Python, your code for printing the Fibonacci Sequence would be:

```python
first = 0
second = 1
sequence = str(first) + ", " + str(second)

numberOfNumbers = input("How many numbers do you want to
    print? ")

for index in range(0, numberOfNumbers):
    next = first + second
    first = second
    second = next
    sequence = str(sequence) + ", " + str(next)
print sequence
```

IN THIS CHAPTER

» **Working with lists**

» **Sorting items in a list**

» **Coding a sorting algorithm in Java**

» **Searching for items in a list**

» **Coding a search algorithm in Java**

Chapter **11**

Adding Lists

Lists are ways of grouping data in coding. Kids encounter lists all the time in their daily lives, and so do you! Classrooms list the names of students in the class. Cookbooks list the ingredients in a recipe. Travelers make lists of what to pack in their suitcases. Students study lists of vocabulary words. Sometimes you create two lists that pair together. Parents list expenses when creating a budget, placing items such as "rent" and "car loan" in one list, and the associated cost in a second list. Dieters create paired lists of food items and their calories. Chapters 8 and 10 includes simple examples of how lists can make your programs a bit more interesting. For example, Chapter 10 shows how you can code a list of classmates that you iterate through and have your program say "hi" to each of your classmates.

TIP

If you aren't familiar with loops, review Chapter 10 before continuing on with this chapter. Loops and lists often go together, so understanding how loops work helps you understand how lists work.

Lists, Unplugged

You can represent a list to your young coder in a lot of different ways. You can write a list of numbers or names on a piece of paper, or even use a deck of cards to represent a list of cards. The important thing for your young coder to understand is that lists are essentially ordered collections of some kind of data. The data can be numbers, names, card values, or even objects. A fun way to get your young coder interacting with lists is to ask her to sort a deck of cards into four piles (one for each suit) and in numerical order.

You could use a variety of different algorithms for this sorting. For example, you could follow these algorithmic steps:

```
For each card in the deck
    Place the card in one of four piles depending on its suit
For each pile of suit cards
    For each card in the suit pile
        Find the smallest numbered card
        Place the card face down in a new pile
```

But you could do a different algorithm too, like this:

```
For each card in the deck
    Place the card in one of 13 piles depending on its number
    value
For each pile of number cards
    Find the pile with the smallest numerical value
    Move the pile to a new row of piles
For each pile of cards
    For each card in the pile
        Place the card face down in the correct suit pile
```

Or you could even have an algorithm like this:

```
For suit of card
    For each card in the deck
        Find the smallest numerical value of the suit
        Place the card face down in the correct suit pile
```

Whichever algorithm you choose to follow, you end up with four piles of cards, sorted by suit and in numbered order from smallest to largest when the cards are face up.

TIP

Having a conversation with your young coder about different ways you physically sort things really helps reinforce the concepts of sorting and lists explained in code later in this chapter!

Introducing Lists

You can think of a list as having data and an arrow to the next piece of data. This means that when you're writing code, you know about the first item in the list, but to access other items in the list your computer has to follow the arrows until it reaches the item you're looking for. For example, if you want the fifth item in your list, your computer has to follow five arrows until it reaches it. This is because your computer is storing each item in your list in a different place! Each arrow knows where the next item is, but that is it! So you can't go from the first item directly to the fifth item; you can only go from the first item to the second item, then to the third, and so on. Figure 11-1 shows an example of how you might want to draw a list.

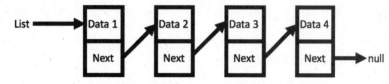

TECHNICAL STUFF

You might have noticed that Figure 11-1 has the word "null" at the end of the list. This is a coding word used to say "nothing." It basically means, there is nothing here following the final item on the list.

Some of the most basic actions to take on lists are creating a list, add an item to a list, remove an item from a list, get the size of a list, get an item at a certain location of a list, and iterate through a list. These six actions allow you and your young coder to do a lot with data sets (aka lists of data).

Using pseudocode

The six basic actions to take on lists are pretty straightforward. Here are examples of each action in pseudocode:

Create a list:

```
List listName
List listName = (item1, item2, ...)
```

Example:

```
List classmates
List classmates = ("Sarah", "Camille", "Steve", "Rebecca")

List classmates = ("Sarah")
```

Add items to a list:

```
listName.add(item)
```

Example:

```
List classmates = ("Sarah")
classmates.add("Luke")
```

Result:

```
classmates = ("Sarah", "Luke")
```

When adding an item to a list, the item that you're adding gets added to the end of the list.

Remove items from a list:

```
listName.remove(item)
listName.remove(position)
```

Example:

```
List classmates = ("Sarah", "Camille", "Steve", "Rebecca")
classmates.remove("Camille")
```

Result:

```
classmates = ("Sarah", "Steve", "Rebecca")
```

Example:

```
List classmates = ("Sarah", "Camille", "Steve", "Rebecca")
classmates.remove(3)
```

Result:

```
classmates = ("Sarah", "Camille", "Rebecca")
```

Get the size of a list:

```
listName.size
```

Example:

```
List classmates = ("Sarah", "Camille", "Steve", "Rebecca")
int size = classmates.size
```

Get an item or position in a list:

```
listName.get(position)
listName.getPositionOf(item)
```

Example:

```
List classmates = ("Sarah", "Camille", "Steve", "Rebecca")
String name = classmates.get(2)
int position = classmates.getPositionOf("Sarah")
```

Iterate through a list:

```
for(item in list)
    item.performAction
```

Example:

```
List classmates = ("Sarah", "Camille", "Steve", "Rebecca")
for(classmate in classmates)
    print "Hi " + classmate
```

Using Scratch

Scratch makes using lists really easy and straightforward! The following sections offer examples of the six basic interactions with lists in Scratch.

Creating a list

Figure 11-2 shows how to create a list in Scratch. Select Make a List under the Data category and give your list a name.

After you create the list, you see a lot of new blocks for your list, as shown in Figure 11-3, as well as the list being displayed on the stage.

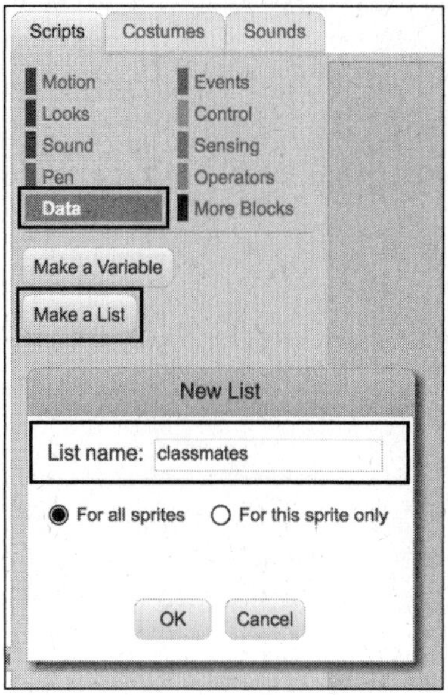

FIGURE 11-2:
How to create a
list in Scratch.

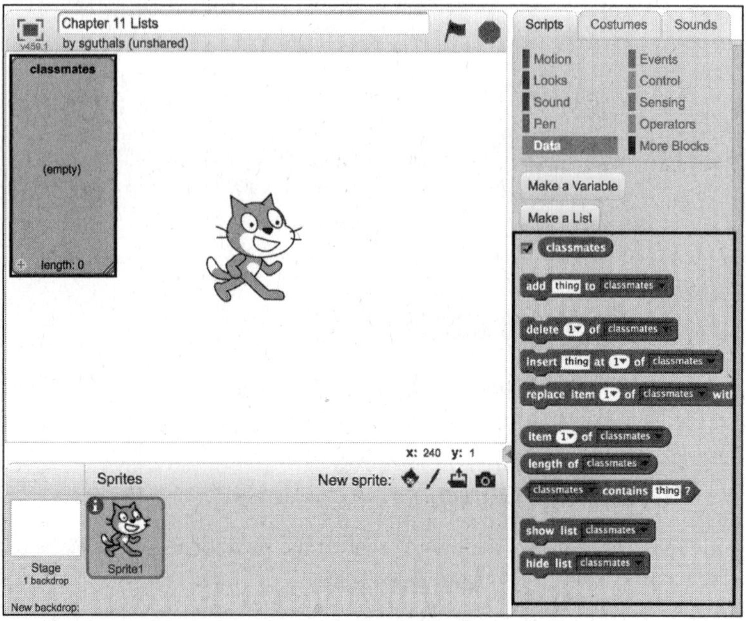

FIGURE 11-3:
All the new code
blocks are added
when you create
a list in Scratch.

Adding items to a list

Figure 11-4 shows how to add four names to the "classmates" list in Scratch. The
list on the stage shows what it looks like after the green flag has been pressed.

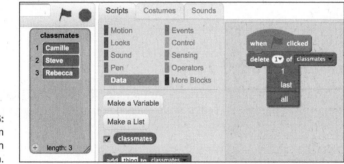

FIGURE 11-4:
Add items to a list
in Scratch.

Removing items from a list

Figure 11-5 shows how to remove one name from the "classmates" list in Scratch. Notice that you can specify removing the first item, the last item, or all the items from the list. You can also specify a specific position to remove by typing any other number instead of using the drop-down list. The list on the stage shows what it looks like after the green flag has been pressed.

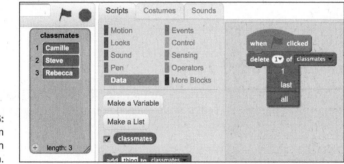

FIGURE 11-5:
Remove item
from a list in
Scratch.

Getting the size of a list

Figure 11-6 shows how to get the size of the "classmates" list in Scratch. The list on the stage shows what it looks like after the green flag has been pressed.

Getting an item at a position in a list

Figure 11-7 shows how to get an item from a certain position from the "class-mates" list in Scratch. Notice that you can specify getting the first item, the last item, or a random item from the list. You can also specify any other position by typing the number instead of using the drop-down list. The list on the stage shows what it looks like after the green flag has been pressed.

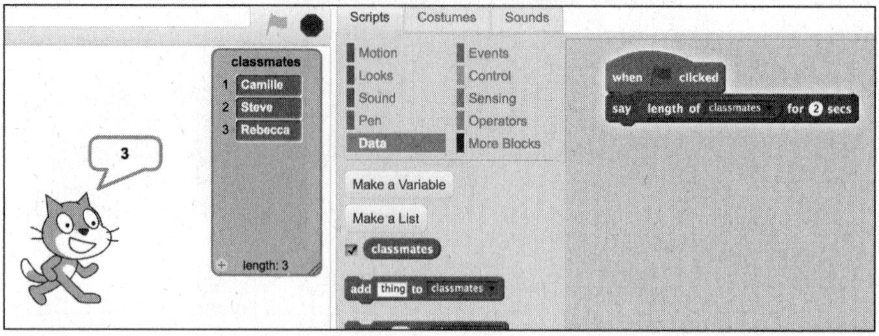

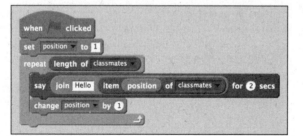

FIGURE 11-6:
Get the size of a
list in Scratch.

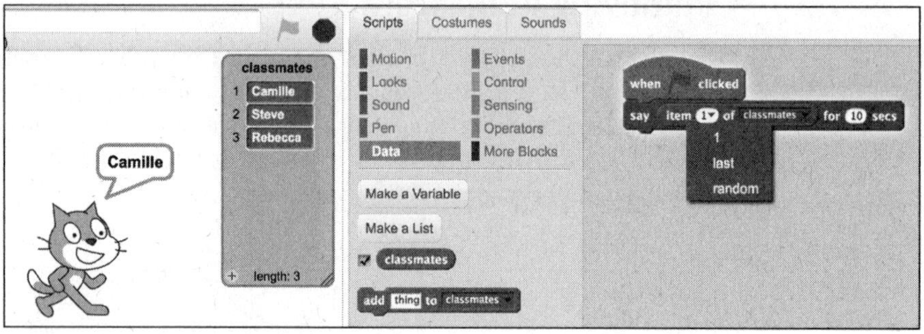

FIGURE 11-7:
Get an item from
a list in Scratch.

Iterating through a list

To iterate through a list in Scratch, you have to use a loop. Figure 11-8 shows an example of a program that says Hello to each person in the classmates list.

FIGURE 11-8:
Iterate through a
list in Scratch.

Using Java

Java has a List class that makes the six basic list operations fairly simple to use in your code. The only thing is that you have to import the List library into your program first. For more on code libraries, check out Chapter 8.

Each example in this section should be surrounded by the basic Java main class, and in this case you need to import the necessary libraries. If you want to test the examples in this section, make sure you create a file called Lists.java in your favorite IDE (see Chapter 3 for more information on coding environments for Java). Your Lists.java file should have the following code:

```java
import java.util.ArrayList;
import java.util.Arrays;
import java.util.List;

public class Lists
{
  public static void main(String [] args)
  {
    // INSERT EXAMPLE CODE HERE

      //You can use this line to print the list to see it
      System.out.println(listName);
  }
}
```

Java also has a generic List class, which you can learn all about on the Java documentation site for lists at https://docs.oracle.com/javase/8/docs/api/java/util/List.html. When you actually create a list, however, you might have to specify what type of list. In this chapter, you see examples of array lists, which are simple lists.

TECHNICAL STUFF

Unlike the pseudocode examples in this book and Scratch, Java (and other text-based languages like Python and JavaScript) start numbering positions in lists at 0. This makes sense if you think about it from a place-value point of view. The first ten numbers are: 0, 1, 2, 3, 4, 5, 6, 7, 8, and 9 — all numbers in the place value for One. This can cause a lot of confusion for young coders when working with lists because it can cause off-by-one errors. An example of an off-by-one error is when the coder thinks they're getting the first item in the list, but used 1 as the position instead of 0. You find more about fixing off-by-one errors in Chapter 13.

TECHNICAL STUFF

Java is a strongly typed language. This means that when working with lists in Java, you have to specify what type the data is inside the list. To specify this, you have to put <Type> next to the declaration of a list. You see this throughout the examples in this section.

Create a list:

```
List<Type> listName = new ArrayList<Type>();
List<Type> listName = Arrays.asList(item1, item2, ...);
```

Example:

```
List<String> classmates = new ArrayList<String>();
List<String> classmates = Arrays.asList("Sarah", "Camille",
    "Steve", "Rebecca");

List<String> classmates = Arrays.asList("Sarah");
```

Add items to a list:

```
listName.add(item);
listName.add(position, item);
```

Example:

```
List<String> classmates = new ArrayList<String>();
classmates.add("Sarah");
classmates.add("Luke");
classmates.add(1, "Camille");
```

Result:

```
classmates = ("Sarah", "Camille", "Luke")
```

When adding an item to a list, you can either add to the end of the list or at a specific position in the list.

REMEMBER

Remove items from a list:

```
listName.remove(item);
listName.remove(position);
```

Example:

```
List<String> classmates = new ArrayList<String>();
classmates.add("Sarah");
classmates.add("Luke");
classmates.add(1, "Camille");
classmates.remove("Camille");
```

Result:

```
classmates = ("Sarah", "Luke")
```

Example:

```java
List<String> classmates = new ArrayList<String>();
classmates.add("Sarah");
classmates.add("Luke");
classmates.add(1, "Camille");
classmates.remove(2);
```

Result:

```
classmates = ("Sarah", "Camille")
```

Get the size of a list:

```java
listName.size();
```

Example:

```java
List<String> classmates = new ArrayList<String>();
classmates.add("Sarah");
classmates.add("Luke");
classmates.add(1, "Camille");
int size = classmates.size();
```

Result:

```
size = 3
```

Get an item or position in a list:

```java
listName.get(position);
listName.indexOf(item);
```

Examples:

```java
List<String> classmates = new ArrayList<String>();
classmates.add("Sarah");
classmates.add("Luke");
classmates.add(1, "Camille");
String name = classmates.get(2);
int position = classmates.indexOf("Sarah");
```

Result:

```
name = Luke
position = 0
```

Iterate through a list:

```
for(indexName = startIndex; condition; iterationAmount)
{
    listName.get(indexName);
}
```

Example:

```
List<String> classmates = new ArrayList<String>();
classmates.add("Sarah");
classmates.add("Luke");
classmates.add(1, "Camille");
for(int position = 0; position < classmates.size();
    position++)
{
  System.out.println("Hi " + classmates.get(position));
}
```

Example:

```
List<String> classmates = new ArrayList<String>();
classmates.add("Sarah");
classmates.add("Luke");
classmates.add(1, "Camille");
for(String classmate : classmates)
{
  System.out.println("Hi " + classmate);
}
```

Result (same for both iteration examples):

```
Hi Sarah
Hi Camille
Hi Luke
```

ARRAYS

Lists are an example of a collection of data, but another common collection type is arrays. *Arrays* are essentially the same as lists, except they're stored on the computer slightly differently (see the first figure). Because computers store all the data for an array right next to each other on the memory card, it makes arrays more efficient than lists when trying to access a specific item. This also means, however, that when you create an array you have to know exactly how many elements you want to have in the array. This code shows you how to create an array of ten elements, where each element is a number. When this code is run, it prints the numbers 1 through 10. Notice that arrays still start at an index of 0, but because the code is putting the value of the index+1 into the position in the array, the numbers printed start at 1.

```
int[] myArray = new int[10];
for(int index = 0; index < myArray.length; index++)
{
    myArray[index+1] = index;
}
for(int index = 0; index < myArray.length; index++))
{
    System.out.println("myArray[" + index + "] = " +
     myArray[index]);
}
```

This code prints:

```
myArray[0] = 1
myArray[1] = 2
...
myArray[9] = 10
```

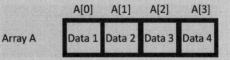

Arrays do have one benefit over lists, however; they can represent two-dimensional data! This can be useful, if you're wanting to represent a checker board or the seats in a classroom or movie theater. You can create a 2D array that represents each row and column of the physical space, such as the rows and columns of a classroom. Then you can iterate through each row and column to call on each student in the class!

(continued)

(continued)

For example, if you want to create a 2D array where you have two rows and three columns, you create it using this code:

```
String[][] myClassroom = new String[2][3];
```

The layout of your array would be drawn as shown in the following figure.

	myClassroom[row][0]	myClassroom[row][1]	myClassroom[row][2]
myClassroom[0][column]	myClassroom[0][0]	myClassroom[0][1]	myClassroom[0][2]
myClassroom[1][column]	myClassroom[1][0]	myClassroom[1][1]	myClassroom[1][2]

Now you put in names for each position in your 2D array, because that is where each student is sitting in the classroom:

```
myClassroom[0][0] = "Sarah";
myClassroom[0][1] = "Camille";
myClassroom[0][2] = "Rebecca";
myClassroom[1][0] = "Steve";
myClassroom[1][1] = "Luke";
myClassroom[1][2] = "Winston";
```

The layout of the classroom (shown as a 2D array) is shown in the following figure.

	myClassroom[row][0]	myClassroom[row][1]	myClassroom[row][2]
myClassroom[0][column]	Sarah	Camille	Rebecca
myClassroom[1][column]	Steve	Luke	Winston

Now you want to go through and say "hello" to each student, saying "hello" to the first row first, and then the second row. You need to use a nested loop, going through each column on the first row, and then going through each column on the second row:

```
for(int row = 0; row < myClassroom.length; row++)
{
    for(int col = 0; col < myClassroom[row].length; col++)
    {
```

```
            System.out.pritln("Hello " + myClassroom[row][col]);
        }
    }
```

This code prints:

```
Hello Sarah
Hello Camille
Hello Rebecca
Hello Steve
Hello Luke
Hello Winston
```

Arrays, especially 2D arrays, can be really useful when writing complex programs. Though this was just a brief introduction, you can find a lot more information on the web!

Sorting Lists

Lists are often full of data that can be sorted. Whether your list is of names of people in a class or a set of numbers, sometimes you and your coder want to have your data in a sorted order. This section describes one common sorting algorithm written in English, and then shows an example of sorting numbers in a list in Java.

Selection sort: An easy sorting algorithm

Though many sorting algorithms get used fairly often in coding, one of the most common ones is called *selection sort*. If you did the unplugged activity of this chapter with your young coder, you might have stumbled upon this algorithm. Basically, in selection sort, you search the entire list for the next smallest item.

Here's how the selection sort works:

1. Iterate through the list until you have found the smallest item and swap it with the first item.

2. Iterate through the list starting at the second item, find the smallest item in the list, and swap it with the second item.

3. Iterate through the list starting at the third item, find the smallest item in the list, and swap it with the third item.

4. Repeat moving your start position and finding the smallest item in the list until your start position is the final item in the list.

Common application: Arranging numbers in order

This section shows how to implement the selection sort algorithm in Java on a list of integer numbers.

```java
import java.util.ArrayList;
import java.util.Arrays;
import java.util.List;

public class sort
{
 public static void main(String [] args)
 {
  List<Integer> numbers = Arrays.asList(6, 8, 3, 4, 5, 10, 13,
  22, 9, 21);

  System.out.println("Unordered: " + numbers);

  for (int startPosition = 0; startPosition < numbers.size();
  startPosition++)
  {
   int positionOfSmallest = startPosition;

   for (int iterator = startPosition + 1; iterator < numbers.
  size(); iterator++)
   {
    if (numbers.get(iterator) < numbers.get(positionOfSmallest))
    {
     positionOfSmallest = iterator;
    }
   }

   int smallestNumber = numbers.get(positionOfSmallest);
   numbers.set(positionOfSmallest, numbers.get(startPosition));
   numbers.set(startPosition, smallestNumber);
  }

  System.out.println("Ordered: " + numbers);
 }
}
```

A challenge for you and your coder is to follow the steps in the Java code and make the comparisons in the list yourself. Figure 11-9 shows one way of tracing the code. It's a little tedious, but basically you match each line of code to making a change to variables on your paper. Then you can make sure you and your coder truly understand why this code matches the algorithm!

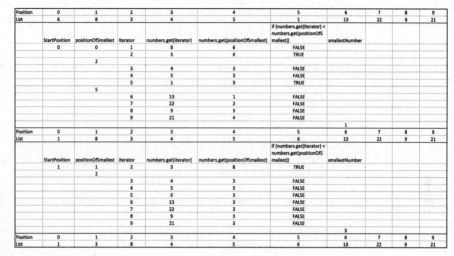

FIGURE 11-9: How the selection sort works in Java.

Searching Lists

Searching through lists is also a very important task that you and your coder might want to have your program accomplish.

Linear versus binary searching algorithms

When it comes to lists, linear search is pretty straightforward. Essentially you start at the beginning of the list, and check to see if the first item is the item you're looking for. If it is, you're done! If it isn't, you move to the next item in the list. And you repeat this sequence until you've either found your item, or you've reached the end of the list and know that your item isn't in the list.

Binary searching is a little more complicated than linear searching. Luckily, you've probably already used the binary search algorithm in your everyday life though. For example, when you're looking for the word "Search" in a dictionary, you probably don't read each word in order until you get to the word "Search." Instead, you flip to the middle of the dictionary and check to see whether the word "Search" comes before the page you opened, or after. You know this because the dictionary is in alphabetical order! If "Search" comes after the page you're on, you flip to a page to the right and repeat the process until you end up on the right page.

This is called binary search, also known as "divide and conquer." When writing the code for this type of search, you literally go to the middle of the list, and then the middle of the side that you know the word is on; each time dividing your search space by half. In your everyday life you might not be exactly at half, but it's close enough to still call it a binary search.

REMEMBER

The only caveat to binary search is that the list must be sorted for the sorting to work. A linear search implementation doesn't require your list to be sorted before searching.

Common application: Finding a phone number

In this section we include the code for finding a phone number in a list of names that are ordered alphabetically. This code is written in Java and, because the names are sorted but the phone numbers are not, this implementation uses the linear search algorithm.

```
import java.util.ArrayList;
import java.util.Arrays;
import java.util.List;
import java.util.Scanner;

public class sort2
{
  public static void main(String [] args)
  {
    Person sarah = new Person("Sarah", "555-7765");
    Person camille = new Person("Camille", "555-9834");
    Person steve = new Person("Steve", "555-2346");
    Person rebecca = new Person("Rebecca", "555-1268");

    List<Person> directory = Arrays.asList(sarah, camille, steve,
    rebecca);

    Scanner scanner = new Scanner(System.in);

    System.out.println("Please enter the phone number so I can
    tell you the name: ");
```

```
    String number = scanner.nextLine();
    String nameFound = "";

    for(int index = 0; index < directory.size(); index++)
    {
     Person personInDirectory = directory.get(index);

     String numberInDirectory = personInDirectory.getNumber();

     if(numberInDirectory.equals(number))
     {
      nameFound = personInDirectory.getName();
      break;
     }
    }

    if(nameFound.equals(""))
    {
     System.out.println("Sorry, the number you are looking for
    does not belong to anyone in this directory");
    }
    else
    {
     System.out.println("The number " + number + " belongs to " +
    nameFound);
    }
   }
}
```

This code relies on another class in a file called Person.java. The code for this file is:

```
public class Person
{
 String name;
 String number;

 public Person(String p_name, String p_number)
 {
  name = p_name;
  number = p_number;
 }
```

```
public String getName()
{
 return name;
}

public String getNumber()
{
 return number;
}
}
```

Chapter **12**

Coding Subprograms

A s your coder has probably noticed, writing code can result in a long sequence of instructions that can become complicated and hard-to-follow. One key to coding is to simplify code as much as possible, making it efficient and reusable. *Efficient* means that the program uses only as many commands as necessary to accomplish a task. *Reusable* means that, for a group of commands that is used more than one time in a program, the group can be defined once and then used many times without writing all the commands each time.

To accomplish these goals, your coder writes *subprograms* — small chunks of code that form just a part of the program and can be reused simply by naming the subprogram, and invoking its use by calling its name. Using subprograms makes programs more efficient by reducing *redundancy* (doing the same thing over and over again) and simplifying code.

Subprograms, Unplugged

What could be more delicious that an unplugged activity that involves dessert? Whether you act it out, or actually get cooking in the kitchen, this activity helps your coders better conceptualize the idea of a subprogram. Begin by inviting your coder to help you create a cake and ice cream dessert (see Figure 12-1). Following are the steps she can consider, along with suggestions for you to help her think about the role of subprograms in the dessert:

1. **Write the steps for making the dessert.**

    These steps make up the *main program*, sometimes called just *main*: making cake, making frosting, making ice cream, and assembling (plating) the dessert.

    Each component — making cake, making frosting, making ice cream — are subprograms that require their own set of steps.

2. **Write the steps for the making cake subprogram.**

    Cake requires you to gather ingredients, specifically flour, eggs, butter, sugar, milk, and baking powder. It also includes a variable ingredient for flavor; for example, chocolate, vanilla, or strawberry. Because different cakes use ingredients in different proportions, your coder may point out that a variable accompanies each ingredient to indicate the quantity of each. (See Chapter 7 for details on variables.) Then you measure and mix ingredients in a specific sequence of steps, and bake the cake in the oven at a specific temperature for a specific time period. You can increase the level of detail of this process as you feel necessary to convey the process of baking a cake.

3. **Write the steps for the making frosting subprogram.**

    Apply the process used in Step 2 to convey the process of making frosting.

4. **Write the steps for the making ice cream subprogram.**

    Apply the process used in Step 2 to convey the process of making ice cream.

5. **Write the steps for assembling (plating) the dessert.**

    List, in order, the steps for putting together the dessert on the plate.

FIGURE 12-1: Making dessert is a program comprised of subprograms for making cake, making frosting, making ice cream, and plating the dessert.

Starting with Pseudocode

Writing a program and its subprograms involves naming each of the parts, defining each part, and calling it (asking it to execute) when you need it.

Here is the unplugged, dessert program written in pseudocode:

```
main dessert
    makeCake
    makeFrosting
    makeIceCream
    plateDessert
end
```

Here are the subprograms to make the dessert program work:

```
to makeCake
    constant flour
    constant eggs
    [more constants]
    var flavor
    [more variables]
    preheat oven to 375 degrees
    add flour to bowl
    add eggs to bowl
    [more instructions]
    beat together
    pour batter into pan
    place pan in oven
    cook for 40 minutes
    remove pan from oven
end

to makeFrosting
    [constants and variables]
    [instructions]
end

to makeIceCream
    [constants and variables]
    [instructions]

end
```

```
to plateDessert
   slice cake
   place cake on plate
   frost cake
   place ice cream on cake
   place cherry on top
end
```

Notice that this format is also how most cookbooks and chef shows are structured: the main program explains the overall process of cooking the dessert, while the subprograms drill down to more specific details about specifically how to make each component.

Creating a Spirograph with Subprograms

Coding coaches, do you remember playing with a Spirograph when you were a kid? If so, you may recall using a pen, some paper, and some gear-like plastic pieces to draw some beautiful geometric art. Spirograph-style art is a simple shape drawn many times, in slightly different positions, to create a new, more complex shape. See Figure 12-2.

FIGURE 12-2:
A Spirograph toy helps kids think about main programs and subprograms in the creation of beautiful, geometric art.

Figure credit: https://www.amazon.com/Kahootz-01006-Spirograph-Design-Boxed/dp/B00CIYXK76/ref=sr_1_6?s=toys-and-games&ie=UTF8&qid=1517179160&sr=1-6&keywords=spirograph+set

Your coder can create computer programs that draw designs similar to those you create with a Spirograph. Encourage her to think about how to create a main program, art, and the subprograms that comprise art.

Pseudocode

Her pseudocode programs could look something like these:

Main Program

```
main art
    clear off previous drawing
    put the pen down
    repeat number
        draw square
        rotate angle
end
```

Subprogram

```
to square
  repeat 4
      forward 100
      right turn 90
  end
end
```

Your coder can easily write her own program and subprograms in a programming language. Each programming language has its own specific way of formatting programs, formatting subprograms, and calling subprograms. Here's how this is accomplished in some common programming languages your coder may use.

Scratch

Scratch calls a subprogram a *block*. To make a block, complete these steps:

1. At the More Blocks category of tiles, click the Make a Block button.

A New Block dialog box opens, as shown in Figure 12-3.

2. At the New Block dialog box, type a name for the block.

Scratch allows any name, including spaces, although it's a good idea to adhere to camelCase naming practices.

FIGURE 12-3:
The New Block
dialog box allows
you to create a
subprogram in
Scratch.

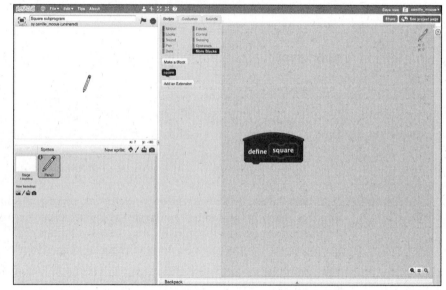

FIGURE 12-3:
The New Block dialog box allows you to create a subprogram in Scratch.

3. Click OK.

A define block tile appears in the Scratch workspace. Additionally, a call subprogram block tile appears in the tile bin of the More Blocks category. See Figure 12-4. (Note also that Scratch Cat has been cut from the stage, and a pencil sprite has been added. The code is being constructed on the pencil sprite.)

FIGURE 12-4:
Define block and call block tiles in Scratch.

4. Attach code tiles to build your define code block.

See Figure 12-5 for an example of command tiles for drawing a square of size 100.

5. Use the call subprogram block in your main program.

See Figure 12-6 for a program that draws a Spirograph-style pattern. The figure also shows the program after it has executed. Note that the main program, activated by pressing the green flag, calls the square subprogram to execute 24 times! Yet the program is very short — now that's efficient code.

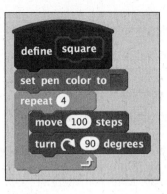

FIGURE 12-5:
Defining a code block, square, to draw a square of size 100 in Scratch.

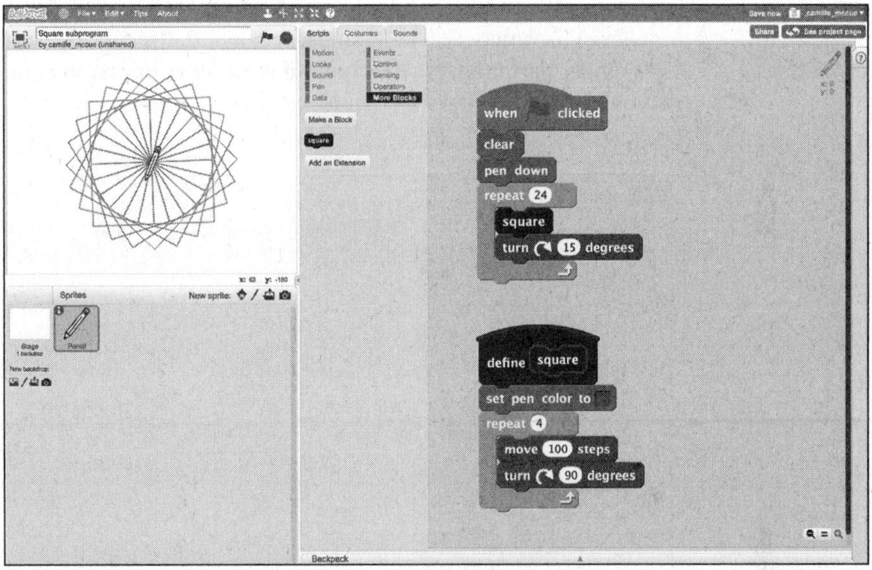

FIGURE 12-6:
The call subprogram tile in the main program runs the square code block.

TIP

Only place inside a block the code that actually needs to be reused. In a drawing program, if the pen color doesn't change, don't place it inside the draw shape block. Otherwise you end up executing lines of code over and over again that don't need to execute. Try to be as efficient as possible in defining a code block.

JavaScript

JavaScript calls a subprogram a *function*. To create a function in Code.org's App Lab, using JavaScript, complete these steps:

1. At the Functions category of tiles, drag a function `myFunction()` tile into the program workspace.

2. Replace the myFunction() placehoder by typing a name for the function.

Use camelCase naming conventions for JavaScript. See Chapter 7 for an explanation of why camelCase is important in JavaScript.

3. Attach commands to define your function.

4. Use the function name to call it from your main program.

See Figure 12-7 for a JavaScript program featuring functions, written in the App Lab, which draws a field of twenty flowers, all the same size and pink color, randomly distributed in the display. Note that there are two functions: one to draw oneFlower(), and one to draw onePetal() of the flower. Here, the main program calls the oneFlower() function, and the oneFlower() function, calls the onePetal() function. The emulator shows the result of executing the program. The empty parentheses at the end of each function name indicates that the function has no parameters.

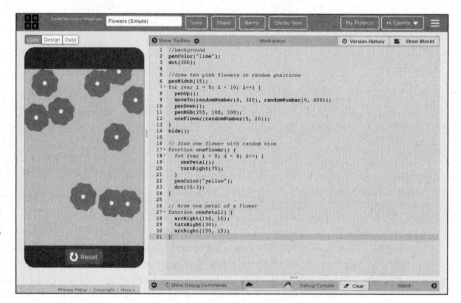

FIGURE 12-7:
Using JavaScript in the App Lab to create a field of flowers using two functions: oneFlower() and onePetal().

Functions should be placed towards the bottom of your program, and function calls should be placed as needed, in the main body of the program.

TIP

Java

The name for a Java subprogram is a *method*. While exploring the intricacies of Java methods is a bit beyond the scope of this book, here is an example that shows your young coder that working with methods is somewhat similar to working with other types of subprograms.

Figure 12-8 shows a program (called a *class* in Java) named Product, written in the BlueJ IDE (see Chapter 3 for details in working in this Java editor). Product has a main program and a multiply method.

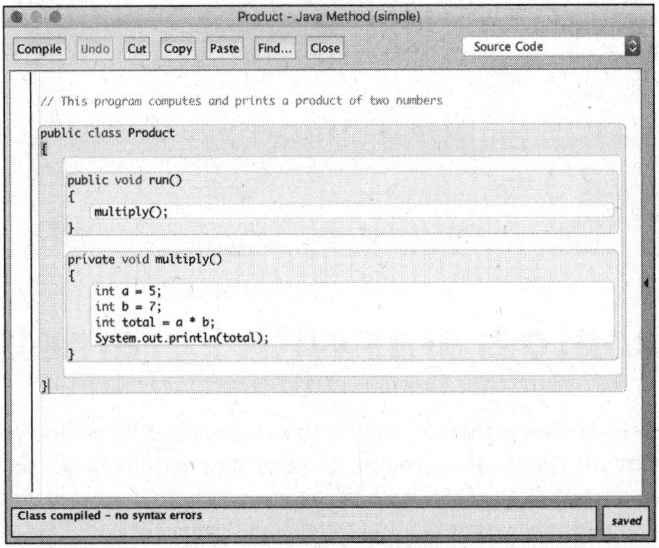

```
// This program computes and prints a product of two numbers
public class Product
{
    public void run()
    {
        multiply();
    }

    private void multiply()
    {
        int a = 5;
        int b = 7;
        int total = a * b;
        System.out.println(total);
    }
}
```

Class compiled – no syntax errors   saved

FIGURE 12-8: Code a method — a subprogram in Java.

1. Code the class name: `public class Product {`.

2. Code the `main` **program.**

This is the section labeled `main`. The main program calls the `multiply` method.

3. Code the `multiply` **method.**

The `multiply` method defines three variables, a, b, and `total`. It computes `total` and prints its value.

4. Close the class with a curly bracket.

Figure 12-9 shows the execution of Product. Notice that the numbers a and b can be changed inside the `multiply` method to result in a new product for `total`. However, there's no easy way to reuse this subprogram without manually changing the variable values inside of it. In the next section, your coder finds out how to apply parameters to make the method more flexible and better suited for reuse.

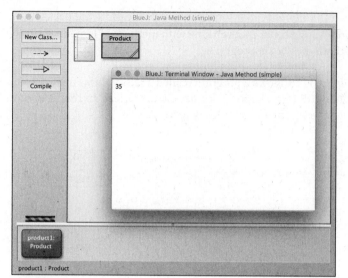

FIGURE 12-9:
Execution of a
program,
including one
method, in Java.

Coding Subprograms with Parameters

Your coder can provide flexibility to her programs by adding parameters to sub-programs. For example, coding a square subprogram allows the program to draw a square of a defined size each time the subprogram is called. But what if you want the square subprogram to draw squares of differing sizes? By adding a parameter to the subprogram you can do just that. A *parameter* is a variable that you pass into a subprogram, which the subprogram uses as it executes. You can pass a param-eter into the square subprogram that tells the code how big to draw the square.

Scratch code block with parameters

Scratch allows you to add one or more parameters to any subprogram block you create. Your coder can begin by making a simple block (see the earlier section "Creating a Spirograph with Subprograms" for the steps on Scratch). Then, your coder can add parameters when she first creates the block, or she can edit the block after it has been created — the process is essentially the same. Here are the steps for editing the square code block previously created:

1. **In the More Blocks category, right-click (Windows) or control+click (Mac) the instance code block tile that you previously created.**

2. **Select Edit from the pop-up menu which appears.**

   The Edit Block dialog box appears.

3. **At the Edit Block dialog box, click the Options tab to expand the options for adding parameters.**

4. **Click the icon for any of the parameter options shown to add that parameter to your block.**

   You can choose Add Number Input, Add String Input, Add Boolean Input, or Add Label Text. When you click an icon to add that parameter, a blank field is added to your instance code block tile. You can add more than one parameter. Figure 12-10 shows the addition of a number input parameter.

5. **Inside the blank field on the instance code block tile, type the variable name of the parameter(s) you're adding.**

   Figure 12-10 shows that the new number input parameter is named size.

6. **Select the Run without Screen Refresh check box.**

   This allows for faster execution of your program.

7. **Click OK.**

   The dialog box closes and the code block tile now shows the added parameter(s).

WARNING

In Scratch, parameters added to code blocks play the same role as variables. When the parameter is added, you can use it just like a variable in your program — although be aware that it doesn't appear in your list of variables in the Data category.

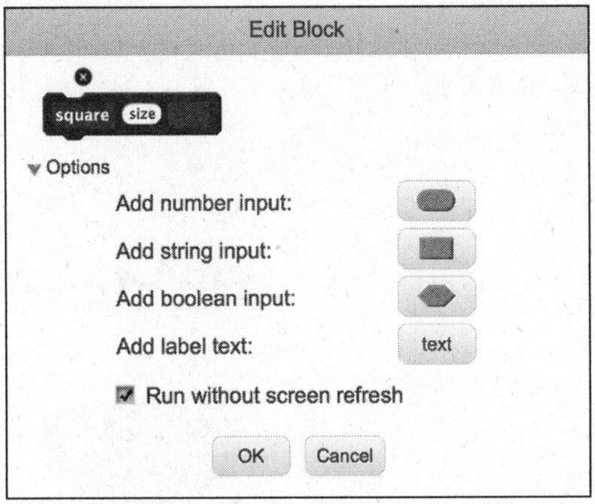

Edit Block

square size

▼ Options

Add number input:

Add string input:

Add boolean input:

Add label text: text

☑ Run without screen refresh

OK   Cancel

FIGURE 12-10: Editing a Scratch block definition to add parameters.

Using your edited block with parameters is easy! Just drag the parameter tile from the code block definition (the big "hat" tile) into your code when you want to use the parameter. The parameter replaces code which you previously defined out-right. Instead of the code tile for move 100 steps, you now have a code tile for `move size steps`. This allows for more flexible usage of the code block because it can now accept a number for the size, sent by the main program, and execute the code block with that size as the side length.

Your main program then calls the parameterized block, sending it a number to use for the size: `square 30` draws a square with side lengths of 30 pixels (see the top figure in Figure 12-11); `square 110` draws a square with side lengths of 110 pixels (see the bottom figure in Figure 12-11).

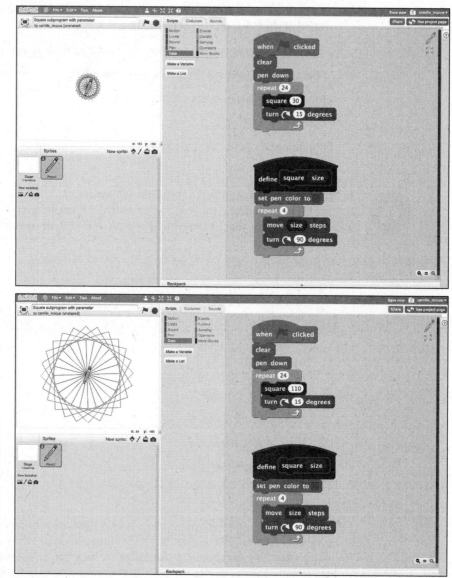

FIGURE 12-11: Executing Spirograph-style Scratch code using a square block with parameter size passed as 30 (top); or with parameter size passed as 110 (bottom).

JavaScript, with parameters

You can add parameters to your JavaScript functions to add flexibility to your programs. To create a function with a parameter in Code.org's App Lab, using JavaScript, complete these steps:

1. **At the Functions category of tiles, drag a function `myFunction(n)` tile into the program workspace.**

   The `n` is a parameter. If you already added a `myFunction()` command without a parameter, you can add the parameter by typing the parameter inside the parentheses. (Or, if you are working in tile mode, press the little horizontal arrows to add or remove parameters from your function.) In text mode, separate multiple parameters using a comma and a space following each parameter.

2. **Replace the `myFunction(n)` placehoder, by typing a name for the function, and a name for your parameter(s).**

   Use camelCase naming conventions for JavaScript. Each parameter is a variable in your program.

3. **Attach commands to define your function.**

   The parameters are referenced by their variable names inside the function.

4. **Use the function name and parameter values to call it from your main program.**

   The parameters values are passed into the function. Parameter values are assigned to the parameter variables and used inside the function.

See Figure 12-12 for a JavaScript program with functions and parameters, written in the App Lab. This program draws a field of twenty flowers of *different* sizes and pink color, randomly distributed in the display. Note that there are two parameterized functions: one to draw `oneFlower(size)`, and one to draw `onePetal(size)` of the flower. Here, the main program calls the `oneFlower(size)` function that has been defined to include a `size` parameter. The `oneFlower (randomNumber(5, 20))` function call sends a random number, from 5 to 20, to the `oneFlower(size)` function; `size` takes on a new value between 5 and 20 each time the function is called. The `oneFlower(size)` function then calls the `onePetal(size)` function. The `onePetal(size)` function receives whatever value its parent subprogram received for `size`. The effect is that flowers of different sizes are drawn onscreen. The emulator shows the result of executing the program.

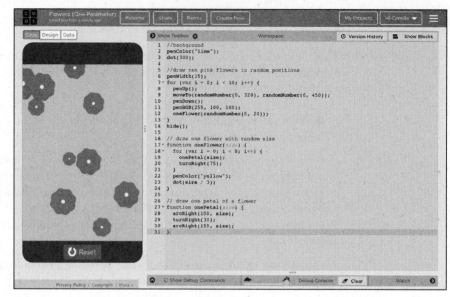

FIGURE 12-12:
Generating a random number and assigning it to a size parameter in a JavaScript function creates variation in the sizes of the resulting flowers.

Java, with parameters

Figure 12-13 shows a Java class named Product, written in the BlueJ IDE (see Chapter 3 for details in working in this Java editor). The class contains one method, Product, which has two parameters, a and b.

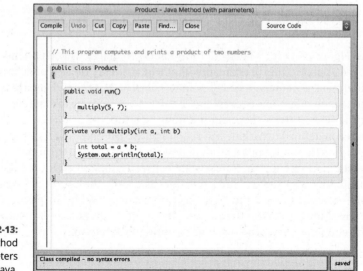

FIGURE 12-13:
Code a method with parameters in Java.

Here's how to code this program:

1. **Code the class name:** `public class Product {.`

2. **Code the main program.**

This is the section labeled `main`. The `main` program calls the `multiply` method, which receives two parameters.

3. **Code the** `multiply` **method, which has two parameters,** `a` **and** `b`.

The `multiply` method defines three variables, a, b, and `total`. Variables a and b are parameters defined as integers. Their values, 5 and 7, are received from the call located in the main program. The `multiply` method computes `total` and prints out its value.

4. **Close the** `class` **with a curly bracket.**

Figure 12-14 shows the execution of `Product`. Notice that the values of the variables a and b can be changed outside of the `multiply` method to result in a new product for `total`. This makes the `multiply` method modular and easy to reuse with different variable values on each use. Parameterizing methods build a more flexible program.

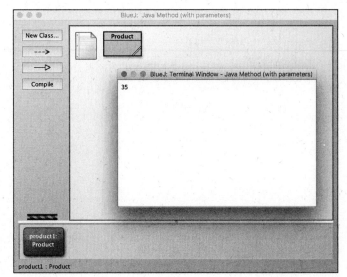

FIGURE 12-14: Execution of a program, including one method with parameters, in Java.

TECHNICAL STUFF

Subprograms can also generate information that they pass onto other subprograms or back to the main program. In Java, your coder sometimes sees the code void. This means that, when the subprogram is called, it's not sending anything back to the program that called it. In other cases, your coder sees a variable type and name following the name of the main program or of a subprogram. That type and name tells you what type of information is going to be received by the program making the call. The subprogram contains a return command indicating what variable value is being returned (passed back to) the program that called it.

4

Applying What You Know

Start practicing one of the most critical aspects of coding — fixing mistakes — and learn about the infamous bugs of debugging.

Create a webpage with HTML, CSS, and JavaScript.

Create a mobile app game with MIT's App Inventor and test it on an Android device.

Write the code for a reaction time game and build the simple machine needed to play it.

Meet Tim Berners-Lee, Bill Gates, and Paul Allen.

Chapter **13**

Fixing Problems by Debugging

B ugs have been causing coders headaches and frustration for decades. Coders spend upwards of 50 percent of their time debugging — *fixing* errors in their code, and not just writing code! This is part of what makes coding so "hard." It's not impossible to figure out — it just takes persistence when the computer is telling you you're wrong.

You can encounter two different kinds of coding bugs: syntax bugs and semantic bugs. *Syntax* bugs are ones where you have written something incorrectly. Maybe you spelled a variable wrong, or you forgot a semicolon at the end of your line of code. These bugs are often easy to fix and result in your programming environment displaying an error message to you. *Semantic* bugs are ones where your logic is incorrect. For example, you're iterating through a list of five numbers and you try to access the sixth element, or you're checking to see whether `variable1` is less than `variable2` in an `if-then` statement, but you accidentally write `variable1 > variable2`. These bugs are often harder to find because they require you to test your code and see what happens, and then trace your code to find where the error is located.

When teaching and guiding young coders through their coding journey, it's important to help them understand that errors, bugs, and mistakes in coding are normal and expected. Performing the debugging process is a huge part of being a coder, and learning strategies, patience, and persistence is critical to coders if they are to succeed in their coding adventures.

If you haven't heard of the infamous Admiral Grace Hopper and how she coined the term "bug" for an error in a computer program, you should definitely read the sidebar about her in Chapter 5!

Debugging, Unplugged

Teaching your young coder about debugging is also about teaching her that computers are very precise. When we're introducing this concept to young coders, we like to present them with the following scenario: If I told you to go to your shoes and put your room on, you could probably figure out that I *meant* to say go to your room and put your shoes on. But if I were to tell a robot to go to its shoes and put its room on, it would literally walk over to its shoes and then *try* to put its room on. . .which is impossible! And it would probably tell you that it cannot complete the action, or maybe even try so hard to "put its room on" that it just crashes.

As a fun activity to do with a group of young coders, you can play a game of "Describe the Picture." In this game each person is given a unique picture drawn on a grid. Each person keeps his picture hidden from his partner. Then, each person is given a blank sheet of grid paper.

In one version of the game, each partner takes a turn describing his picture to his partner using only descriptive language (not showing them the image). He has five minutes to describe the picture while his partner tries to re-create it on the grid paper. Then they switch who is describing and who is drawing. At the end of the ten minutes they show each other their drawings. Most of the drawings will be incorrect, and at that point you can talk about what went wrong and how hard it is to be precise!

In another version, you can add an element of debugging to the end of the game. Rather than describing the picture to their partners, each person writes a series of steps that his partner should follow to re-create the picture. For example, if a coder is given the picture shown in Figure 13-1, then he has these steps to re-create the picture:

1. Draw a rectangle at the top center of the page.

2. Draw another longer rectangle underneath that rectangle.

3. Draw a circle under that rectangle.

4. Draw another, bigger circle under that circle.

5. Draw another, bigger circle under that circle.

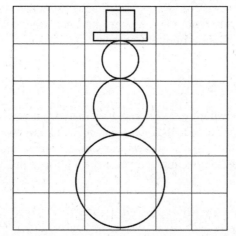

FIGURE 13-1:
An example of a picture on a grid to re-create in an unplugged activity.

However, based on these steps, his partner could also create the image shown in Figure 13-2. After each partner completes their steps and draws their partner's drawing, they can work together to improve their list of steps — essentially debugging the error in their steps. For example, partners may decide that adding specifics such as "below," "touching but not overlapping," and, "with centers aligned along the y-axis" may improve their instructions.

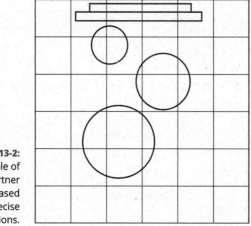

FIGURE 13-2:
An example of what the partner might draw based on imprecise instructions.

Finding Common Syntax Errors

One of the hardest parts about debugging is finding where the program is displaying the errors in your code, and then interpreting them. Each programming language and coding application has slightly different ways of displaying and describing error messages. This section gives some examples of error messages that you might see in different programming languages, where to find them in an example application, and how to interpret them.

Scoping errors

A scoping error is one where you've created a variable and you try to access the variable, but the part of the code that you are in doesn't know about it. Scopes can be described by looking at what is between curly braces, or within the "mouth" of a block-based language. For example, if you write a for loop in Java it would look like this:

```java
for(int index = 0; index < 10; index++)
{
    System.out.println(index);
}
```

The index variable only lives within the scope of the for loop. So that means, when you print the index variable within the curly braces of the for loop, the computer knows what variable you want to print, and can accurately print it. However, if the code looked like this:

```java
for(int index = 0; index < 10; index++)
{
    System.out.println("In scope:" + index);
}
System.out.println("Out of scope:" + index);
```

The line that tries to print the index that is outside of the curly braces would throw a scoping error. The error in Java would be:

```
java:lineNumber: error: cannot find symbol
    System.out.println("Out of Scope: " + index);
                                          ^

  symbol: variable index
  location: class className
1 error
```

This error would appear when you try to compile your Java code.

Though it's pretty difficult to get a syntax error in block-based languages because the blocks are already created for you, it's possible to get a scoping error. For example, in App Inventor, you could create a local variable called myName and set a label to that variable. However, if you only had one variable that was local, and you tried to set a label to that variable outside of its own "mouth," it would show a scoping error — there would be no variables available for that block. Figure 13-3 shows an example of this error in App Inventor.

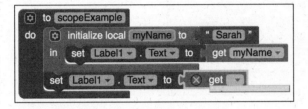

FIGURE 13-3:
An example of a
scoping error in
App Inventor.

Typing errors

Typing errors can happen to the best of us! Especially for young coders who don't have a lot of experience typing on a keyboard, or who may not be the best spellers, typing errors can be fairly common. Common typing errors are misspelling variables and methods, but another type of typo can be mis-capitalization. For example, in a simple Python program that assigns a value to a variable, and then attempts to print the variable:

```
myName = 'Sarah'
print (myname)
```

The error is that the variable has camelCasing when it's defined, but then has only lowercase when used in the print function. The error you would get if you ran the program would be:

```
Traceback (most recent call last):
  File "example.py", line 2, in <module>
    print myname
NameError: name 'myname' is not defined
```

Scratch, on the other hand, is a language that really tries to protect the user from typing errors. For example, Figure 13-4 shows a simple program; it's impossible to make the same error as you can with Python (mis-capitalizing the variable name), because you don't re-type the variable names each time with Scratch; you simply use the variable block that is created when you first created the variable. But a potential mis-capitalization is checking the value of the variable. Notice that the value was set to Sarah, but the if-then statement checks to see whether the value was sarah. In a language such as Python or Java this error would make the if-then condition evaluate to false, but in Scratch it evaluates to true, making the sprite say "Hello there!" when the green flag is clicked.

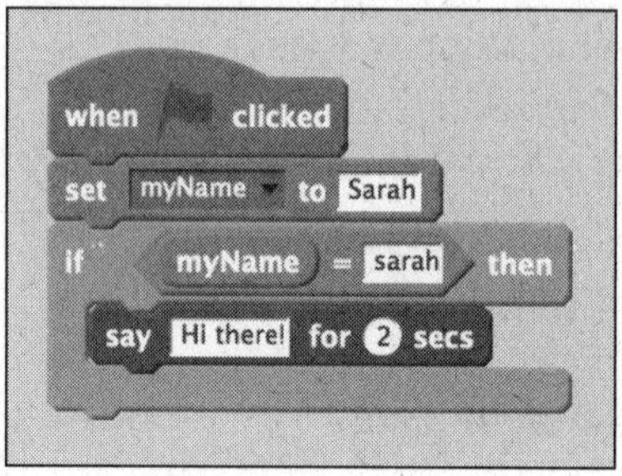

FIGURE 13-4:
An example of a typing error in Scratch that is caught by the app.

TIP

When you're coding and you run into an error that identifies a variable that is unknown, check spelling and capitalization!

Incorrect data types

Another syntax error to watch out for is using incorrect data types. This can happen only in strongly typed programming languages, like Java. For example, say you had the following program:

```
int month = "11";
int day = "15";
System.out.println("My birthday: " + month + "/" + day);
```

The errors that you would get when compiling your program is:

```
java:lineNumber: error: incompatible types: String cannot be
    converted to int
    int month = "11");
            ^
java:lineNumber: error: incompatible types: String cannot be
    converted to int
    int day = "15");
          ^
2 errors
```

Usually the error messages regarding incorrect data types are straightforward; however, understanding what data types are the correct ones to use can be a tricky subject for young coders. For example, the error messages in the code example indicate that the coder attempted to assign a string type (11 and 15 are strings because they have quotation marks around them) to a variable that is an integer type, which is a number.

Finding Common Semantic Errors

Unlike syntax errors, semantic errors are often more difficult to capture. This is because semantic errors are typically errors in the programming logic, rather than something that you typed incorrectly. This section has a couple of examples of semantic errors that you and your young coder might encounter in a few different programming languages.

Infinite loops

Infinite loops are loops that never end! They go on infinitely. This can be a problem because it might seem like the code just isn't working, but really the program is just running forever and ever.

Using Java

If you wrote a small Java program where you wanted to print the numbers 0 through 9, you might write something like this:

```
for(int index = 0; index < 10; index--)
{
   System.out.println(index);
}
```

But there is an error in this code! Instead of updating the index to be index + 1, the code updates the index to be index − 1! So the code does the following:

```
index = 0
Is index < 10? Yes
Print index 0
index = index − 1 index = −1
Is index < 10? Yes
Print index −1
index = index − 1 index = −2
```

```
Is index < 10? Yes
Print index −2
index = index − 1 index = −3
Is index < 10? Yes
Print index −3
```

This continues forever, because it's impossible for index to be greater than or equal to 10. So when you run the Java code, the program continues to print forever, until you kill the program!

Using Scratch

Although infinite loops can be a problem, some programming languages deliberately have implemented infinite loops to make some pretty neat effects! For example, in Scratch there is a forever block. Figure 13-5 shows two programs that are very similar. The left figure shows a program that checks to see whether the mouse pointer is touching the sprite. If it is, then the sprite meows. The problem is that the if-then block is checked only once — at the moment when the green flag is pressed — and it's never checked again. The right figure shows the same program, but with a forever loop block around the if-then block. Now, after the green flag is clicked, the if-then block keeps asking, forever, whether the mouse pointer is touching the sprite. This makes it a program that always makes the sprite meow when the mouse pointer touches it until the red stop sign is pressed (which is the same as killing the program).

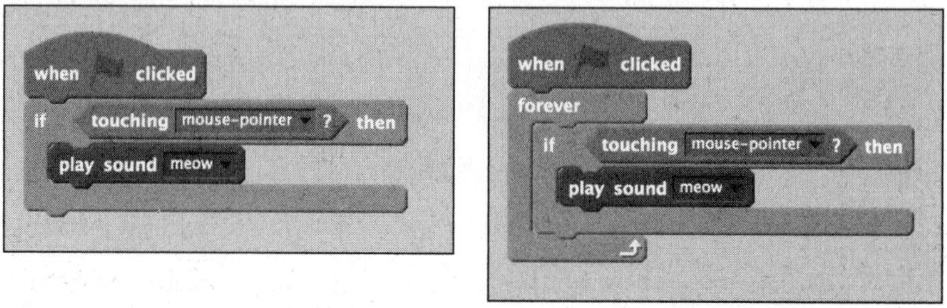

FIGURE 13-5:
An example of a
Scratch program
that doesn't do
what is intended
because there
is no forever
loop (left); an
example of a
Scratch program
benefiting
from infinite
loops (right).

Off by one

Another very common error to run into is called an off by one error. This is very common when dealing with lists and iterating through lists. For more information about lists, check out Chapter 11.

Using Scratch

Scratch, as usual, handles off by one errors for the user without really indicating there's a problem. For example, Figure 13-6 shows a program that loops through a list of pets and has the sprite say Hi petName, where petName is replaced with the item from the list (either Luke, Winston, or Princess). The loop repeats four times, but there are only three items in the list. Instead of completely breaking, on its last iteration, Scratch prints Hi with nothing after it (as shown in Figure 13-6).

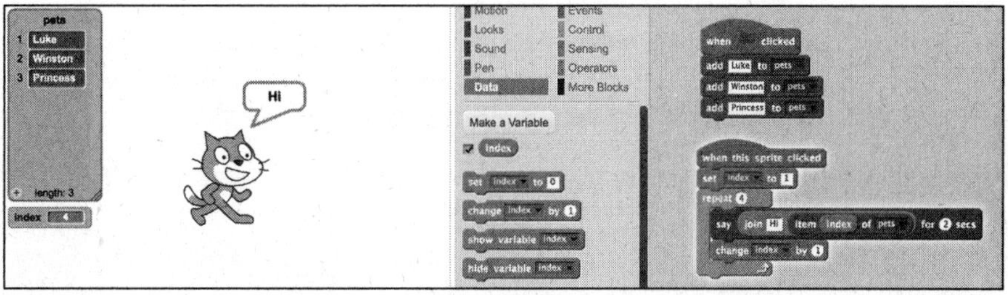

FIGURE 13-6:
An example of a Scratch program with an off by one error.

Using Python

Other programming languages are not as forgiving. For example, in Python you might have the following program to say hello to the three pets:

```
pets = ['Luke', 'Winston', 'Princess']
for x in range(1, 3):
    print ('Hi ' + pets[x])
```

If you run this program, the output would be:

```
Hi Winston
Hi Princess
```

The reason 'Hi Luke' doesn't print is because lists in Python start at 0, not at 1. The correct code would be:

```
pets = ['Luke', 'Winston', 'Princess']
for x in range(0, 3):
    print ('Hi ' + pets[x])
```

TECHNICAL STUFF

If you're confused by any of the Python list examples, make sure to check out Chapter 11. For example, the range function used in Python:

```
range(0, 3)
```

Represents the elements 0, 1, and 2 because the range function *includes* the first number but *excludes* the second.

Another version of an off by one error in Python would be if you went beyond the length of the list. For example:

```
pets = ['Luke', 'Winston', 'Princess']
for x in range(0, 4):
  print ('Hi ' + pets[x])
```

This causes even more of an issue, because instead of simply missing an element in the list, you're trying to access an element that never existed in the first place. The output for running this code is:

```
Hi Luke
Hi Winston
Hi Princess
Traceback (most recent call last):
  File "filename.py", line 4, in <module>
    print ('Hi ') + pets[x]
IndexError: list index out of range
```

There is an actual error, because the data for pets[4] doesn't exist, so the computer cannot resolve it; therefore it doesn't know what to do.

REMEMBER

Off by one errors can be really tricky for young coders, especially if they're switching between languages where lists start at 1 versus lists that start at 0.

Strategies for Debugging

When you and your young coder are trying to debug, sometimes no error messages give you insight into the problem. This section has a list of strategies for debugging programs where you don't get an error message, or the error message doesn't give you enough information.

Turning sections on and off

One of the best ways to debug is to disable sections of code so that you have small sections to test.

Using Scratch

In Scratch, you might have a lot of scripts that start when the green flag is pressed. This can cause problems if some of the scripts cancel out or affect the other scripts. For example, Figure 13-7 shows three scripts associated with one sprite. The problem that the user notices is when the mouse pointer is touching the sprite, it does not meow. To try to figure out the problem, the coder might disconnect all the scripts and only have one script connected at a time, like in Figure 13-8. Then they see that the code for the mouse pointer touching the sprite works correctly, but that there is another problem (the code that stops all sounds forever). By connecting and disconnecting the blocks, the coder can identify the problem.

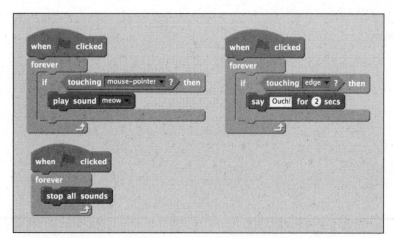

FIGURE 13-7:
An example
Scratch program.

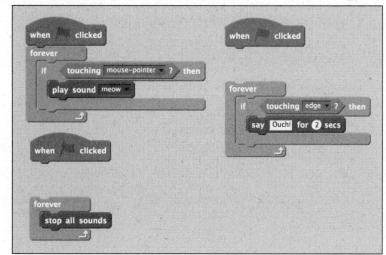

FIGURE 13-8:
An example of
turning off
sections in
Scratch to identify
a bug.

Using App Inventor

Other block-based languages like App Inventor make turning sections on and off even easier! For example, in Chapter 15 there is a Puppy Play Day mobile game that you can create. Figure 13-9 shows how if you right-click a code block, you can disable that block. In this example, you might want to make sure the initial property settings work before creating the lists and hiding the items. Then, after you confirm the properties are set properly, you can enable the call to setupLists to make sure that works. Then you can enable the call to hideItems to make sure that works.

REMEMBER

By turning off all sections and then turning each one on one at a time, it's easier to find bugs.

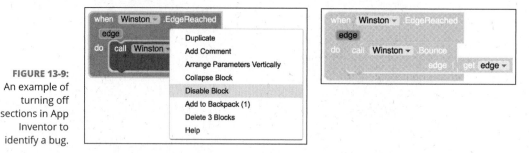

FIGURE 13-9: An example of turning off sections in App Inventor to identify a bug.

Using Python

Text-based languages have a similar way of turning sections on and off — you only have to comment out the lines of code. In Python, you can comment out a single line of code like this:

```
#print 'Hi'
```

And you can comment out multiple lines of code like this:

```
'''
for x in range(0, 4):
   print ('Hi ' + pets[x])
'''
```

Commenting out code is how you "turn off" or "disable" parts of your code when you're in a text-based language.

Testing sample data

A common bug that coders run into is not testing data to make sure that the program works. This can especially be a problem if you're writing programs that take user input. It's important to make sure you and your young coder think about what kind of input you're expecting, and test to make sure the input is handled correctly.

You might have a program that gets input from the user and prints what the user types, like this Python code:

```
name = raw_input('What is your name? ')
print ('Hi ' + name)
```

It's important to test to make sure that if you put the following types of input, they still do what you, as the coder, expect:

```
Sarah
Sarah Guthals
13
11/15
Sarah 55 Guthals
```

By mixing letters, spaces, numbers, and other symbols like / you're ensuring that your program performs as expected. This type of testing is *unit testing* and ensures that small portions of your program execute correctly with varying input.

Adding output messages

One of the most challenging aspects of coding is that the code is abstract and sometimes the data is hidden. This is especially tricky when you have complex data or are performing complex operations on data. By adding a number of output messages in your code, you can indicate when certain sections of code have been reached, or you can show the current values of certain variables at various points during execution.

An example of adding output messages to a program to gain insight in Python follows. Here, your goal is to write a program to solve an algebraic expression. For example:

```
x = input('Provide a number for x: ')
y = input('Provide a number for y: ')
```

```
first = 2*x
second = 6*y
sum = first - second

print '2x + 6y = '
print (sum)
```

There is an error in this program; instead of adding the first and second elements, the coder is accidentally subtracting. Though this error is fairly obvious because this example is small, it shows how a simple typo could completely change the output. If you run this code, you get results like:

```
Provide a number for x: 2
Provide a number for y: 3
2x + 6y =
-14
```

This is clearly wrong. 2*2 + 6*3 = 4 + 18 = 22, not –14. One way of debugging this code is to add output messages at each point. For example, you could change your code to:

```
x = input('Provide a number for x: ')
print ('x: ')
print (x)

y = input('Provide a number for y: ')
print ('y: ')
print (y)

first = 2*x
print ('first: ')
print (first)

second = 6*y
print ('second: ')
print (second)

sum = first - second

print "2x + 6y = "
print sum
```

Then, when you run the code you get the following output:

```
Provide a number for x: 2
x:
2
Provide a number for y: 3
y:
3
first:
4
second:
18
2x + 6y =
-14
```

Then the coder can see that x, y, first, and second are all correct. This must mean that it's just when the sum is calculated that there is an error.

Walking Away

Although there might be other ways to debug for different languages and programming environments, one universal strategy is to walk away from your code. Sometimes, when you stare at the same code for hours, you just aren't seeing the obvious problems. By walking away from your program and giving yourself a 20-30 minute break, you can gain perspective. One of Sarah's professors liked to call this the Gilligan's Island strategy because he would walk away and watch an episode of Gilligan's Island before returning.

Many expert coders can tell you stories of how they worked on debugging a program for over 5 hours, they went home and went to bed, and when they woke up they knew exactly what the problem was and were able to fix it in a matter of minutes. Camille finds that walking her dog, Pepper, unclutters her own thinking and allows her to approach the problem with fresh eyes and a clear mind. This isn't magic. It's letting your brain relax and approach the problem in another way.

REMEMBER

For a lot of young coders, walking away from a problem can be really difficult. They don't want to give up and they are already frustrated because the program isn't working as they expected. When frustrated, this is the most important time to walk away.

Chapter **14**

Creating a Webpage

aking a website can be a really fun way to get your coder showing off his skills. Though websites can be easily created on sites like Wix.com or Squarespace.com without any coding, having the flexibility and knowledge to be able to create something unique and personalized cannot be replaced. Websites are written using three main languages: HTML, CSS, and JavaScript.

This chapter guides you through making a website where you and your young coder can showcase some of your favorite things — animals, programs you have written, video games, you name it! This chapter is written to be read in order; however, if you're looking for specific guidance on how to add something to a webpage, you can navigate directly to that section.

If your young coder shows a special affinity for creating websites, check out *Creating a Web Site: Design and Build Your First Site!*

Getting Set Up

To start making a website, you should get your programming environment set up. This chapter walks you through making your first webpage by using a very simple programming environment — TextEdit. The examples in this chapter are on a

Mac; however, the instructions are almost the same if you're coding on a Windows machine using Notepad.

WARNING

Don't use a word processor (such as Word) to create the code for your HTML page; only use a text editor — TextEdit or Notepad — and edit in plain text mode.

Follow these steps to get your programming environment setup:

1. **Create a new folder called "Website."**

   You can create this on your desktop, or inside of any other folder on your computer.

2. **Open TextEdit.**

   Leave the pop-up window open while you complete the next couple setup steps.

3. **Choose TextEdit ⇨ Preferences, and select the New Document tab at the top of the dialog box that appears.**

   Make sure that new documents will be created in plain text, not rich text (see Figure 14-1).

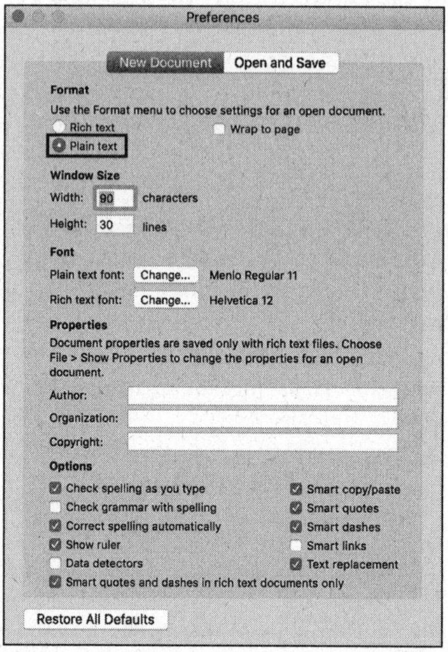

FIGURE 14-1:
New documents should be created as plain text.

4. **Continuing in the Preferences dialog box, click the Open and Save tab and make sure the Display HTML Files as HTML Code Instead of Formatted Text box is checked, as shown in Figure 14-2.**

This ensures that your HTML code appears *as* a formatted webpage (as opposed to your code appearing as code *on* a webpage).

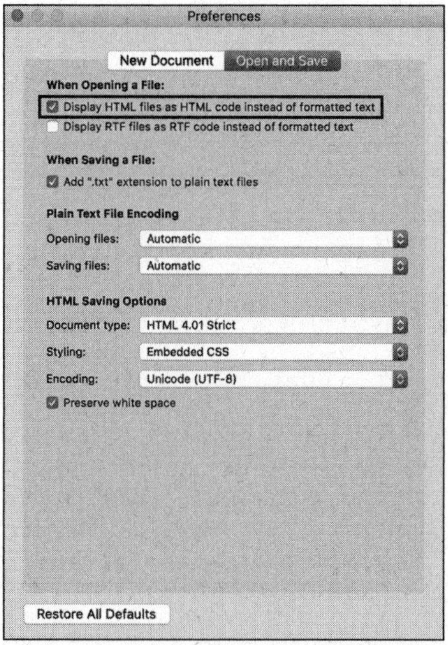

FIGURE 14-2:
Opening HTML
documents
should show
code, not
formatted text.

5. **Close the Preferences dialog box.**

6. **At the TextEdit window that appeared when you first opened the program, navigate to the new Website folder that you created in Step 1 and click New Document, as shown in Figure 14-3.**

A new, blank document opens, as shown in Figure 14-4.

7. **Save this blank document by pressing ⌘+s or choosing File ⇨ Save.**

In the Save dialog box, as shown in Figure 14-5, name your file website and change the file type to Webpage (.html), make sure you're saving the files to your Website folder, and click Save.

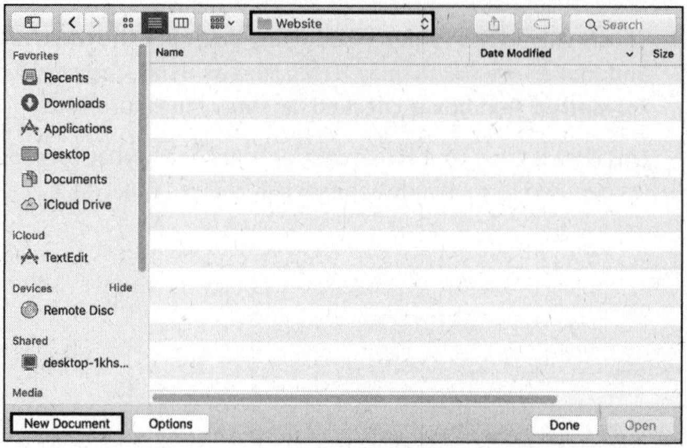

FIGURE 14-3:
An example of
opening a new
TextEdit
document into
the Website
folder.

FIGURE 14-4:
An example of
the new TextEdit
document.

You now see a new file in your Website folder called `website.html`. This folder is where you put any companion files, such as images, that you want to include on your website. If you double-click the `website.html` file, a new blank web browser window opens and displays your (currently empty!) page as shown in Figure 14-6. The URL of this website is the file path of where your `website.html` file is located on your computer.

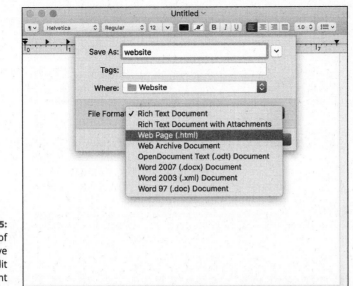

FIGURE 14-5:
An example of
how to save
your TextEdit
document
as HTML.

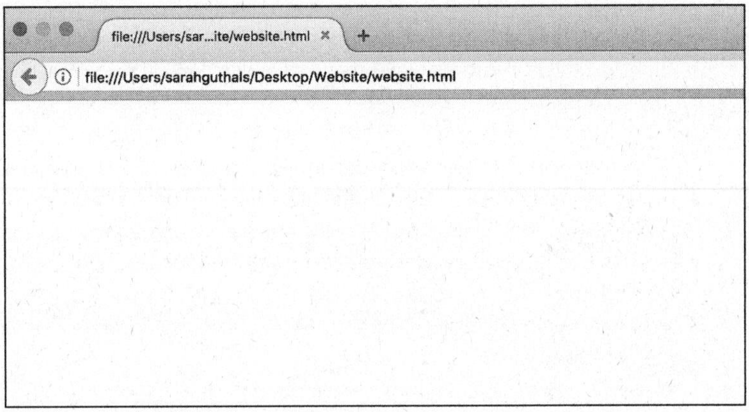

FIGURE 14-6:
Blank website
after creating
your website.html
file.

Now you are all set up to create your first webpage. Setting yourself up like this makes it significantly easier to get everything working after you start adding in graphics and maybe even other HTML files!

TECHNICAL
STUFF

If you close your `website.html` file and need to open it again, you have to make sure to open it with TextEdit. You can do that by opening TextEdit and finding the file. You can also find the file in your finder, right-click it, and choose Open With ⇨ TextEdit, as shown in Figure 14-7.

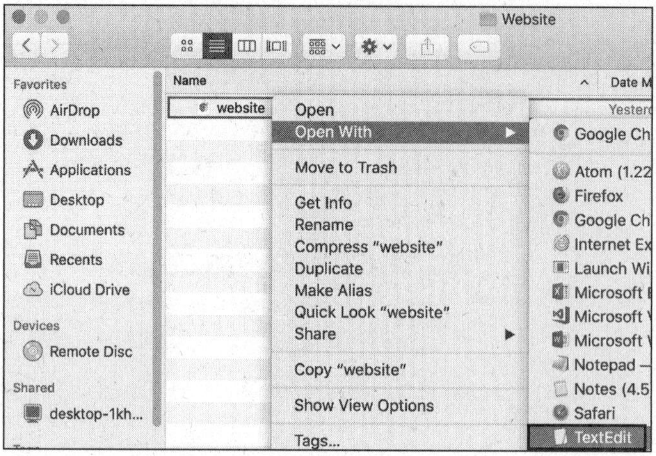

FIGURE 14-7:
To open an HTML file in TextEdit, right-click and choose Open With.

SIR TIMOTHY BERNERS-LEE: INVENTING THE WORLD WIDE WEB

Sir Timothy Berners-Lee is a living legend, widely known as the "Inventor of the Web." But how did this master of coding get his spark of ingenuity to create something that is now so fundamental to daily life?

Tim Berners-Lee was born in London in 1955 to tech-savvy parents who worked on the first commercially built computer, the Mark 1. As a child, he loved electronics and his model railway. As he points out, "I made some electronic gadgets to control the trains. Then I ended up getting more interested in electronics than trains." That early interest in using electronics to remotely control the movement of trains would later contribute to Tim's ideas regarding using code and electrical signals to remotely control the movement of information.

Tim earned his degree in physics from Oxford, and began his first job working as an engineer, creating typesetting software for printers. Tim then traveled to Switzerland to work for CERN — the facility filled with engineering devices and researchers exploring the tiniest matter that makes up the universe. An important part of Tim's work at CERN was to share information among researchers located in different places. Putting his knowledge of type, text, and technology to work, he came up with method for using *hypertext* to share written content electronically. The Internet itself had existed for more than two decades as a way to send information back and forth between computers, using a set of rules called a *protocol* — specifically the Transmission Control Protocol. But Tim's brilliant idea was joining hypertext with the Internet to create a visual interface for viewing, selecting, and sharing information in an easy-to-navigate, user-friendly format. He also knew that he needed to come up with a way to locate information among many hundreds (now billions!) of computers, so that a user's request could track down the desired information from where it was stored. This sort of "Internet address book" is called the DNS, the *domain name system*.

By 1990, Tim crafted the three technologies that are the foundation of the web (specifically HTML, URLs, and HTTP). He also wrote the code for the first browser, the "viewer" for webpages. As Tim said, "I just had to take the hypertext idea and connect it to the Transmission Control Protocol and domain name system ideas and ta-da! — the World Wide Web."

For his important work, Tim was knighted by Queen Elizabeth II in recognition of his "services to the global development of the Internet." So the next time your young coder browses the web, tell him that it was Tim Berners-Lee who put together several existing technologies to create that web — a whole new innovation that has entirely transformed our world!

Figure credit: http://www.telegraph.co.uk/content/dam/technology/
2016/08/04/6454294_Tim_Berners-Lee_director_of_the_World_
Wide_Web_Consortium_trans_NvBQzQNjv4BqRQ0aJoQj5FX45KYe
47MsqGlpGoFNnTqgG-x1RiaPKlg.jpg

Creating a Basic Webpage Layout

Almost every website uses two main languages: HTML and CSS. HTML is basically the structure of your page; details like where different parts show up and how big their areas are. CSS is basically the look and feel of your page; details like specifying fonts and sizes of your text and how sections are aligned. The next two sections walk you through the basics of both of these languages and how to incorporate them into your website.

The skeleton: HTML basics

Making a webpage always starts with a very basic skeleton. HTML is considered a "markup" programming language, as opposed to a true coding language. You can think about HTML as the skeleton or frame of a building. HTML is a set of tags that are written with the symbols ‹ and › with specific words between them to tell the web browser what goes in that area of the site.

Almost every section of a website has an open and close tag. Open tags are written as ‹tagName› and close tags are written as ‹/tagName›. This tells the web browser where the start and end of the section is.

TIP

Indenting everything within an open and close tag helps you and your young coder keep track of what sections are embedded in other sections.

In these next sections, we show the basic tags that you use throughout your website, and where it is appropriate to put them.

HTML tag

The HTML tag is required for every website and is always surrounding everything else that is in your website.

```
<html>
...
</html>
```

Head tag

The head tag contains *metadata*. This chapter doesn't go into details about metadata, but it's basically additional information about your website that you might want the web browser to know.

```
<head>
...
</head>
```

Body tag

The body tag indicates everything that is inside of the window of the web browser. All the text for the webpage goes inside the body tag.

```
<body>
...
</body>
```

Title tag

The title tag is used within the head tag to give your website a title. The title of a website appears on the title bar in the web browser.

```
<title>
...
</title>
```

Header tag

Header tags make large headers for your website. Header tags have different levels, starting with h1 as the biggest header and going down to h6 as the smallest. Any header you use goes inside the opening and closing body tags.

```
<h1>
...
</h1>
```

Paragraph tag

Paragraph tags are used to write smaller text, typically below a header.

```
<p>
...
</p>
```

Break tag

Break tags are used to force something onto a new line. Break tags don't have an open and close tag; there is only one. This is because it just creates a new line and there is nothing that can be embedded within the tag.

```
<br>
```

Div tag

Div tags are used to create sections within your webpage. You can embed any other tags within a div tag. They basically let you separate your page into sections, making it easier to stylize entire parts of your webpage, which you can read about in the next section on CSS.

```
<div>
...
</div>
```

Putting all the HTML tags together

Now that you have had an introduction to each of the basic HTML tags, you can put it all together in your website.html file in TextEdit to create a simple, first version of your website.

```
<html>
  <head>
    <title>My First Website</title>
  </head>

  <body>
    <h1>Your Name Here</h1>
    <div>
      <p>
        A short paragraph describing the kinds of things
        you like to do and what your favorite programming
        language is.
      </p>
      <p>
        Paragraph two has a line break. So this is on
        the first line
        <br>
        and this is on the next line, but it is all
        within one paragraph tag.
      </p>
    </div>
  </body>
</html>
```

If you open your website.html file in a web browser, you see a webpage similar to the one in Figure 14-8.

Take note of these few things about the HTML code and the displayed website:

>> The title can be seen on the tab in Figure 14-8.

>> The title and header tags have the text on the same line as the tags, while the html, head, body, and paragraph tags have the text (or sub-sections) on separate lines, indented. Either way is valid for all tags, the decision to put everything on the same line is for clarity for the coder.

>> Even though the text in the code for the first paragraph is on multiple lines, when it is displayed in the web browser everything is displayed on one line. This is because the text is within one paragraph tag with no break tags.

>> The div tag in this example doesn't change anything, but it keeps both paragraphs in the same section. Later in this chapter you might want to make sure that everything within the div tag has a blue background color, which would be much easier if they were all within one tag.

>> The difference between separating text with paragraph tags and with a break tag is similar to what you would expect in a word document. The paragraph tag gives a larger space between the two sets of text, while the break tag is just like a new line within a paragraph.

>> Though not shown in this example, you can use multiple break tags to create more space between the two lines of text.

TIP

One of the best websites to reference when making a website is w3schools.com. For example, on https://www.w3schools.com/html you can find a menu with a sample of how to do almost anything in HTML! It also includes information about CSS and JavaScript, the other two languages you read about in this chapter!

The aesthetics: CSS

Webpages aren't just sections with simple formatting; you can do so much with formatting and styling! CSS (Cascading Style Sheets) is almost always included in website coding. CSS is basically an additional formatting language used to describe the style of HTML code. Sometimes CSS code is written in a separate file with a .css extension, but you can also embed it in your HTML file either in the head tag, or within each individual tag.

This section shows how to use CSS to add a style tag to your HTML file within the head tag of your HTML code. To get started, make sure your HTML code matches this code here:

```
<html>
  <head>
```

```
    <title>My First Website</title>
    <style>

    </style>
</head>

<body>
    <h1>Your Name Here</h1>

    <div>
      <p>
        A short paragraph describing the kinds of things
        you like to do and what your favorite programming
        language is.
      </p>
      <p>
        Paragraph two has a line break. So this is on
        the first line
        <br>
        and this is on the next line, but it is all
        within one paragraph tag.
      </p>
    </div>
  </body>
</html>
```

You add all the code in the examples in this section between the open and close style tags. After you add the CSS to the style tag, you need to tell the HTML sections which classes of CSS styling they should be following. Each example also includes HTML code that you would need to include. The bolded section of the HTML code is the portion required to apply a certain style to that section.

Fonts

You can specify the font of the text for different sections. When specifying a font, you need to let the viewer's browser have alternative options if the exact font you want isn't available. You do this by adding a comma between each alternative font that the browser can choose. You also have the option of just giving the browser a type of font and let it choose the best font in that category. If the font name is more than one word, the name needs to be enclosed in quotes.

CSS examples:

```
p.serif {
   font-family: "Times New Roman", Times, serif;
}
p.monospace {
   font-family: "Courier New", monospace;
}
```

HTML examples including CSS:

```
<p class="serif">This paragraph is Times New Roman"</p>
<p class="monospace">This paragraph is Courier New"</p>
```

Font styles

You can also specify the style of font you want to use. These examples show normal, italic, and bold.

CSS examples:

```
p.normal {
   font-style: normal;
   font-weight: normal;
}

p.italic {
   font-style: italic;
   font-weight: normal;
}

p.bold {
   font-style: normal;
   font-weight: bold;
}

p.italicBold {
   font-style: italic;
   font-weight: bold;
}
```

HTML examples including CSS:

```
<p class="boldItalic">This paragraph will be bold and italic</p>
```

Font size

Font size can be measured in pixels.

CSS examples:

```
p.big {
   font-size: 40px;
}

p.normal {
   font-size: 14px;
}

p.small {
   font-size: 5px;
}
```

HTML examples with CSS:

```
<p class="small">The text in this paragraph will be really
          small! Might be good for a caption under an image.</p>
```

Text alignment

Text in your webpage can be aligned differently within the section that it's in.

CSS examples:

```
p.left {
  text-align: left;
}

p.center {
  text-align: center;
}

p.right {
  text-align: right;
}
```

HTML examples with CSS:

```
<p class="left">This paragraph will be left-aligned, just like
        words in a book.</p>
<p class="center">This paragraph will be center-aligned, might
        be good for titles and headers.</p>
<p class="right">This paragraph will be right-aligned.</p>
```

Combining multiple styles in one section

You can combine multiple styles within a single style category or you can apply multiple style categories to one section.

CSS examples:

```
p.italic {
    font-style: italic;
    font-weight: normal;
}

p.serif {
    font-family: "Times New Roman", Times, serif;
}

p.fancyParagraph {
    font-style: italic;
    font-weight: bold;
    font-family: "Courier New", monospace;
}
```

HTML examples with CSS:

```
<p class="italic, serif">This paragraph will be italic and Times
        New Roman</p>
<p class="fancyParagraph">This paragraph will be italic, bold,
        and monospace</p>
```

Applying styles to entire categories

For every example in this section, the style can be applied to an entire category of tag instead of just a specific class.

CSS examples:

```
p {
    font-style: normal;
    font-weight: normal;
    font-family: "Times New Roman", Times, serif;
    font-size: 14px;
    text-align: left;
}

h1 {
    font-style: normal;
    font-weight: bold;
    font-family: "Times New Roman", Times, serif;
    font-size: 30px;
    text-align: center;
    text-decoration: underline;
    text-transform: uppercase;
}
```

HTML examples with CSS:

```
<h1>Every header that is H1 will be bold, Times New Roman, 30px,
          centered, underlined, and all uppercase letters.</h1>
<p>Every paragraph will be normal text, Times New Roman, 14px
          and aligned to the left.</p>
```

Organizing sections on the webpage

You can do more than just modify text on a page; you can also organize entire sections with margins, alignments, and position. Typically, you use organizational styles in div tags, described in the HTML section earlier in this chapter.

CSS examples:

```
p.hidden {
    display: none;
}

h1 {
    font-weight: bold;
    font-size: 30px;
    text-align: center;
    text-decoration: underline;
    text-transform: uppercase;
```

```
}

div.header {
  width: 100%;
  position: fixed;
  top: 0;
  margin: auto;
  height: 75px;
}

div {
  margin: auto;
  top: 75px;
  position: fixed;
  text-align: center;
}
```

HTML example with CSS:

```
<div class="header">
  <h1>My Awesome Website</h1>
</div>

<div>
  <p>My favorite programming language is Java!</p>
  <p class="monospace">System.out.println("Hello world!");</p>

  <p>
    One of my favorite things to do is write the
    <p class="monospace">Hello World!</p>
    program!
  </p>

  <p class="hidden">No-one knows I'm here!</p>
</div>
```

This CSS and HTML code displays a website similar to Figure 14-9.

TIP

The "hidden" attribute added to the final paragraph in this code example can be particularly useful when you have a portion of the website that you want to have hidden at first, and then revealed after the user does something (such as click a button). An example of this is when you enter your username and password incorrectly on a website. A new div tag appears, typically with red text, that lets you know that the username or password are incorrect. This div tag with the text is there all along; it's just hidden and only made visible when you input the wrong credentials.

FIGURE 14-9:
This is the
example of a
website that has
structure added
to it with div tags.

You can find additional text styling and more at W3Schools; specifically go to `https://www.w3schools.com/css` where you find a list of all the categories of styles on the left, with the ability to test a number of styles within each category.

Getting Fancy with Color and Graphics

Most websites are more than just a white background and black text. When you add color and graphics to your webpage, you can really make the page unique and your young coder can start to get very creative.

Adding color to your page

You can add color to your webpage in a couple ways: text color and background color. This section shows how to do both of these.

TIP

If you ever want to do something specific when building a website, search online for an example. For example, if you want to specifically have a header that has a red line underneath it, and a blue background color, you can start searching for "html header color underline and color background" in Google and you would find examples! For example, the first result for that query is a W3Schools link with how to create a red underline.

Text color

You can specify a text color in one of three ways: color name, hex value, and RGB value. One of the best ways to choose a color is to use W3Schools' color picker at `https://www.w3schools.com/colors/colors_picker.asp`. You can either choose a color from the wheel at the top or click the color bar under Or Use HTML5 to bring up a pop-up window with even more specific colors. After you choose a color, the website shows you what different text looks like on that color, as shown in Figure 14-10. You get the color name (red), hex value (#ff0000), and RGB value (rgb [255, 0, 0]). If you continue to scroll down the page, you find colors that are slightly lighter and darker than the one you chose.

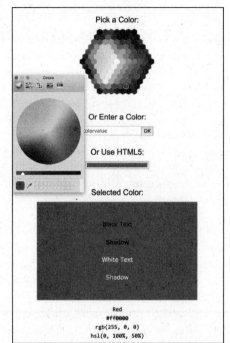

FIGURE 14-10:
W3Schools.com offers an extensive color picker.

The following code shows how to incorporate color into your webpage.

CSS examples:

```
div {
  color: MediumSeaGreen;
}

h1 {
  color: #ff6347;
}

p {
  color: rgb(255, 165, 0);
}
```

RGB AND HEX COLOR CODES

Though HTML has come a long way, and you can often use the English name of a color to set your text colors (like "Black"), there are still two other ways to represent colors that give you more control over the exact color you're choosing. RGB and hex color codes have significantly more detail about the color than "Black" does.

RGB stands for *Red, Green, Blue*. Computers represent essentially all colors using varying amounts of each of these three base colors. It's similar to when you're painting and you have two parts white and one part red, you get pink; if you have three parts white and one part red, you get an even lighter pink. Each color can have a value between 0 and 255. If R, G, and B are all set to 0, it would be represented as (0,0,0) and the color displayed is black. If R, G, and B are all set to 255, it would be written as (255, 255, 255) and the color displayed is white. If your RGB value is (255, 0, 0) then the color would be pure red; if it was (0, 255, 0), it would be pure green; if it was (0, 0, 255), it would be pure blue. Any other value in between would create a variation of red, green, or blue. For example, (102, 0, 204) is purple (a bit of red, no green, and a lot of blue). The best way to discover these colors is to play around with the values, or use color pickers (refer to Figure 14-10).

Hex, on the other hand, stands for *hexadecimal*, and is a number system that uses 16 digits (different from the decimal 10 digits) to represent all possible values. The 16 digits are 0-9 and A-F. (Converting between different base numbering systems is beyond the scope of this book, but you can find more information about that in the numerous tutorials online about converting between numbering systems.) For the purposes of colors, hex is yet another way to represent red, green, and blue values. Hex color codes are typically 6 digits long and start with a pound # sign. Each color is represented using two digits that represent 0 through 255. In Hex, 0 is 00 and 255 is represented as FF. So, if you want black, the hex code is #000000; white is #FFFFFF; purple is #6600CC (because 66 in hex is converted to 102 in decimal and CC in HEX is converted to 204 in decimal).

Regardless of how you choose to represent color in your webpage, whether through the English name, the RGB value, or the hex code, a lot of websites can help you find the color you're looking for. You can also use all three color code types throughout your webpage, as shown in some of the examples in this chapter.

HTML example with CSS:

```
<h1>Red Header</h1>
<div>
  Green Text
```

```
</div>
<p>Yellow Paragraph</p>
```

Figure 14-11 shows what these look like.

Red Header

Green Text

Yellow Paragraph

FIGURE 14-11: Three different ways of specifying text color.

Background color

Background color in different sections on your website can be really useful, not only for allowing you and your young coder to get creative and unique with your webpage, but also for debugging! Adding a different background color to each section can help you determine whether a section is in the right place on the page. The background color style supports color name, hex value, and RGB value, similar to text color.

CSS examples:

```
div {
   color: MediumSeaGreen;
   background-color: rgb(0, 0, 255);
}


h1 {
   color: #ff6347;
   background-color: lightblue;
}


p {
   color: rgb(255, 165, 0);
   background-color: #000000;
}

body {
   background-color: yellow;
}
```

HTML example with CSS:

```
<h1>Red Header, light blue background</h1>
<div>
  Green Text, blue background
</div>
<p>Yellow Paragraph, black background</p>
```

Figure 14-12 shows what these look like.

Introducing graphics

Having colors and text styles can make your webpage unique, but a lot of the creativity comes with adding graphics!

REMEMBER

When you add graphics, you have to make sure the graphics you're including are in the same folder as your HTML file. Remember, you should be using images that are legal to use. See Chapter 6 if you have any questions about finding and downloading graphics.

Images can be sized with CSS or directly in the HTML tag. If you use CSS, you need to specify the image size; that overwrites the size that you specify within the tag. For example, in the following code, the `kitten.jpeg` image is 100x100 pixels if the CSS code is present, and 150x150 pixels if the CSS code is removed.

TIP

You can also add background images to your webpage. In your CSS, you simply add the code:

```
body {
  background-image: image.png
}
```

However, background images can be tricky! Oftentimes they're dark and make it hard to read text on the page. You can make background images stretch to the size of your webpage, or have them repeat over and over to fill the space. For a full list of what you can do with images and background images, visit w3schools.com.

CSS examples:

```
img {
    height: 100px;
    width: 100px;
}

img.seeThrough {
    opacity: 0.5;
}
```

HTML examples with CSS:

```
<img class="seeThrough" src="smile.gif"/>
<img src="puppy.jpg"/>
<img src="kitten.jpeg" width="150" height="150px"/>
```

The code in this example creates the webpage shown in Figure 14-13.

FIGURE 14-13:
Example of a
webpage with
images in
your page.

TECHNICAL
STUFF

Notice that the image tag in HTML doesn't require an open or close tag. Instead, it's all just one tag. That is because the data for the image is all within the tag itself. It doesn't make sense to put text, or other sections, within an image. If you want to have text overlaid on an image, you can do that using the *z-index* (a process in which you can stack images and text on top of each other). You can find out more at `https://www.w3schools.com/howto/howto_css_image_text.asp`.

Adding Hyperlinks

Hyperlinks from your page to any other page on the Internet are actually pretty simple to include! Basically you use one new HTML tag:

```
<a href="url">...</a>
```

Oftentimes you have text between the two anchor (a) tags; however, you can also put images or even entire sections there! You can also stylize hyperlinks on your website with CSS. For example, you can have the color of the link change when the page visitor has clicked the link, or change color when the page visitor hovers over it. You can also specify if you want the hyperlink to open into a new tab in the web browser.

CSS examples:

```
a:link {
    color: blue;
    text-decoration: none;
}

a:hover {
    color: blue;
    text-decoration: underline;
}

a:visited {
    color: red;
    text-decoration: none;
}
```

HTML examples with CSS:

```
<div>
    <p>My favorite programming language is Java!</p>

    <p class="monospace">System.out.println("Hello world!");</p>
```

```
<p>
  One of my favorite things to do is write the
  <a href = "https://en.wikipedia.org/wiki/%22Hello,_
World!%22_program">
    <p class="monospace">Hello world!</p>
  </a>
  program!
</p>

<a href="https://en.wikipedia.org/wiki/Dog" target="_blank">
  Open the Wikipedia article on puppies in a new tab!
</a>

<a href="https://en.wikipedia.org/wiki/Cat">
  <img src="kitten.jpeg"/>
</a>
</div>
```

This code creates the website shown in Figure 14-14. Notice that the Wikipedia page on dogs has already been visited and the page visitor is hovering over the Hello World link.

FIGURE 14-14:
Example of a
webpage with
hyperlinks.

Going Interactive with JavaScript

Adding JavaScript to your webpage is just as simple as adding CSS! First, you add a new script tag:

```
<script>...</script>
```

This script tag can be placed in the head tag or the body tag. For consistency and to ensure any JavaScript functions you create are available, keep them in the head tag.

You can write simple one line JavaScript commands within a script tag, or you can create functions that are called from the HTML. You can affect the HTML and CSS with JavaScript, as well as other examples presented throughout this book. If you get stuck, W3Schools has examples of almost everything you and your young coder would want to do with JavaScript and a website!

Adding buttons

One of the best ways to make your website interactive is to add buttons! This section gives a few examples of incorporating buttons into your site to cause information to pop up on the screen.

```html
<html>
  <head>
    <title>My First Website</title>

    <script>
      function sayWinston() {
        window.alert("My name is Winston");
      }
    </script>
  </head>

  <body>
    <h1>My Awesome Website</h1>

    <img src="puppy.jpg" width="100" height="100"/>
    <br>
    <button onclick="sayWinston();">
      Get the puppy's name
    </button>
  </body>
</html>
```

This example creates the website shown in Figure 14-15. When the button is clicked, the pop-up window appears.

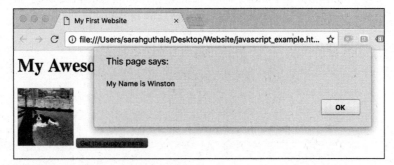

FIGURE 14-15:
Example of a webpage with a button that creates a pop-up window.

You can change the body of the HTML code from the previous example to make it so that your visitors click the image instead of the text.

```
<body>
  <h1>My Awesome Website</h1>

  <button onclick="sayWinston();">
    <img src="puppy.jpg" width="100" height="100"/>
  </button>
  <br>
  Get the puppy's name by clicking on the picture
</body>
```

This example creates the website shown in Figure 14-16. When you click the image of the puppy, the pop-up window appears.

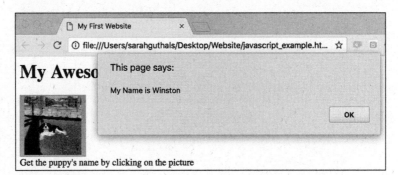

FIGURE 14-16:
Example of a webpage with a picture that, once clicked, opens a window.

Changing your page with buttons

Not only can you add buttons that create pop-up windows, but you can also have your buttons change what is actually being shown on your webpage! Here is an example of changing text, images, and buttons.

```html
<html>
  <head>
    <title>My First Website</title>

    <script>
      function showCat() {
        document.getElementById('kitten').style.display =
"block";
        document.getElementById('noKitten').style.display =
"none";
        document.getElementById('title').innerHTML =
"My Puppy and Kitten!";
      }

      function hideCat() {
        document.getElementById('kitten').style.display =
"none";
        document.getElementById('noKitten').style.display =
"block";
        document.getElementById('title').innerHTML =
"My Puppy!";
      }
    </script>

  </head>
  <body>
    <h1 id="title">My Puppy!</h1>

    <img src="puppy.jpg" width="100" height="100"/>
    <br>
    <div style="display:none" id="kitten">
      <img src="kitten.jpeg" width="100" height="100"/>
      <br>
      <button onclick="hideCat();">
        Click to hide the kitten!
      </button>
    </div>
```

```
    <div id="noKitten">
      <button onclick="showCat();">
      Click to show the kitten!
      </button>
    </div>
  </body>
</html>
```

This code creates the website shown in Figure 14-17. On the left is what the page looks like when first opened. On the right is what the page looks like after the Click to Show the Kitten! button is clicked.

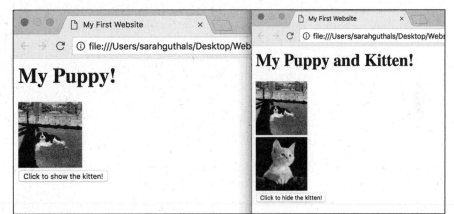

FIGURE 14-17: Example of a webpage that uses JavaScript to change the page.

Combining HTML, CSS, and JavaScript

Using everything presented in this chapter, you and your coder can create a simple website similar to the one shown in Figure 14-18. If you get stuck, don't forget to check out W3Schools.com!

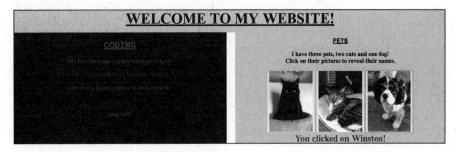

FIGURE 14-18: Example of a webpage you could create with this chapter.

The entire HTML file (with the HTML, CSS, and JavaScript code) is here:

```
<html>
  <head>
    <title>My First Website</title>
    <style>
      p.monospace {
        font-family: "Courier New", monospace;
        font-size: 20px;
      }
      p.aboutCode {
        color: green;
      }
      p {
        font-size: 20px;
      }
      h1 {
        font-family: "Times New Roman", Times, serif;
        font-style: normal;
        font-weight: bold;
        font-size: 50px;
        text-align: center;
        text-decoration: underline;
        text-transform: uppercase;
      }
      h2.code {
        font-family: "Courier New", monospace;
        font-style: normal;
        font-weight: bold;
        font-size: 30px;
        text-align: center;
        text-decoration: underline;
        text-transform: uppercase;
        color: green;
      }
      h2.animals {
        font-family: "Arial", sans-serif;
        font-style: normal;
        font-weight: bold;
        font-size: 20px;
        text-align: center;
        text-decoration: underline;
        text-transform: uppercase;
      }
```

```
      div.header {
        width: 100%;
        top: 0;
        height: 75px;
        margin: auto;
        background-color: lightblue;
      }
      div.codeArea {
        width: 49%;
        top: 200;
        height: 50%;
        float: left;
        text-align: center;
        background-color: black;
      }
      div.petArea {
        width: 49%;
        top: 200;
        height: 50%;
        float: right;
        text-align: center;
        background-color: pink;
        font-weight: bold;
        font-size: 15px;
        margin-left: 2px;
      }
      div.petName {
        font-size: 30px;
      }
      img {
        height: 200px;
        width: 150px;
      }
  </style>

  <script>
    function showPrincess() {
      document.getElementById('petName').innerHTML =
"You clicked on Princess!";
      document.getElementById('petName').style.fontSize =
"30px";
      document.getElementById('petName').style.color =
"black";
    }
```

```
    function showLuke() {
        document.getElementById('petName').innerHTML =
"You clicked on Luke!";
        document.getElementById('petName').style.fontSize =
"30px";
        document.getElementById('petName').style.color = "grey";
    }
    function showWinston() {
        document.getElementById('petName').innerHTML =
"You clicked on Winston!";
        document.getElementById('petName').style.fontSize =
"30px";
        document.getElementById('petName').style.color =
"brown";
    }
  </script>
</head>
<body>
  <div class="header">
    <h1>Welcome to My Website!</h1>
  </div>

  <div class="codeArea">
    <h2 class="code">Coding</h2>
    <p class="aboutCode">
      My favorite programming language is Java!
    </p>
    <p class="monospace aboutCode">
      System.out.println("Hello World!");
    </p>
    <p class="aboutCode">
      One of my favorite things to do is write the
    </p>
    <a href= "https://en.wikipedia.org/wiki/%22Hello,_
World!%22_program">
      <p class="monospace">Hello world!</p>
    </a>
    <p class="aboutCode">
      program!
    </p>
  </div>

  <div class="petArea">
    <h2 class="animals">Pets</h2>
    <p>
```

```
            I have three pets, two cats and one dog!<br>
            Click on their pictures to reveal their names.
        </p>
        <div>
          <button onclick-"showPrincess();">
            <img src="princess.jpg">
          </button>
          <button onclick-"showLuke();">
            <img src="luke.jpg">
          </button>
          <button onclick-"showWinston();">
              <img src="winston.jpg">
          </button>
          <br>
          <div id="petName"></div>
        </div>
      </div>
    </body>
</html
```

Chapter **15**

Building a Mobile Game

Young coders often spend a lot of their time playing games on mobile devices. One of the most powerful experiences for a young coder is to create a mobile game! In this chapter, you're introduced to MIT App Inventor, a browser, block-based programming environment where you can make actual Android mobile apps and games!

To get more in-depth information than we can give in this chapter, see *Building a Mobile App: Design and Program Your Own App!*

Getting Started with MIT App Inventor

To get started with MIT App Inventor, you need a Google account. Then follow these steps to set up your programming environment:

1. **Go to appinventor.mit.edu and click Create Apps in the top-right corner of the webpage.**

2. **Sign in with your Google account.**

3. **Give permission for Google to share your email address with App Inventor, as shown in Figure 15-1.**

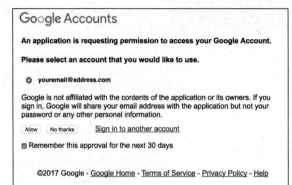

FIGURE 15-1:
Allow Google to share your email address with MIT App Inventor.

4. **Accept the Terms and Services for App Inventor and click Continue when you're ready.**

5. **Dismiss the survey and other items that pop up so that you can get started!**

    You now see a view where all your projects are listed, as shown in Figure 15-2.

You're now ready to start designing and writing your first mobile app!

FIGURE 15-2:
The view of all your projects in App Inventor after you log in.

Community and support within MIT App Inventor

App Inventor was first released in 2010, and the community of coders and educators has grown. Make sure you're signed in and then click Gallery. Figure 15-3 shows the gallery where you find projects and tutorials that other coders have made and published. You and your coder can contribute to these too!

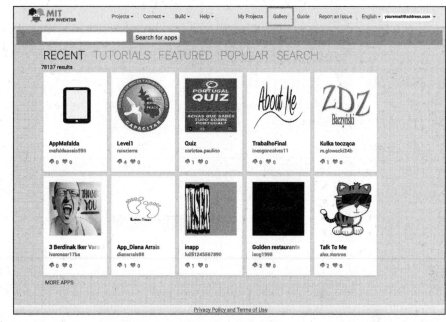

FIGURE 15-3:
The view of the
App Inventor
gallery.

In addition to the community gallery, MIT has created a number of resources for individuals and classrooms. For example, if you head to `http://appinventor.mit.edu/explore/ai2/tutorials.html` you find over 30 tutorials divided by difficulty level and an option to filter by topic (such as game).

There are also a ton of resources about using App Inventor, setting everything up, troubleshooting, and documentation. All this can be found at `http://appinventor.mit.edu/explore/library`. Although this page is a bit less user-friendly — basically a list of links — it can be a great place to start if you have a question or experience any trouble.

The community isn't just created by MIT; there are also a number of books that you can find on App Inventor and forums where you can ask questions and get very specific answers on the App Inventor website (http://appinventor.mit.edu) under Resources. There are also specific resources for educators, which you can find at http://teach.appinventor.mit.edu/. Be sure to explore all the resources when getting your young coder acquainted with the software.

The layout of MIT App Inventor

Before you get started on your first mobile game, take the time to get acquainted with the programming environment. There are two areas your coder will spend time in: Design View and Code View.

To get to Design View, click Start New Project in the top left of the programming environment. Name your project "myFirstApp." The Design View opens as shown in Figure 15-4.

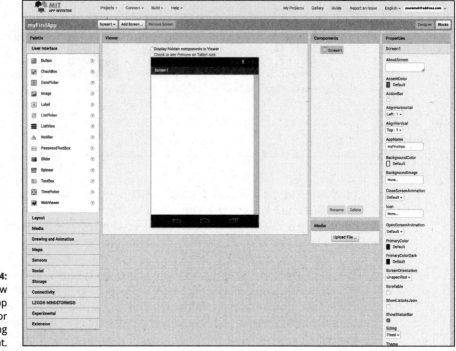

FIGURE 15-4: The Design View of the App Inventor programming environment.

Note these six areas:

>> **Menu Bar:** The menu bar across the top has the title of your app, options for multiple screens, and a toggle button for Designer and Blocks.

>> **Palette:** On the left is a list of options for things to add to your app.

>> **Viewer:** The viewer is basically what you see on your mobile device after you test your app. This is where you organize all the components to add to your app.

>> **Components:** The components list shows all the elements in your app. Sometimes components are invisible, so this is an important view to know everything in your screen.

>> **Media:** Under the Components view is a Media view where any sounds or images that you have uploaded to your app appear.

>> **Properties:** If you click a component in the Components view, then the properties for that component is listed in this view. You can also change properties in this view, too.

Then, to see the Code View as shown in Figure 15-5, click the Blocks button on the very right of the Menu Bar.

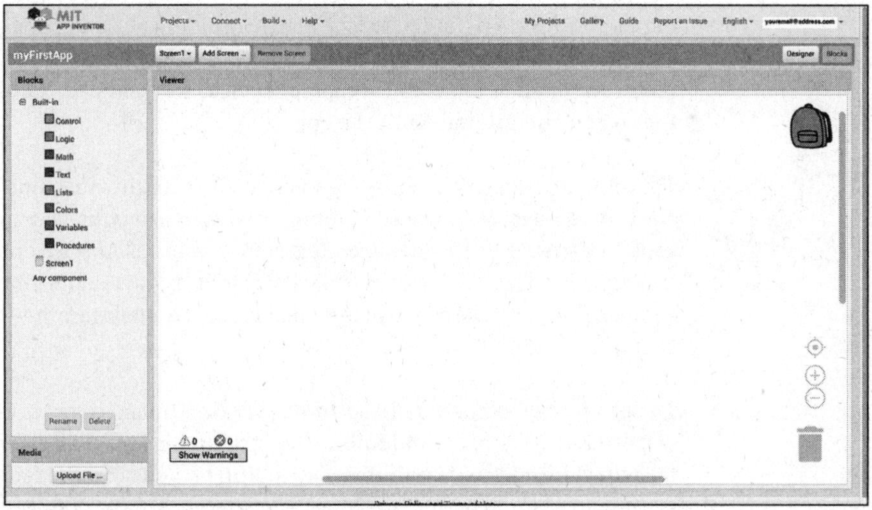

FIGURE 15-5: The Code View of the App Inventor programming environment.

>> **Menu Bar:** Just like in the Design View, the menu bar allows you to switch screens or go back to the Design View.

- >> **Blocks:** This view has all the coding blocks (also referred to as tiles). There are generic blocks, but if you have a component in your design, there also are blocks specifically for that component.

- >> **Media:** This view has all the sounds and images that you have uploaded to your app.

- >> **Coding Area:** The coding area is where you drag the coding blocks to actually make your app respond to your users.

Using an Emulator versus a Real Device

Before getting started on making your first app, make sure your coder has a way to test her app, either on a real mobile device or on an emulator. This section walks you through using the emulator or a real device, and the rest of this chapter gives examples of using an Android device connected to Wi-Fi on a Mac, using Chrome.

Using the Android Emulator

The Android Emulator is a great resource if you and your young coder are developing mobile apps on a Windows or Mac computer (not a Chromebook or other type of netbook). The emulator is basically a fake Android device that you can run on your computer. It looks like a mobile device, and you use your mouse to "touch" the screen and interact with the app.

WARNING

The emulator doesn't always work very well. It might crash and require you to restart. If you decide to use the emulator with your young coder, there will be lessons in patience with software. Remember, a lot of App Inventor was written by students at MIT, and although they have done an incredible job, there isn't a large company of software engineers dedicated to maintaining and creating this software.

To set up your emulator, head to `http://appinventor.mit.edu/explore/ai2/setup-emulator.html` and follow the instructions on that page. This process can take upwards of 20-30 minutes, depending on your Internet connection. If you're setting up more than one machine, for example a classroom, be sure to download, install, and test the emulator at least one day before you plan for your young coders to test with it. Although the process of setting up new software is one that is useful to learn, this software in particular can be frustrating and can discourage young coders from wanting to continue building.

After you finish the installation process, create a basic app to make sure everything is up and running properly. (See "Testing on the emulator and Android device" section coming up.)

Using a real Android device

If you have access to an Android device — tablet or smartphone — you can actually test your mobile apps on the device itself! Your device doesn't need a cellular plan, but ideally it has Wi-Fi access.

You need to download MIT AI2 Companion App to your device. If you have Wi-Fi, you can download it from the Google Play Store and enter a 6-digit code to test your app. The instructions for this option can be found at `http://appinventor.mit.edu/explore/ai2/setup-device-wifi.html`.

If you don't have access to Wi-Fi, use a USB cord to connect your device to your computer and install the MIT AI2 Companion App to your device. All the instructions for setting up your device this way can be found at `http://appinventor.mit.edu/explore/ai2/setup-device-usb.html`.

After you finish setting up your Android device, you can then create a basic app to make sure everything is up and running properly. (See the next section.)

Testing on the emulator and Android device

This section helps you create a very simple app to make sure your emulator or device is working properly before developing your mobile game.

Make sure you're logged in at `http://ai2.appinventor.mit.edu/` and that you're looking at the same screen as in Figure 15-6. Then follow these steps:

1. **Under the Palette column, click the Layout category and drag a HorizontalArrangement to the Viewer, as shown in Figure 15-7.**

2. **Under the Components column, rename the HorizontalArrangement1 to Images and under the Properties column change the Width to Fill Parent.**

   Your Viewer, Components, and Properties should match Figure 15-8.

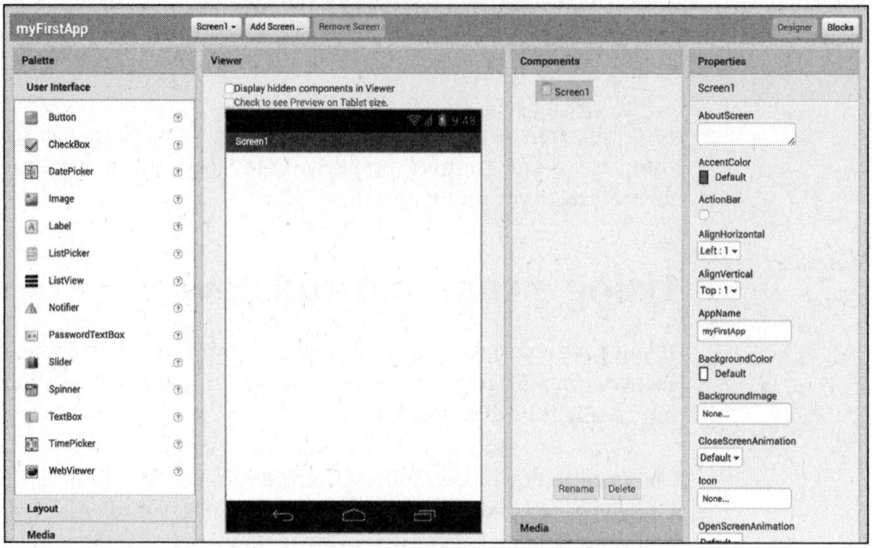

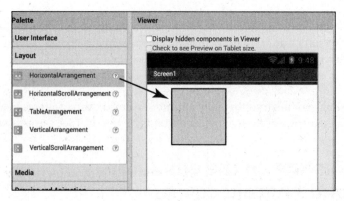

FIGURE 15-6:
The view of myFirstApp before you create the testing app.

FIGURE 15-7:
Adding a horizontal arrangement to your app screen.

3. **Find three images to upload into your app.**

If you need advice on finding images, revisit Chapter 6.

4. **Under the Palette column, click the User Interface category and drag three buttons into the horizontal arrangement you created in Step 2.**

You should see three buttons like in Figure 15-9.

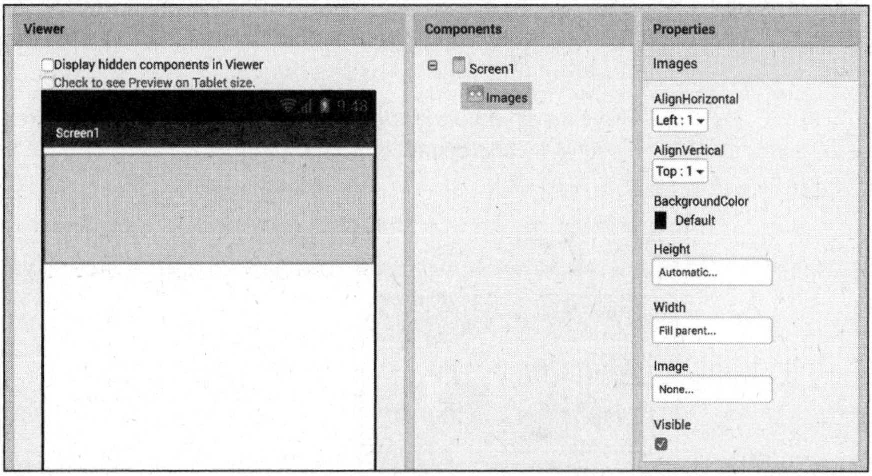

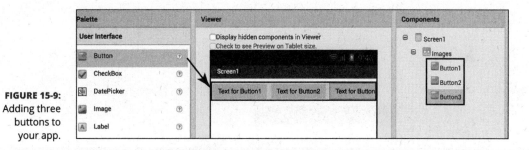

FIGURE 15-8:
Setting up the properties for your horizontal arrangement.

FIGURE 15-9:
Adding three buttons to your app.

5. **Upload the three images you found in Step 3 to the Media column. Then, make these changes for each button:**

   - Change the name of the button to a name that identifies the image.

   - Change the width to 75-100 pixels.

   - Change the height to a ratio that would match that width for the images you chose.

   - Set the image for each button to be one of the images you uploaded.

   - Remove all of the text for the button.

   Your images should look something like Figure 15-10.

6. **Add a second HorizontalArrangement that is the width of the parent and name it "Labels" and do the following:**

   - Add a Label called "SayHello."

   - Make sure the properties of SayHello has a FontSize of 30, TextAlignment centered, and the Text is blank.

- Make sure that the properties of Labels has an AlignHorizontal centered and a Width of Fill Parent.

Your design should look like Figure 15-11. Don't worry that your Labels arrangement is empty.

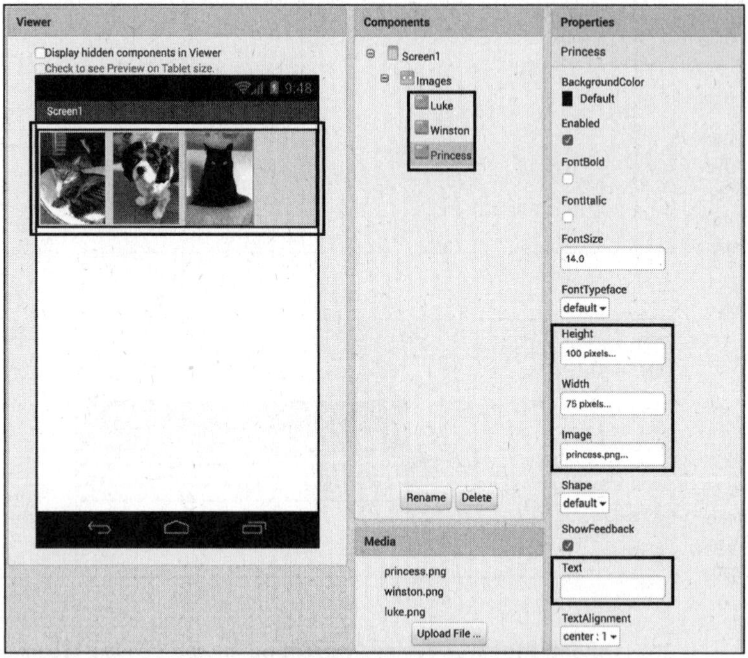

FIGURE 15-10:
Setting up the
properties for
the buttons.

FIGURE 15-11:
Adding a label
to your app.

7. **Click Blocks in the Menu Bar and write code to make your app do something.**

Notice that the code block (tile) options available are specifically applicable to the components you have added.

8. Add three pieces of code to make your program work:

- Click each button and drag a When button.Click block into your Coding Area.

- Click SayHello and drag a Set SayHello.Text to into each When button.Click code block.

- Click Text and drag an empty text block to the end of each Set SayHello. Text to block.

Your final code should look similar to Figure 15-12.

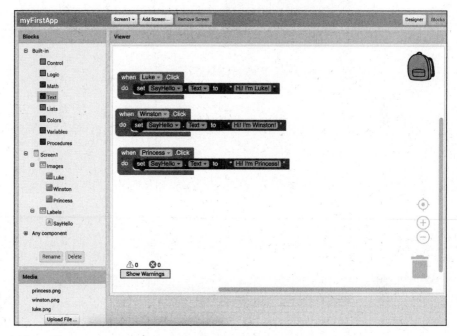

FIGURE 15-12:
The code for
your first app.

9. Click Connect at the top of your screen and choose your option:

- AICompanion if you're using a real Android device connected over Wi-Fi.

- Emulator if you're using the Android Emulator.

- USB if you have your Android device connected via USB.

Figure 15-13 shows all the options for testing your app.

When you test your app, click each button and see the label change! Figure 15-14 shows how the app looks after the user has clicked the first image. Figure 15-15 shows how the app looks after the user has clicked the second image. Figure 15-16 shows how the app looks after the user has clicked the third image.

FIGURE 15-13:
The options for
testing your app.

FIGURE 15-14:
Your first app
working on an
Android device,
shown when the
user clicks the
first image.

Throughout your App Inventor development there will probably be times when you've updated your app design or code but your changes aren't reflected on the device or emulator. When this happens, click Reset Connection (refer to Figure 15-13). If that doesn't help, click Hard Reset.

Encourage your young coders to make minor changes to the first app to help them better understand the design and coding environments. Some fun ideas are

>> Add sounds to play when the buttons are clicked.

>> Make the pictures change to other pictures when clicked.

>> Play a video below the label when a button is clicked.

Now that you've created and tested an app, you're ready to build your game!

FIGURE 15-15:
Your first app
working on an
Android device,
shown when the
user clicks the
second image.

FIGURE 15-16:
Your first app
working on an
Android device,
shown when the
user clicks the
third image.

Designing Mobile Apps

Before you and your coder get started building an app, it's a good idea to plan the app — in this case, a game — you want to build. When we're teaching young coders to make mobile game apps, we often have them make paper prototypes of their games first, then go onto App Inventor to actually create the game.

A paper prototype is basically a low-tech version of your app. You can create one with actual paper or with software (for example, PowerPoint or Google Slides). When using actual paper, one fun way to get your young coder excited about it is to draw an Android device where he can draw on the "screen." For example, if you were to make a paper prototype of the app shown in Figures 15-14 through 15-16, you might have four different sheets. On each sheet you would have the three images. On one of the sheets, you would have no words shown; on one, you would have "Hi! I'm Luke!;" on one, you would have "Hi! I'm Winston!;" and on the last, you would have "Hi! I'm Princess!" Then you would have a description on the bottom or back of the sheet to explain how to see that view. For example, on the first sheet you might have a description that says "This is how the app looks when you first open it and you haven't pressed any buttons yet." And on the last sheet you might have "This is how the app looks when you have clicked the button with Princess on it."

REMEMBER

Taking time to think about, draw, and design how all the components interact with each other can be very useful before coding because you can find problems with your app before you've spent time building it. This is a software engineering trick that large companies do as well. For example, when first designing the myFirstApp in the previous section, Sarah imagined that each of the images were just images, not buttons. But then she realized she needed a way to trigger an event to change the text below the images. That's when she realized that each image needed to be a button, not just an image.

Though this chapter has a very specific game to build, when building your next game or app, remember to go through the design process with your young coder!

This chapter gives you the steps to create a simple game called "Puppy Play Day," where you fling a puppy sprite around the screen and try to collect treats and avoid baths! To build this game, you need the following components:

» A canvas

» A sprite with an image of a dog

- » Three sprites with images of dog treats

- » Three sprites with images of bath tubs

- » A HorizontalArrangement with six labels for tracking a score

- » A HorizontalArrangement with two labels for tracking the timer

- » A HorizontalArrangement with three buttons for the difficulty level

- » A clock component (which is invisible)

The game you make will look similar to Figure 15-17.

FIGURE 15-17:
The Puppy Play
Day app on an
Android device.

Adding the Components in Design View

The first part of designing your app is adding all the components to the app. When building an app from scratch, this might be an iterative process. However, if you and your young coder have sketched how you want your app to work using a paper prototype, then you probably know everything that you need to add to the screen.

REMEMBER

Iterative means that it repeats over and over. In this case, the iterative process of developing an app means that you might build a small version first, test it on your device, add a new feature, test, and so on. It could also mean that after completing your app, you might decide that you want to add something more, or change it, even months afterwards!

These steps guide you through each component that needs to be added:

1. **From the Drawing and Animation category, drag a Canvas into your app.**

    - Rename it PlayArea.

    - Change the Height to 80 percent and the Width to FillParent.

2. **Find three images to use in your app: a puppy, a dog treat, and a bathtub.**

    Make sure you follow the guidelines in Chapter 6 for finding legal images to use. The size of your image files should be less than 4MB for each image.

3. **Upload your three images to the Media section on App Inventor.**

4. **Add seven ImageSprites from the Drawing and Animation category into your Canvas.**

    - Rename the ImageSprites treat1, treat2, treat3, tub1, tub2, tub3, and puppy.

    - Set each image to Height 50 pixels, Width 50 pixels, and Picture to the appropriate image from the ones you uploaded in Step 3.

5. **From the Layout category, add a HorizontalArrangement below the canvas.**

    - Rename it Scores.

    - Set AlignHorizontal to Center, AlignVertical to Center, Height to 5 percent, and Width to Fill Parent.

6. **From the User Interface category, add six labels to the Scores HorizontalArrangement.**

    - Rename them TreatLabel, Treats, BathLabel, Baths, ScoreLabel, and Score.

    - Change the text for three of the labels to Treats, Baths, and Total Score and make them FontBold.

    - Change the text for the other three labels to 0.

7. **From the Layout category, add another HorizontalArrangement below the Scores HorizontalArrangement.**

   - Rename it Timer.
   - Set AlignHorizontal to Center, AlignVertical to Center, Height to 5 percent, and Width to Fill Parent.

8. **From the User Interface category, add two labels to the Timer HorizontalArrangement.**

   - Rename them TimerLabel and Countdown.
   - Change the text for TimerLabel to Time Left and make it FontBold.
   - Change the text for Countdown to be nothing.

9. **From the Layout category, add one more HorizontalArrangment below the Timer HorizontalArrangement.**

   - Rename it Levels.
   - Set AlignHorizontal to Center, AlignVertical to Center, Height to 10 percent, and Width to Fill Parent.

10. **From the User Interface category, add three buttons to the Levels HorizontalArrangement.**

    - Rename them Easy, Medium, and Hard.
    - Change the Easy button text to Easy and the BackgroundColor to Green.
    - Change the Medium button text to Medium and the BackgroundColor to Yellow.
    - Change the Hard button text to Hard and the BackgroundColor to Red.

11. **From the Sensor category, add a clock to your screen.**

    The clock doesn't show up on your screen because it's invisible. You can leave the name Clock1, but make sure TimerEnabled is unchecked.

Figure 15-18 shows a sample of what your Design View should look like. You might notice that your three buttons are not visible on screen. That is okay because when you code your game, the Levels HorizontalArrangement shows and the Timer HorizontalArrangement is hidden. Then, when your player chooses a level, the Levels HorizontalArrangment is hidden and the Timer HorizontalArrangement is shown.

Coding Your Mobile App

Now that your young coder has all the components in place for the Puppy Play Day app, it's time to start coding them! This section guides you through coding the game app in an iterative process. It's important that your young coder learn to code in small portions, and test the functionality often. It's a cycle — code – test – code – test – code – test — until you're playing the game you wanted to build! Coding is never "complete." You can always add more features, polish existing functionality, or make changes. So the iterative process of development is one that allows you to make decisions about the code you're building as you build it, and then make a decision as to when it is complete enough. Click the Blocks button on the right of your Menu Bar to get started with coding your game.

Getting your puppy moving

The first step is to get your puppy moving around the screen. In this game, you fling your puppy around the screen. Follow these steps to make your puppy explore the play area:

1. **Click the puppy ImageSprite in the Blocks column and drag a When Puppy.Flung block into your coding area.**

2. **From the puppy category, drag a Set Puppy.Speed to block into the When Puppy.Flung block, and set the speed to 10 by clicking together a Math number block to the Set Puppy.Speed to block.**

3. **From the puppy category, drag a Set Puppy.Heading to block below the Set Puppy.Speed to block. Then hover over the parameter Heading in the When Puppy.Flung block and drag the Get Heading block to click to the Set Puppy.Heading to block.**

   See Figure 15-19 to make sure you have your When Puppy.Flung block set up correctly.

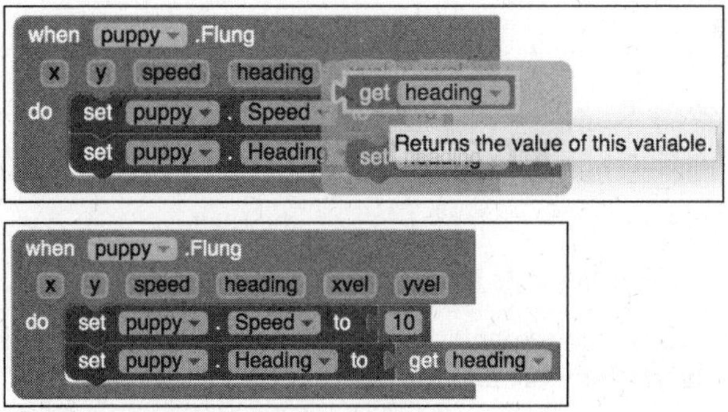

FIGURE 15-19:
Getting the
direction that
the player flung
the puppy to use
to move the
sprite (top); the
code needed to
make the puppy
move when you
fling it with your
finger (bottom).

4. **From the puppy category, drag a When Puppy.EdgeReached block into your Coding Area.**

5. **From the puppy category, drag a Call Puppy.Bounce Edge block into the When Puppy.EdgeReached block. Hover over the Edge parameter and click a Get Edge block into the When Puppy.EdgeReached block.**

   You now have a new code block in your coding area similar to Figure 15-20.

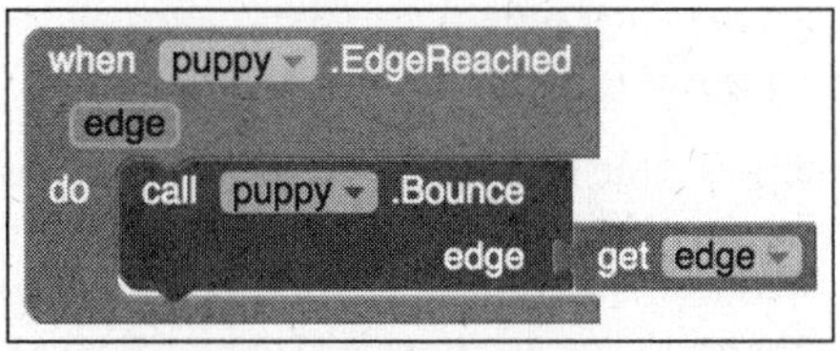

FIGURE 15-20:
Coding the puppy
to bounce off the
edge of the
screen.

6. **Test your code.**

   Make sure that when you touch the puppy and fling your finger that the puppy ImageSprite moves around the screen. If the puppy reaches an edge, it should bounce.

Setting up your start screen and variables

Now that your puppy can move, you need to set up the rest of your game. Follow these steps to get your start screen correct and the lists you use to make coding easier. For a review on how lists work, visit Chapter 11.

1. **From the Screen category, drag a When Screen1.Initialize block into your coding area.**

2. **Set the following properties inside of the When Screen1.Initilize block:**

   - Set Treats.Text to 0; make sure 0 is a Math number block, not a String block.

   - Set Baths.Text to 0; make sure 0 is a Math number block, not a String block.

   - Set Score.Text to 0; make sure 0 is a Math number block, not a String block.

   - Set Clock1.TimerEnabled to false; false is in the Logic category.

   - Set Timer.Visible to false; false is in the Logic category.

   - Set Levels.Visible to true; true is in the Logic category.

3. **Create two new variables called treats and tubs and set them to be Empty List from the Lists category.**

4. **Create a new procedure called setupLists and add each treat to the treats list and each tub to the tubs list.**

   The treat (1, 2, and so on) blocks can be found in each of the ImageSprites under the Blocks category.

5. **Call the setupLists procedure at the end of your When Screen1.Initialize block.**

   The Call setupLists procedure block can be found under the Procedures category.

6. **Create a new procedure called hideItems that makes all the treats and tubs hide when the program first starts.**

   From the Control category, drag two For Each Item in List blocks into the hideItems procedure. From the Variables category, drag the Get Global Treats and Get Global Tubs blocks to be the list that the loops will iterate through. From the Any Component category, choose Any ImageSprite and drag a Set ImageSprite.Visible of Component . . . To . . . block into each of the loops. Hover over Item to get the Get Item block to connect to Of Component and from the Logic category drag a False block to connect to To. Then call the hideItems procedure from the When Screen1.Initilize block.

   Figure 15-21 shows all the code that you added to initialize the screen and set up all your variables is shown.

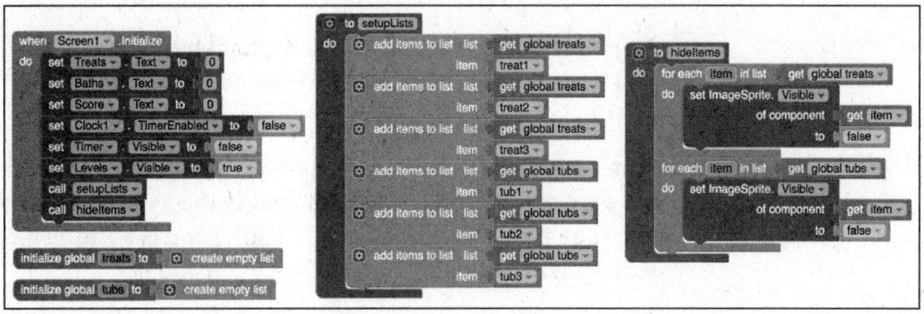

FIGURE 15-21:
The code needed
to make the
puppy bounce off
of the edge of the
screen.

7. **Test your code.**

   Now when you test on your Android device or emulator, you see only the puppy onscreen and it still bounces around when you fling it. You should also not see the Timer labels anymore.

Coding random placement of items

Now that you have your puppy roaming around the screen and the items hidden, you can make the items appear randomly around the play area. When the puppy touches an item, it can increase the score for that type of item, and make the item move to another random place on the play area! Follow these steps to check for placing the items randomly:

1. **Create a new procedure called randomPlacementSetup.**

2. **Drag two of the For Each Item In List blocks into the randomPlacement-Setup procedure.**

3. **Drag a Get Global Treats and Get Global Tubs to click into the List connection on the two loops from Step 2.**

4. **From the Any Component ⇨ Image Sprites category, drag a Set ImageSprite.Visible Of Component To into each of the loops from Step 2.**

5. **Hover over the item in each loop from Step 2 and drag a Get Item block into Of Component for each of the Set ImageSprite.Visible Of Component To blocks from Step 4.**

6. **From the Logic category, drag a True block into to of the Set ImageSprite.Visible Of Component To blocks from Step 4.**

7. **From the Any Component ⇨ Image Sprites category, drag a Call ImageSprite.MoveTo For Component X Y block into each of the loops from Step 2.**

8. **Hover over the item in each loop from Step 2 and drag a Get Item block into For Component for each of the Call ImageSprite.MoveTo For Component X Y blocks from Step 7.**

9. From the Math category, drag a Random Integer From 1 to 10 into both X and Y for each Call ImageSprite.MoveTo For Component X Y blocks from Step 7.

10. From the PlayArea blocks, drag a PlayArea.Width into both Random Integer From 1 to 10 blocks attached to the Xs, replacing the 10s. Drag a PlayArea.Height into both Random Integer from 1 to 10 blocks attached to the Y connection, replacing the 10 placeholder.

11. Create a new procedure called setupStart, which is called when the level button is chosen.

12. Call the randomPlacementSetup from inside the new setupStart procedure.

13. For each componenet, set the following properties:

- Set Timer.Visible to True.

- Set Levels.Visible to False.

- Set Clock1.TimerEnabled to True.

- Set Treats.Text to 0; Math number 0, not String.

- Set Baths.Text to 0; Math number 0, not String.

- Set Score.Text to 0; Math number 0, not String.

14. From each button, drag a When Button.Click Do block into the coding area, and call setupStart from inside the block.

All the code you added in this section is similar to Figure 15-22.

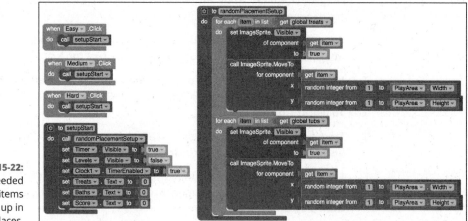

FIGURE 15-22: The code needed to make the items show up in random places.

15. Test your code.

Now when you press any button (Easy, Medium, or Hard), the items appear in random places onscreen.

Coding collision with items

The items aren't very useful unless you can actually collect them! Luckily, the code for collecting each item is almost exactly the same. Follow these steps to make sure you can record the items being collected:

1. Drag a When Treat1.CollidedWith Other Do block into your coding area.

2. From the Control category, drag an If Then block into the When Treat1. CollidedWith Other Do block.

3. From the Logic category, drag an = block to the If part of the If Then block from Step 2.

4. Hover over the Other in the When Treat1.CollidedWith Other Do block and connect a Get Other block to the left side of the = block from Step 3.

5. From the puppy component, drag a Puppy block to the right side of the = block from Step 3.

6. Inside of the If Then block, add a Set Treat1.Visible to False block.

7. Below the block added in Step 6, add a Set Treats.Text To block.

8. From the Math category, connect a + block to From the Set Treats.Text To block from Step 7.

9. From the Treats category, add a Treats.Text block to the left side of the + block from Step 8.

10. From the Math category, add a number block with 1 to the right side of the + block from Step 8.

11. From the Treat1 category, drag a Call Treat1.MoveTo X Y block below the block added in Step 7.

12. Add a Random Integer From 1 To PlayArea.Width to X and Random Integer From 1 to PlayArea.Height to Y.

13. From the Treat1 category, drag a Set Treat1.Visible To True as the last block in the When Treat1.CollidedWith Other Do block.

The Treat1 collision code is similar to Figure 15-23.

14. Duplicate the entire block of code you just created (refer to Figure 15-23) by right-clicking and choosing Duplicate from the menu.

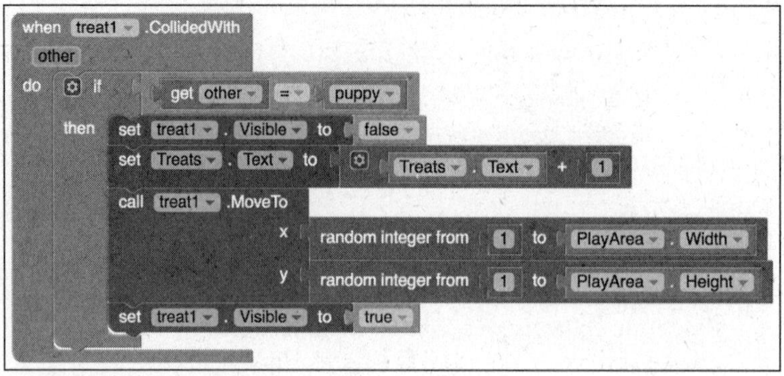

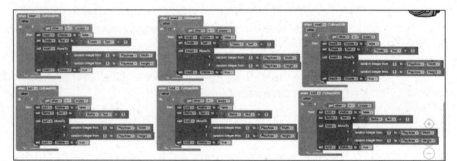

FIGURE 15-23:
The code needed
to detect the
collision of the
puppy and treat1.

15. Change treat1 to treat2 in every instance of the duplicated blocks of code.

16. Duplicate the code four more times, changing to each treat3, tub1, tub2, and tub3.

For each of the three blocks of code for each tub, make sure you also change Treats to Baths for the blocks Set Baths.Text To Baths.Text + 1.

The six new blocks of code that you added are shown in Figure 15-24.

FIGURE 15-24:
The code
needed to detect
the collision of
the puppy and
each item.

17. Test your code.

Now when the puppy hits any of the items, they disappear and reappear in a different location. The numbers in the scores for Treats and Tubs also increase, depending on which type of item the puppy collided with.

Levels, timers, and final score

Now you make each level slightly different for the user, keep track of time, and give the user a final score when time runs out. Just follow these steps to finish your mobile game:

1. **For each of the When Button.Click Do blocks of code, add a Set Puppy. Speed To block and Set Countdown.Text To block.**

2. **For the Easy button block, set the puppy's speed to 5 and the countdown text to 20.**

   Make sure to set the speed and text to the Math number block 5 and 20, not a String.

3. **For the Medium button block, set the puppy's speed to 10 and the countdown text to 15.**

   Make sure to set the speed and text to the Math number block 10 and 15, not a String.

4. **For the Hard button block, set the puppy's speed to 15 and the countdown text to 10.**

   Make sure to set the speed and text to the Math number block 15 and 10, not a String.

   The Easy level has the puppy move slower, making it easier to control the sprite with flinging and the countdown 20 seconds, giving the player more time to collect more items. Figure 15-25 shows the changes to these blocks.

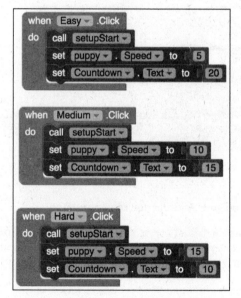

FIGURE 15-25:
The code needed
to change the
game based on a
level choice.

5. **From the Clock1 category, drag a When Clock1.Timer Do block into the coding area.**

6. Set Countdown.Text to Countdown.Text – 1.

7. From the Control category, drag an If Then block below the block from Step 7. Set the condition to Countdown.Text = 0.

8. Inside the If Then block, call hideItems, then set the following properties:

- Set Clock1.TimerEnabled to False.

- Set Timer.Visible to False.

- Set Levels.Visible to True.

- Set Score.Text to Treats.Text – Baths.Text.

- Set puppy.Speed to 0; Math number 0, not String.

Figure 15-26 shows the code to add to count down the time and show the player the final score.

The total score is the number of treats you collected minus the number of baths. You lose points for every bath you make the puppy take and earn points for every treat you give the puppy!

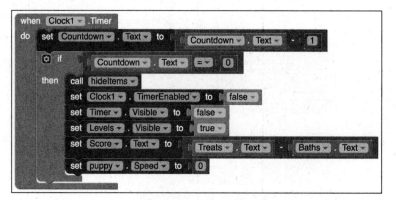

FIGURE 15-26: The code needed to countdown the timer and show the final score.

9. Test your game on your Android device or emulator.

Now you can choose a different level, which changes the speed of the puppy and the countdown timer. You can collect treats and tubs and your score reflects that. When the timer runs out, the game resets.

Distributing Your Apps

After you and your young coder finish making your app, you can share it with anyone who has an Android device. Just go to your list of Projects (Projects ⇨ My Projects), check the box next to the app you want to publish, and click Publish to Gallery, as shown in Figure 15-27.

FIGURE 15-27:
The view from the Projects list to publish your app to the Gallery.

Fill out the form by uploading an image and providing a description as shown in Figure 15-28. This is where you can put any attributions of media that you might have used in your app. Click the Publish button when you're ready.

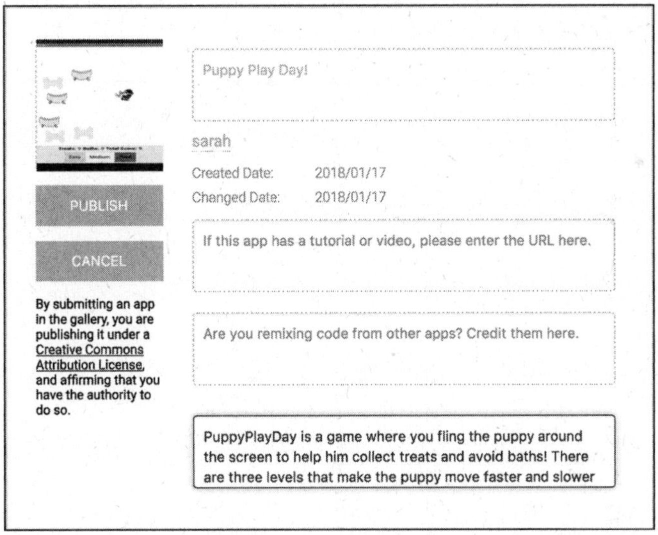

FIGURE 15-28:
The form to fill out when you want to publish your app.

The screen you're taken to, after you publish your app, has a share link, which you can share with your friends who might want to check out your code. They can then click Open The App and remix it to try it on their own! You can see the app built in this chapter at ai2.appinventor.mit.edu/?galleryId=6447403443683328.

To share your app with friends who just want to play your game, you have two options.

» **Generate a temp QR code.** This code allows your friends to download your app. Open your app and choose Build ⇨ App (provide QR code for .apk). In the pop-up window is the QR code, which you can share with your friends. Using any QR code scanner, they can scan the QR code, open the link that is associated with the QR code, and a download starts. After the download is complete, they can open the app and play your game! The game is available until they delete it, even though the QR code expires in two hours.

» **Download your app files and distribute them to your friends.** You can do this by choosing Build ⇨ App (save .apk to my computer). Then you can upload the file to Google Drive (or any other accessible server), make sure it's accessible for anyone to view the file, and then distribute the link to the file. When your friends open the link on their Android device, the app starts downloading. You can download the game made for this chapter by visiting https://www.thewecan.zone/build-mobile-app and clicking the Puppy Play Day App button.

Chapter **16**

Programming Simple Electronics

L earning to write code is a skill that young coders apply in many different ways. Creating apps and websites are some of the most familiar and visible digital products they can produce with their newfound skills.

You can also encourage them to use their coding talents in writing programs to control hardware devices, too! Hardware consists of electronics and other components such as motors, lights, and speakers. Controlled by code, the hardware can be constructed to build everything from robotic rovers and drones to wearable gadgets and musical instruments. This chapter guides you in helping kids create and code a simple electronic device. Using a micro:bit electronics board (or just emulating one on the computer), your young coder can build fun toys, gadgets, and games!

Gathering Your Hardware

The alarm project presented in this chapter can be completed on a computer without the use of any outside materials or devices. But it's a lot more fun if you obtain a micro:bit electronics board and actually build it!

The micro:bit board

A micro:bit is a tiny, programmable computer that's about half the size of a credit card. It contains the following components:

>> A microcontroller, which is a small computer on a single integrated circuit. This includes 16K RAM (memory) with Bluetooth Low Energy wireless networking

>> A Bluetooth smart antenna

>> A micro USB connector

>> A battery connector

>> A 3-axis accelerometer

>> A 3-axis magnetometer (acting as a compass and metal detector)

>> Three IO (input/output) digital/analog ring connectors

>> One power ring connector and one ground ring connector

>> A 20-pin edge connector

>> Two programmable buttons

>> Twenty-five individually programmable LED lights

The variety of components make the micro:bit a flexible little board that you can program for a wide range of applications.

The BBC (British Broadcasting Corporation) in the United Kingdom distributed a free micro:bit board to around a million tweens in an effort to get British kids coding and inventing!

Buying the board and components

Getting the hardware you need — a micro:bit board (and a couple of companion accessories) — is as simple as placing an order on Amazon. Here are the recommended items for this project:

>> **BBC micro:bit go kit:** This kit contains one micro:bit electronics board; one USB cable; one battery holder; and two AAA batteries. It retails for around $20. See Figure 16-1.

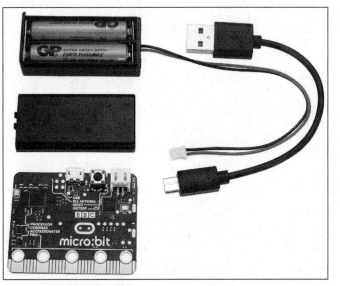

>> **Test leads with alligator clips:** You need two test leads ("wires"). A pack of ten retails for around $7, or you can just borrow a couple from an electronics enthusiast. See Figure 16-2.

>> **Electronic buzzer:** You need one simple buzzer that possesses two connecting wires. Look for a DC buzzer rated for 3 to 24V. These vary greatly in cost and sound quality. They sell for around $3 to $6 each. See Figure 16-3.

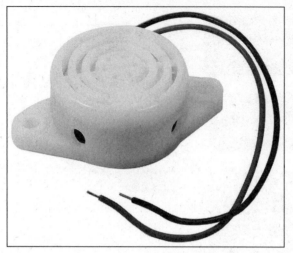

Accessing the Software

Your coder can use a variety of languages to program the micro:bit. One easy way to create the alarm is to code it in JavaScript using the IDE at the Microsoft Make Code site located at https://makecode.microbit.org. Your kid can code using either text mode or tile (block)–based mode.

Navigating the interface

The micro:bit IDE features a few key areas your young coder can use to program his device (see Figure 16-4):

>> **A selector for moving between tiles (blocks) and JavaScript**, located at the top of the IDE. Both options offer coders a list of commands that can be used to write programs. Your coder can switch back and forth between tiles and JavaScript.

>> **A micro:bit emulator**, located on the left of the IDE. This shows how the real micro:bit board will behave when its program is executed. The emulator features an A button, a B button, and an A+B button (if that event handler is included in your kid's code). If you include code that is activated by the accelerometer, such as shake, then the emulator shows a shake button. If you attach component electronics to the pins, the emulator shows the wires connected to the external component. Below the emulator is a play/stop button, a restart button, and a slo-mo button, which looks like a snail, to control its operation.

>> **Categories which organize code commands**, located in the center of the IDE. Categories consist of Basic, Input, Music, Led, Radio, Loops, Logic, Variables, Math, and Advanced. Your coder selects a category to display all the commands related to that category.

>> **A programming area to write the program**, located on the right of the IDE. Your coder can drag tiles (blocks) or JavaScript commands into the area to compose his program. He can also type commands directly into the programming area.

>> **A Download button**, located on the bottom-left of the IDE. Press this button to download your program onto your computer.

>> **An area for saving your program**, located at the bottom-center of the IDE. Type the name of your program in the field and press the Save button to save your program.

>> **View buttons**, located at the bottom-right of the IDE. Use these to adjust your view of the program area. Press the + button to zoom in or press the – button to zoom out.

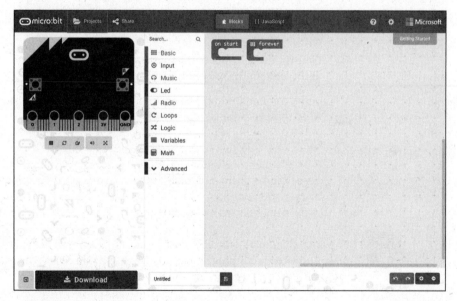

FIGURE 16-4:
The IDE for coding the micro:bit at the Microsoft Make Code site.

Writing and using a program

Writing programs for the micro:bit is similar to using any tile-based programming language. Your coder drags tiles (or JavaScript commands, if he chooses) from the categories into the program area. He then snaps the tiles together to assemble a program.

Running a program on the emulator

You and your coder can test a program on the micro:bit emulator to see how it executes before transferring it onto the micro:bit board. Click the play button under the emulator to run your program. You don't have to complete your program to run it on the emulator — try out sections as you program to test their operation.

Running a program on the micro:bit board

When your coder is ready to run a program on the micro:bit board, follow these steps:

1. **In the IDE, name and save the program.**

2. **In the IDE, click the Download button.**

A .hex file downloads to your computer (usually into your Downloads folder).

3. **Using the cable, connect the micro:bit board to your computer: connect the micro:bit board to the micro USB end of the cable and connect your computer to the USB end of the cable.**

When connected, an icon representing the micro:bit device appears on your desktop.

4. **Transfer the .hex file to the micro:bit by dragging it from your computer to the icon for the micro:bit device.**

During transfer, the micro:bit indicator button (on the device) blinks quickly. When the blinking stops, the transfer is complete.

5. **Power the board.**

The micro:bit is an electronic device and requires power to operate. Your coder can power the board by leaving it connected to your computer via USB cable. Or, to make the device portable, he can attach the battery pack to the micro:bit (and disconnect it from your computer).

REMEMBER

The micro:bit stores only the most recent program transferred to it. If your coder makes updates to his program in the IDE, he should repeat the steps to update the program stored in memory on the micro:bit.

TIP

Your coder will probably create a lot of cool projects with micro:bit! To access saved projects, as well as see additional example projects, click the Projects icon at the top of the micro:bit IDE.

BILL GATES AND PAUL ALLEN: FOUNDING MICROSOFT

Your young coder has probably heard the name Bill Gates, but it's likely due to his immense wealth. The story, though, of how Bill and his lifelong friend, Paul Allen, built a giant computer company, Microsoft, which generated that wealth. . . now *that's* the real story!

Bill Gates and Paul Allen grew up together in Seattle, attending the Lakeside school where they spent all of their free time programming a computer — although that computer differed greatly from any computer your coder would see today. According to Gates, it was, "a teletype that connected over the phone lines with a GE time-sharing computer." To run a program, Bill and Paul had to connect the computer to a phone line, and then upload their code using a paper tape system! Their work was time-consuming and the two teenagers learned everything they could about computer programming and building computers. Bill and Paul also got started in their very first entrepreneurial venture: forming a company called Traf-O-Data at which they wrote code to analyze traffic for Washington state.

Photo credit: http://ww2.hdnux.com/photos/03/31/05/889161/3/1024x1024.jpg

In 1974, the first personal computer kit, the Altair 8800, hit the market. Bill knew that he wanted to capitalize on this technological revolution, so he and Paul moved to Altair's

(continued)

(continued)

headquarters in Albuquerque, New Mexico, and struck a deal writing BASIC (an early programming language) to sell with the Altair. The duo soon formed a new company, Microsoft, and continued seeking new opportunities to write software for the evolving personal computer market.

A few years later, Microsoft partnered with IBM — the largest personal computer manufacturer at the time. Microsoft wrote an *operating system* (the main computer code) for the IBM PC. IBM agreed to sell Microsoft's operating system with every PC shipped, and to pay Microsoft for every sale. Bill and Paul earned a fortune in the deal, and went on to create more software to run on many more brands of personal computers, growing Microsoft ever larger. Their releases included the Windows operating system, the first widely distributed, graphical OS for personal computers. Microsoft also developed the Office Suite, a group of programs that includes a word processing program, a spreadsheet program, a slide presentation program, and other tools that help computer users be more productive. Frequent improvements and additions to their products, from the Internet Explorer browser to the Surface Pro, led to Microsoft's status as the world's largest software maker (as of 2016).

What started out as teen enthusiasm for coding and computers evolved into a successful entrepreneurial venture that became a worldwide brand. Just think about what your young coder and his friends might accomplish!

Don't Wake Baby Gadget

Sarah is a new mom, and as Camille can attest, nothing is more frustrating than getting a baby to sleep, only to have someone or something bump into his carrier. Can a potential babysitter move stealthily enough to avoid disturbing baby? You can code a simple device to find out!

TIP

This gadget is really just a simple motion-sensitive alarm. Challenge your coder to think of other uses and names for the gadget. What about, "Closet Monster Alarm," "Don't Wake the Kraken," "Backpack Motion Sensor," or "Annoying Sibling Alert" — there are so many possibilities!

Flowcharting the program

One way to begin designing a program to operate on your micro:bit is to draw a flowchart of its intended operation. Figure 16-5 shows a simplified version of one possible flowchart design for the Don't Wake Baby Gadget. See Chapter 2 for more information on flowcharting programs.

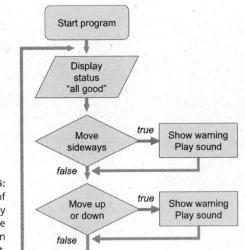

FIGURE 16-5:
Flowchart of
Don't Wake Baby
program to be
implemented on
the micro:bit.

Here are the possible steps your coder can take for this program:

1. Start program; display status "all good."

The program starts and immediately displays a graphic image (such as a smiley) representing an "all good" status.

2. Move sideways decision and consequences.

The program then executes a decision (an if-then conditional) to determine whether the device has been moved side to side. Motion in the x-direction, in the y-direction, or both indicates side-to-side movement. (Note that the accelerometer is really sensing a "rotation along the x-axis or along the y-axis" as opposed to straight-line motion along either axis. See Figure 16-6.) If the decision results in true, then a warning message and an alarm sound are executed. If the decision results in false, the program moves sequentially to the next step.

3. Move up-or-down decision and consequences.

The program then executes a decision (an if-then conditional) to determine whether the device has been moved up or down. Motion in the z-direction indicates up or down movement (against or with gravity). See Figure 16-6. If the decision results in true, then a warning message and an alarm sound are executed. If the decision results in false, the program moves sequentially to the next step.

4. Continue executing in forever loop.

The last step is a return to the start of the program as part of a forever loop. See Chapter 10 for help on loops.

FIGURE 16-6:
The micro:bit
board
accelerometer
measures
changes in
movement
along the x, y,
and z-axes.

Accelerometer location

Writing the code

The following sections outline the steps for one possible program your coder can write for the Don't Wake Baby device.

Step 1: Start program; display status "all good"

See Figure 16-7.

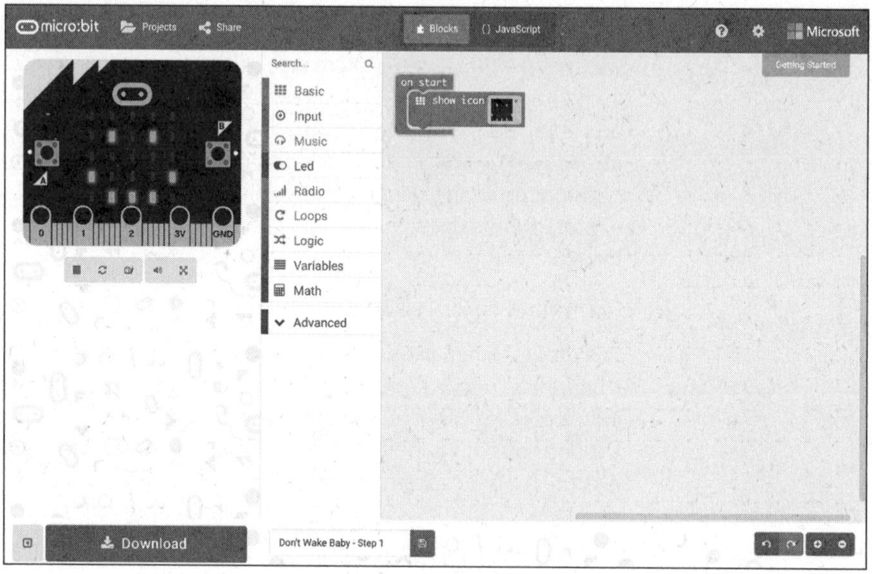

FIGURE 16-7:
Starting the
program and
display status
"all good"
with a smiley.

1. From the Basic category, drag an `on start` command.

2. From the Basic category, drag a `show icon` command and insert it inside of the `on start`. The `show icon` command can take the form of any image that represents an "all good" status. A smiley face icon is used here.

TIP

Drag any unwanted command tiles into the central tile categories area of the IDE. This gets rid of, or "recycles" them, and removes them from the program area.

Step 2: Move sideways decision and consequences

1. From the Variables category, select Make a Variable. Name the variable `sideMove` and click OK. See Figure 16-8.

New variable name:

sideMove

Ok ✓   Cancel ✗

FIGURE 16-8: Create a new variable called `sideMove`.

2. From the Variables category, drag a `set variable` command. Place it next in sequence below the `show icon` command of the smiley face. Click the tab on the command tile to change the variable name to `sideMove`. See Figure 16-9.

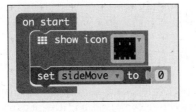

FIGURE 16-9: Add the `set variable` command next in sequence.

3. From the Input category, drag an `acceleration (mg)` command. Attach it next to the `set sideMove` command. Click the tab on the command tile to set the acceleration axis to `x`. See Figure 16-10. When the program runs, `sideMove` stores the constantly updated value of the x-acceleration.

4. From the Logic category, drag an `if-then` conditional command. Place it next in sequence. See Figure 16-11.

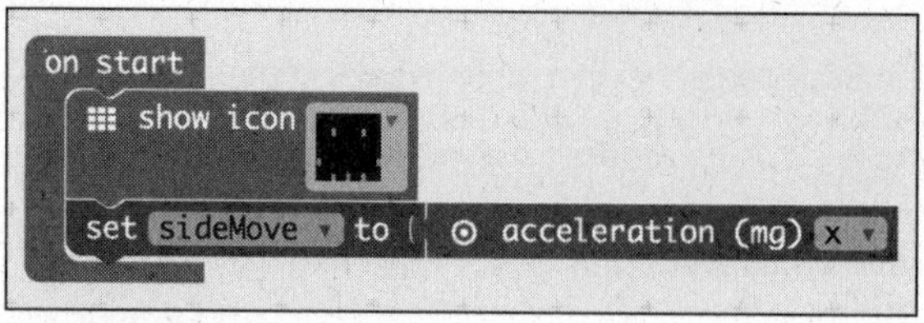

FIGURE 16-10:
Attach the
x-acceleration
command to
set variable.

```
on start
    show icon  [icon]
    set sideMove ▾ to (  ⊙ acceleration (mg) x ▾
```

FIGURE 16-11:
Add the if–then
conditional
command next
in sequence.

```
on start
    show icon  [icon]
    set sideMove ▾ to (  ⊙ acceleration (mg) x ▾
    ⚙ if  (  true ▾
    then
```

5. From the Logic category, drag an or logic command. Attach it next to the if command. See Figure 16-12. This or command is the condition of the if statement: If either of the commands in the or command are true, the if returns a Boolean value of true and then executes the then consequence.

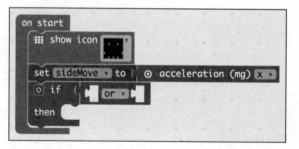

```
on start
    show icon  [icon]
    set sideMove ▾ to (  ⊙ acceleration (mg) x ▾
    ⚙ if  (  [ ] or [ ]
    then
```

FIGURE 16-12:
Attach the or
command to if.

6. From the Logic category, drag two inequality comparison commands. Attach the first inequality preceding the or command, and leave it as a less than (<) symbol. Attach the second inequality following the or command; click the tab and change it to a greater than (>) symbol. See Figure 16-13.

7. From the Variables category, drag two sideMove variables. Drag each sideMove variable into the first position of each inequality. In the first inequality, type the number -200, so that the command reads sideMove < −200. In the second inequality, type the number 200, so that the command reads sideMove > 200. See Figure 16-14. When the micro:bit is at rest, there is no movement in any direction, so there is no movement sideways (movement in the x or y direction).

With no movement, sideMove = 0. Moving (technically, tilting) the micro:bit to the left creates a large, negative x-acceleration. Moving (tilting) the micro:bit to the right creates a large, positive x-acceleration. The command, sideMove < –200 or sideMove > 200, produces true when the micro:bit detects this movement. Adjust the value of the numbers to increase or decrease the sensitivity of the device.

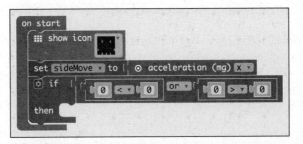

FIGURE 16-13: Attach the two inequality comparison commands.

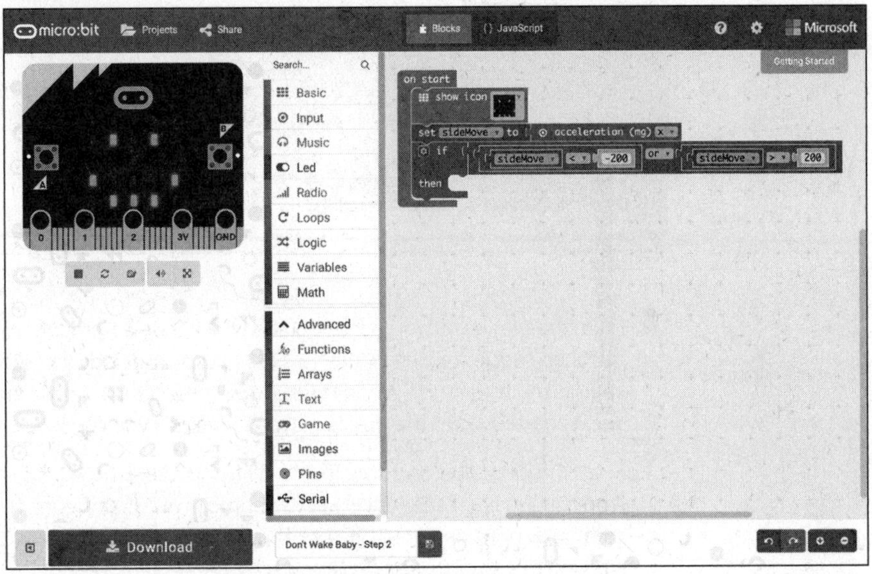

FIGURE 16-14: Add inequalities into the or command to test for sideways motion.

8. From the Basic category, drag the showString command. Drag it into the then command. Type any string of text you want to show when the device is disturbed; for example, OH NO, as shown in Figure 16-15. When operational, this text will be displayed as a scrolling message on the LED lights of the micro:bit. The text replaces the smiley image.

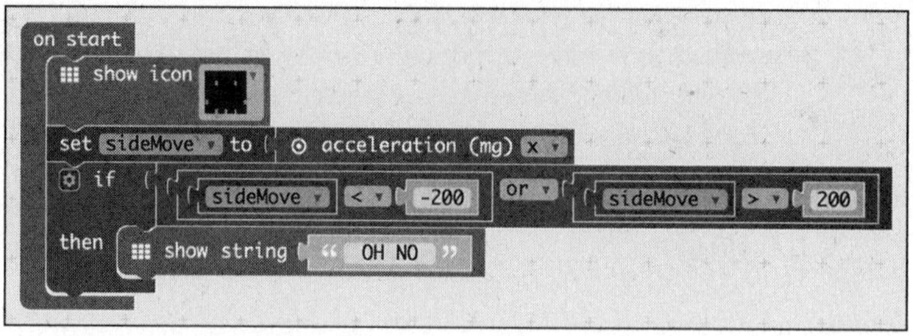

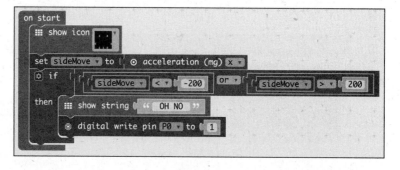

FIGURE 16-15:
If the device is moved sideways, show alert text string.

9. From the Pins category, drag the `digital write pin P0 to` command. Place it next in the `then` sequence. Set the number to 1. See Figure 16-16. This command sends power to ("turns on") the P0 pin. A component attached to this pin, and to ground, is then powered. Once a speaker is connected to the device, it will be powered.

FIGURE 16-16:
Digital write pin P0 to 1 sends power to the pin.

10. From the Music category, drag the `start melody` command. Place it next in the `then` sequence. See Figure 16-17. Select any melody you want. Set the `repeating` frequency. When the alarm is moved the P0 pin is powered, and a speaker attached to the device plays the melody you choose.

11. From the Pins category, drag the `digital write pin P0 to` command. Place it next in the `then` sequence. Set the number to 0. See Figure 16-18. This command halts power to ("turns off") the P0 pin. A component attached to this pin, and to ground, is then not powered.

TIP

You can test your device as coded so far. First, download the code to the micro:bit (see the earlier section "Running a program on the micro:bit board"), connect all the components (see the later section, "Connecting hardware components"), and finally move the micro:bit board to see whether it works the way you expect. Then return to Step 3 and continue on.

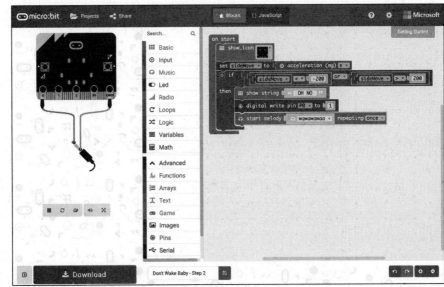

FIGURE 16-17:
Start melody
plays a song.

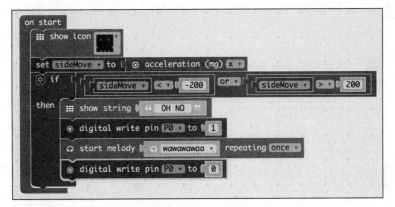

FIGURE 16-18:
Digital write
pin P0 to 0
halts power to
the pin.

Step 3: Move up-or-down decision and consequences

>> Code the micro:bit response to vertical motion as shown in Figure 16-19. Note that the code is similar to the code created in Step 2 for sideways motion. For vertical motion, create a variable called upDnMove and set it to z-acceleration. When z-acceleration is -1024 mg, the device is level — not moving up or down — and is only experiencing the downward acceleration due to gravity. Set the inequalities as follows: upDnMove < −1200 or sideMove > −850. This produces true when the micro:bit detects vertical movement. Adjust the value of the numbers to increase or decrease the sensitivity of the device.

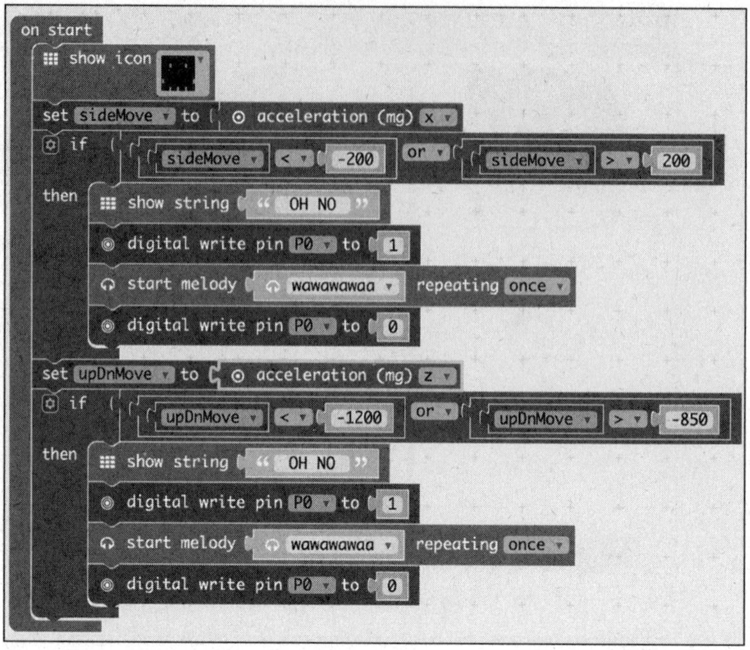

FIGURE 16-19:
Create a block for vertical motion.

You can test your device after Step 3, too. First, download the code to the micro:bit (see the earlier section "Running a program on the micro:bit board"), connect all the components (see the later section, "Connecting hardware components"), and finally move the micro:bit board to see whether it works the way you expect. Then return to Step 4 and continue on.

Step 4: Continue executing in forever loop

>> Drag all tiles from the `on start` command to separate them from `on start` — but leave everything in the program area. Then delete the `on start` command from the program (drag it into the command tiles area to get rid of it), but be sure to keep everything else! From the Basic category, drag a `forever` loop command into the program area. Drag your entire program block inside `forever`. Now, when the program runs, it executes forever until you press the stop button on the emulator or disconnect the physical device from the battery. By executing the program in a `forever` loop, it is constantly checking for motion, and can respond at any future time when it occurs. See Chapter 10 for help on infinite loops.

Your program is now complete! In Figure 16-20, the emulator shows that the program is running and the alarm has been activated. Although you can't hear the alarm sound, you can see that the LEDs are in the process of scrolling the warning message, "OH NO."

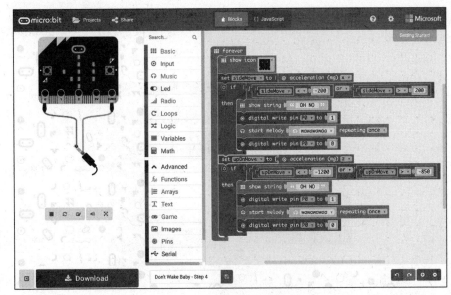

FIGURE 16-20:
Replace
on start
with a forever
command.

**TECHNICAL
STUFF**

Your coder may be wondering why there's no code block to respond to motion in the y-direction. It's unlikely that someone could move the device perfectly along a single axis. Coding for motion along two axes probably covers the movement the micro:bit will experience, and reduces the overall program length. But encourage your coder to code the remaining axis if he wants to do so! The code block for the y-axis is similar in form to the code block for the x-axis.

Downloading code to the micro:bit

Download the code to your micro:bit — see "Running a program on the micro:bit board" earlier in this chapter for directions.

REMEMBER

Each time you make changes to your code, you must transfer (download) the updated code to your micro:bit device.

Connecting hardware components

After your coder has transferred his program to the micro:bit, follow these steps to connect the hardware components (Figure 16-21):

1. **Attach one end of one wire (red) to Pin 0 on the micro:bit. Attach the other end of the same wire to the "hot" (red) lead of the speaker.**

2. **Attach one end of a different wire (black) to Ground on the micro:bit. Attach the other end of the same wire to the "ground" (black) lead of the speaker.**

3. **Power the micro:bit, either by cabling via USB to the computer, or cabling it to the battery pack.**

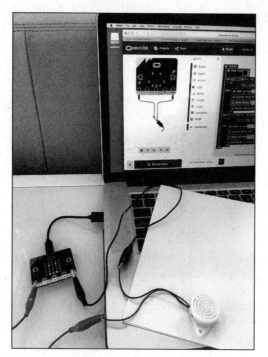

FIGURE 16-21:
Micro:bit,
speaker, and
alligator wires.
Dragging your
downloaded
program to the
Microbit icon on
the computer
desktop transfers
the program to
the device.

Testing the device

Test your Don't Wake Baby device by moving the micro:bit board! If the device doesn't operate as you want, troubleshoot some possible problems. Check that the wires are connected properly, and that the batteries are fresh. If the board shows an image, but you hear no sound, try a different speaker component. If the board is sluggish or too sensitive in responding to motion, adjust your code and remember to transfer the updated code to the board. During transfer, you should see the micro:bit indicator light blinking — if it doesn't, the program isn't downloading to the board.

Ideally, encourage your coder to test often throughout the development process, to ensure that each new chunk of code is producing the desired results on the micro:bit. Don't forget that code additions and edits must be saved, and the new code must be downloaded to the micro:bit.

After fully operational, play with the device and see whether it's possible to move so gently and smoothly that you can prevent the alarm from sounding!

Trying Wacky and Fun Variations

Think about the many exciting devices you can program using your micro:bit. What other toys, gadgets, and games, can your coder invent? Consider designing and building some of these fun possibilities:

>> **A Bop-It toy:** Bop-It gives an instruction and the user must complete the instruction in a limited time frame. For instance, one sound effect (or LED readout) can serve as the instruction for shaking the toy vigorously, while a different sound effect (or LED readout) can serve as the instruction for pressing a button. The accelerometer and buttons afford opportunities to create many practical — and whimsical — devices! Your coder can create a wide variety of conditionals, selected to execute randomly, to serve as the instructions. She can also create a timer to create time pressure, as well as variables to track score!

>> **A dice game:** With no external components required, your coder can code a dice game in which each shake or button press produces a dice face using the LED lights. Five micro:bit "dice" together can replicate a Yahtzee! game.

>> **A cryptographic device:** By writing code that makes use of simple math functions and basic logic, your coder can create a fun Caesar cipher for encrypting (code-making) and decrypting (code-breaking) messages.

>> **A see-and-say toy:** The original See-and-Say toy consisted of an arrow that rotated around a central axis, pointing to an animal that made its correspond-ing sound. Can your coder reproduce a similar device in which the micro:bit rotates around a central axis and uses compass heading input to select and produce a specific sound output?

>> **A meteorological tool:** Every good weatherperson needs to measure and report temperature. Your coder can code his micro:bit to function as a thermometer, measuring and displaying temperature in degrees Celsius. Challenge him to record a daily weathercast (and post it to YouTube!) using his very own custom-designed and coded micro:bit thermometer. (With a bit of additional code and the micro:bit compass, he can also report wind direction.)

>> **Two-player pong:** Your coder can take advantage of commands in the Game category to create a tiny ping-pong game. Now that's a blast from the past that we parents can relate to!

>> **A reaction time game:** Think back to when you were the age of your coder. Remember the science experiment in which a ruler is dropped and you try to grab it as it falls? Or do you recall moving at lightning speed to avoid a speeding red dodge ball during PE in the gym? Engaging in reaction time activities is something our kids love to do. Your coder can build a simple head-to-head electronics game to see who is reaction time Jedi among her

friends. The game produces visual or audio prompts, coded using a random delay time followed by a display of LEDs or production of a sound. Once complete, two players can compete by pressing the A or B button as each player attempts to be the first to react to the micro:bit prompt. Coders can create and use variables to keep score, and a `for` loop to construct a complete game of five or ten total rounds.

>> **A wacky light-controlled instrument:** A theramin is a real instrument with an eerie, science fiction sound patented in 1928. The instrumentalist plays the theramin without ever touching it. Challenge your coder to design, code, and build a "touchless" instrument from his micro:bit and some external components! Consider coding the micro:bit light sensor to respond to flashlights or bulbs, each rated for a different visible light emissions. The consequences of reading different light levels can be playing different musical notes. If eight light levels are produced, your code can play an entire scale!

TIP

For coders who find working on the cryptographic device exciting, encourage them to check out the NSA Day of Cyber website at `https://www.nsadayofcyber.com`. There, you coders can explore what it's like to work in cybersecurity — a very hot career field in which professionals secure computer systems and valuable data from cyber criminals.

5

The Part of Tens

IN THIS PART . . .

Find out about the ten do's and don'ts of choosing a curriculum to guide your young coder.

Explore the ten ways to keep coding learning going.

Chapter 17

Ten Do's and Don'ts for Selecting a Kids Coding Curriculum

Selecting a coding curriculum is a critical task. If you're a parent who is homeschooling your child, you have quite a few options available for coding curricula. If you're a parent of a school-faring kiddo, you may not actually select a curriculum, but instead simply try to assist your child in working with whatever material she's exploring in class.

Coaches and teachers in camps and schools may have some flexibility in selecting a curriculum, especially those working in independent settings. Coaches and teachers instructing for larger public schools, however, may be required to use specific curriculum prescribed by their school districts and state departments of education. This is also true of instructors teaching in online settings. Whatever your circumstances, this chapter can help you find and implement a coding curriculum that is engaging and provides just the right level of difficulty for your young coders!

DO Find the Right Entry Level

So many options are available for coding curricula — so where do you start? Countries including The United Kingdom, Estonia, Australia, France, and others have committed to coding by making it an integral part of their national school curriculum for K-12 students. Most of these countries are developing their own curriculum, getting their students started as young as Kindergarten!

Getting started in elementary grades

In the early grades, many countries focus curricula in two areas: unplugged computational thinking and introductory, tile-based coding.

Unplugged computational thinking addresses the logic of computing using games and role-playing away from the computer. CS Unplugged (http://csunplugged.org), developed in New Zealand, is an outstanding curriculum of unplugged activities you can perform indoors or outdoors, using inexpensive, everyday objects. Topics range from Binary Numbers, to Searching Algorithms, to Error Detection (as shown in Figure 17-1). By focusing on the logic of computation, as opposed to writing code, students build mental models of ideas separate from any particular coding paradigm. Some topics are actually quite complex and are best suited for high schoolers!

FIGURE 17-1: CS Unplugged provides a free, away-from-computer computational thinking curriculum.

Figure credit: http://csunplugged.org/error-detection/#Photos

Introductory, tile-based computing is most frequently conducted in Scratch. Scratch has a *low floor* — meaning it's easy to step into using it. It's also a great starter language for many others reasons: it's free, it's accessible on and offline, it's forgiving, and it's fun! And its many language choices ensure that kids all over the world can find an interface with which they're familiar. With regard to curriculum, Scratch offers an endless treasure trove of free tutorials and millions of shared, completed programs which serve as examples for new coders. There are also many excellent books, including several in the *For Dummies* lineup, which provide step-by-step lessons in Scratch. Additionally, the ScratchEd community of educators makes a free (and fabulous!) Scratch starter curriculum, Creative Computing, available at `http://scratched.gse.harvard.edu/guide/`.

Getting started in the middle grades

In the early grades, many countries focus curricula in two areas: For a broad range of coding curriculum options, Code.org provides multiple, free, online courses rich in content and fantastically fun! Courses begin with CS Fundamentals as young as Kindergarten, and progress through AP Computer Science Principles (see Figure 17-2) for high schoolers. Parents, coding coaches, and educators find these offerings especially appealing for the middle grades, with spillover into upper elementary and early high school. Both tile-based and line-based coding are included, and Code.org's curriculum makes it easy to move between the two. Fun, modern explanatory videos (many with celebrities and young professionals in the industry), clearly scaffolded concepts, hands-on games, and engaging programming projects make Code.org curriculum offerings ideal for a wide range of levels. Code.org also provides the adult in charge a free, superb management system for assigning topics and tracking learner performance.

Getting started in high school grades

If you're working with older novices who are just getting started with coding — or extended their knowledge base in new directions — you can't beat the excellent, free curriculum offerings from CodeHS, as shown in Figure 17-3. Presented through a tidy, easy-to-use online portal, CodeHS presents a wide range of coding courses, addressing many line-based programming languages. Course curricula addresses everything from Python to Java to Virtual Reality, and targets upper middle schoolers and high schoolers. Parents, coding coaches, and educators appreciate the organization of the topics and subtopics in each course, as well as excellent learning management system for tracking learning performance. Simple, explanatory videos, examples, and coding tasks build from easy to very challenging.

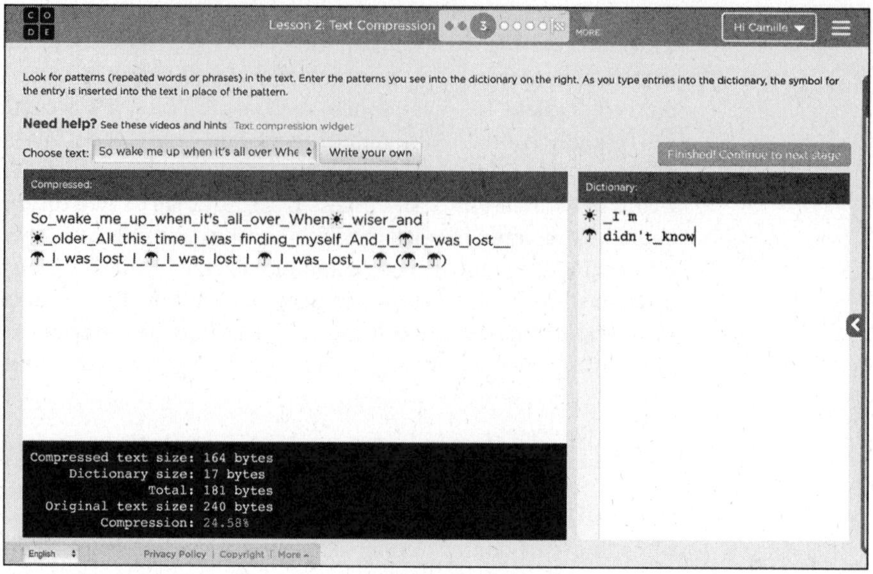

![Screenshot of Code.org Text Compression widget showing Lesson 2: Text Compression]

FIGURE 17-2:
Code.org provides outstanding, online curriculum in coding and related CS topics, spanning grades K-12.

Figure credit: https://studio.code.org/s/csp2/stage/2/puzzle/3

![Screenshot of CodeHS course listing for Camille McCue]

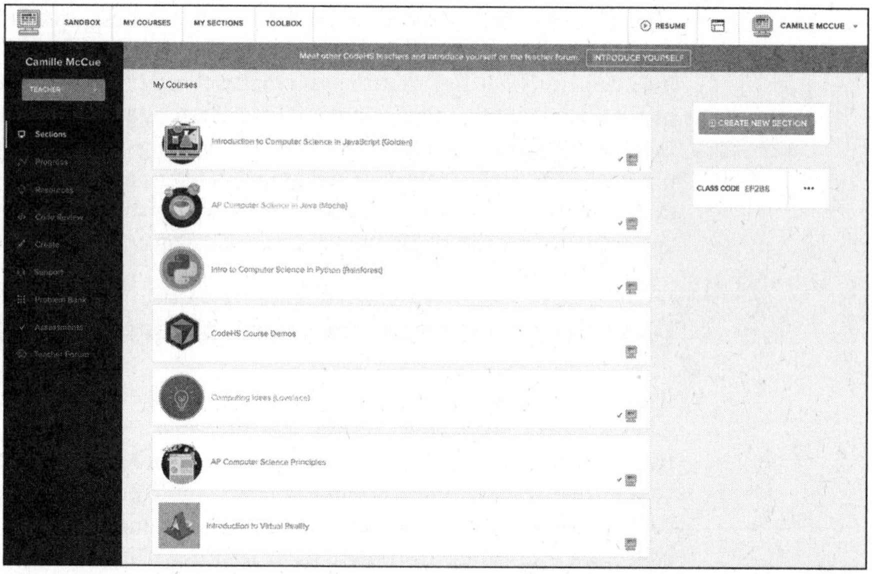

FIGURE 17-3:
Curriculum from CodeHS covers a wide range of languages and themes in multiple free, well-designed, online courses.

Figure credit: https://studio.code.org/s/csp2/stage/2/puzzle/3

TIP

Most coding curricula are implemented on a laptop (of any type) using a web browser. Few curricula (and coding languages) are available on mobile devices, although an exciting new offering, Swift Playgrounds (https://www.apple.com/everyone-can-code/), is offered for kids of all ages on the iPad. Best of all, Swift

Playgrounds (see Figure 17-4) lays the foundation for coders to progress to Swift — a full-tilt professional programming language, developed by Apple, and rooted in Objective-C.

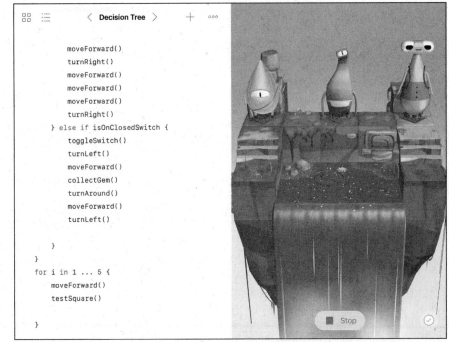

FIGURE 17-4:
Swift playgrounds is an exciting new coding curriculum, available on the iPad.

Figure credit: *https://images.techhive.com/images/article/2016/07/swift-playgrounds-ios10-characters-100671813-orig.png*

DON'T Assume Cost Equals Quality

Beyond the free resources outlined in this chapter, numerous other curriculum offerings for computer science instruction come at a cost. You should know, though, that such offerings vary greatly in price and it's not necessarily the case that more expensive products equate to learning computer science in better, cheaper, or faster ways.

For instance, thousands of free how-to videos on YouTube and other online portals provide CS instruction, showing a variety of languages and other related topics. Some videos are crafted by professionals and teaching institutions. Videos organized into logical collections, accompanied by supporting curriculum, such as those provided free by Khan Academy (`https://www.khanacademy.org/computing/computer-science`), are especially useful. MIT OpenCourseWare (https://ocw.mit.edu/index.htm) also provides free computer science courses recorded in actual lecture halls at the university. Other free instructional videos are created by enthusiasts who simply want to share their knowledge — and while not always "professional" in their production quality, they can be very useful.

Very reasonably priced courses are also available through providers including Coursera (https://www.coursera.org) and Udemy (https://www.udemy.com). These providers and others present instructional videos and accompanying curriculum for a per-course or monthly fee.

Many universities and private companies also offer coding training or boot camps. For adults, this training is packaged as degree or certificate programs, and for kids, it's offered as summer camps. While these programs can be excellent, they're typically quite pricey, so we recommend you conduct substantial research to ensure that the money you spend is truly for quality instructors and instruction.

DO Balance Lessons with Free Exploration

Whatever curriculum you choose (or find your young coder assigned), it's important to encourage kids to balance guided lessons with free exploration. We've observed that our students can be trucking along, doing just great on understanding new concepts, one at a time until asked to combine multiple programming concepts or attempt a messy, not-so-obvious problem. Even as you diligently teach or support a fully fleshed out computer science curriculum, be sure to encourage your coder to go off the beaten path occasionally. As young coders attempt to build complete programs (even very short ones), they sometimes run into roadblocks: misconceptions about how to apply code they do know, as well as missing information about code they don't yet know. Providing young coders these experiences — and coaching them through them — are soft skills equal in value to the actual coding content of prescriptive lesson plans. Ultimately, your role in helping learners feel supported in applying newly acquired skills in novel contexts is important in building their resilience in programming.

DON'T Instantly Dismiss Teaching Languages

Alice, Scratch, and MicroWorlds EX are teaching languages. Unlike programming languages such as JavaScript, Python, Java, and C++, teaching languages aren't used in professional programming contexts. Professional coders often dismiss the usefulness of teaching languages as they believe that such languages are too simplistic to build a realistic understanding of coding. However, we feel that meeting new coders where they are in terms of their knowledge base sometimes requires an easier and more welcoming starting point than the professional languages provide. Most significantly, teaching languages have well-crafted companion curricula that have been specifically written to teach new coders how to code. Providing new coders a doable experience in a teaching language may afford the lower floor they need to step into programming. In time, young coders can then continue advancing their skills and step up eventually to a professional programming language.

Another nontraditional option for getting started with programming is an offering called EarSketch (https://earsketch.gatech.edu). Geared towards high school students, EarSketch (see Figure 17-5) invites coders to approach programming through a music-based interface. Coders "compose" programs in Python or JavaScript, but the tasks they perform focus on producing music by constructing beats, manipulating loops, and applying audio effects. The curriculum is free, web-based, and approved by the College Board.

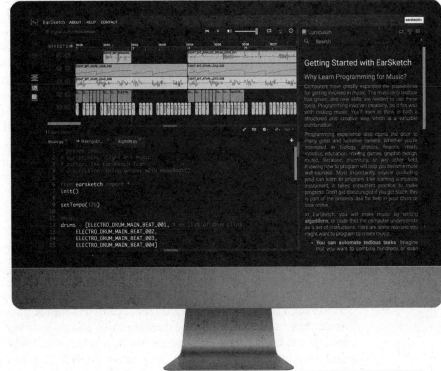

FIGURE 17-5:
EarSketch teaches coding through music production.

DO Consult CSTA for Guidance

Trying to determine what computer science concepts should be taught, when those concepts should be introduced, and in what sequence is daunting. Fortunately, the Computer Science Teachers Association (CSTA) has done the hard work of figuring out all this for you! CSTA (http://www.csteachers.org) is the non-profit governing body that promotes and supports computer science education and computer science teachers. You can check out computer science curriculum frameworks, research, advocacy efforts, conference information, and more at the CSTA website. CSTA is a great source you can consult whenever you need an independent, scholarly perspective on supporting computer science education.

DON'T Buy "Coding" Toys for Babies

There are a few great code-themed toys for preschoolers and Kindergartners. Bee-Bot programmable robots and apps such as The Foos are not only fun and instructional, but wonderfully age-appropriate. However, many blog posts and "toy recommenders" would have you believe that coding curriculum must be implemented shortly after birth or else your child will be behind for life. Preposterous! Don't feel compelled to spend money on coding toys for babies and toddlers — it's a ruse and a waste of your resources. There's also some evidence that over-emphasizing technology in lieu of interpersonal interaction — as well as excessive screen time — is counterproductive for children's development. Reading books, running, playing with blocks, doing puzzles, singing, sorting, imagining, tinkering, and counting are productive, low-cost skill-building activities for children ages one to three. No coding required.

DO Emphasize the Soft Skills

Mathematics, computational thinking, logic, coding, network architecture, software development, hardware, and user interface design are the hard skills of computer science. It's equally important for your young coder to develop the soft skills of computer science including collaboration, communication, creativity, critical thinking, researching, negotiation, troubleshooting, planning, and persistence. Most curricula emphasize the hard skills and that's great! But the number one job you can perform as a coding coach, parent, or teacher is supporting soft skill development in your coders. A spillover bonus is that successfully building these skills serves kids well in every other area of their lives!

DON'T Let Kids Get Stuck in a Loop

There's a story a teacher tells about 3D printing dog tags as a first design project in the classroom. The teacher laments how, after successfully printing the tags, students continue for weeks to perfect their tags, making slight variations, but never learning new skills nor taking risks to design and print something entirely new. It's easy for all of us to relax into a comfort zone, repeating the skills and processes with which we're familiar instead of venturing into unknown territory. As an adult guide to your young coder, notice his progression each week, and — if he appears to be stuck in a loop — help him learn a new coding concept to grow his skill set. No one needs 300 dog tags!

DO Present the Bigger Picture

Coding curricula do sound jobs of presenting well-sequenced concepts and practice activities in their respective languages. You can help your coder situate her work but helping her think through ways in which expert coders, and other professionals who code, view the bigger picture of coding and more generally, computer science. How do medical doctors use code? Radiologists are increasingly relying on the combination of human experience and algorithms that look for anomalies in X-ray images to identify cancer. How do pilots use code? Aerospace engineers write code to read sensors and adjust airplane control structures, as well as engine power, for takeoff and landing autopilot algorithms. How does the IRS use code? The IRS uses algorithms that search for the excessive appearance of certain digits in tax returns to flag possible fraud (really! Look up Benford's Law for more information). The applications of computer science are all around you and your coders. Just look and you'll find them everywhere!

DON'T Stereotype Coders

There is no singular "coder" profile, although pop culture may have you believe otherwise. Sarah is a Latina who has a school teacher for a mom, and didn't know what coding was until she entered college. Still, she persisted and became an engineer and engineering educator! During most of Camille's precollege years, she was one of the few girls programming a computer at home and competing in Saturday morning math contests. But both of her parents had STEM backgrounds (and her grandmother supervised the production of electronics during WWII!), so she felt supported in pursuing her interests.

Coding is not the exclusive domain of any age, ethnicity, background, gender, or orientation. Any interested person can get started in coding and improve his or her skills with time and dedication. No matter what attributes your young coder possesses, you can convey that coding is doable, fun, and worthwhile. As coding is becoming more prevalent in schools and informal education venues, the diversity of its participants will grow and more kids will see people "like themselves" who are passionate about coding. Curricula such as AP Computer Science Principles were specifically crafted to encourage a generation of coders that is inclusive of everyone. Enlist as many people as you can to create a diverse infrastructure to support and encourage the kids you teach and mentor. (There's some evidence that a child's peer group is the most influential factor in sustaining his or her growth in STEM so seek out ways to get your child's friends involved in coding, too!) Ultimately, you can help the young coder in your life by reinforcing diversity and championing the belief in "Coding for All!"

Chapter **18**

Ten Ways to Keep the Coding Learning Going

Though your goal might be to keep your young coder engaged in coding for years to come, it's important to recognize that to do that, it might mean encouraging young coders to see how newly developed skills fit into the rest of their lives. In this chapter, you find tips for keeping the spark of curiosity and creativity alive with your young coder, sometimes by not coding at all!

Unplugged

As you find throughout this book, unplugged activities are great ways to introduce coding concepts to young coders without the need of a computer at all. The benefit of unplugged activities is that you can encourage your young coder to take a step back and really understand a concept well. Unplugged activities can also be done in groups and a lot of them can be done anywhere, even on a long road trip! You can find unplugged activities in a few places, but the two most popular sites are CSUnplugged and Code.Org's unplugged page.

On CSUnplugged (csunplugged.com) you find an entire book available for download or hard copy in English, with some chapters downloadable in over 20 other languages. In addition to the book, activities are targeted for ages 5–12 on a variety of topics such as data representation, algorithms, and cryptography. Most activities are truly unplugged and have simple PDFs that can be downloaded and printed, and CSUnplugged has created a number of videos to support the learning of these concepts as well.

On Code.Org's unplugged page (`https://code.org/curriculum/unplugged`) you find a number of activities aimed at teachers who might be leading the activity in the classroom. Code.Org offers lesson plans, answer keys, assessments, and videos to support the teacher and the students. Similar to CSUnpluged, Code.Org has a book that you can download; the unplugged activities are parts of the curriculum that includes coding activities. For example, the algorithms unplugged activity called "Dice Race" is the first lesson in Course E and the tenth lesson in Course 3. You can therefore choose if you just want to introduce your young coder to specific concepts, or want them to go through an entire curriculum.

Research Pioneers of Computing

Throughout this book you have the opportunity to learn a lot about some of the pioneers of computing. One of the best ways to inspire your young coder and to keep her excited and interested in continuing their learning adventure is to give her role models to look up to. One of Sarah's favorite versions of this was when she was a teaching assistant in Oakland, CA for a diverse class of 10–13 year olds. The educator had a "Wall of Coders" that had pictures of people of all ages, ethnicities, abilities, genders, backgrounds, and so on. These coders were pioneers such as Ada Lovelace, to more recent contributors like Alan Turing and Katherine Johnson, to current leaders such as Elon Musk. On the first day of class, the instructors took pictures of the students and inter-mixed them on the Wall of Coders. Each morning, the class would choose one of the famous pioneers and have a brief discussion about them.

The benefit of having young coders learn about the history of computing and the direction it's headed is they can start to realize that contributions and contributors come in all shapes and sizes. Some people are mathematicians who contribute algorithms; others are hardware engineers. The future of this industry is vast and diverse, and giving your young coder that openness to realize he can explore any aspect of the world with coding and computers is priceless.

Go Lateral from Code

A common misconception about being involved in software development is that you have to be the one coding to do something interesting. In today's digital world, there are so many aspects to developing technology that there are opportunities for young coders to pursue other technological contributions without it being only about the code. Aesthetic, engineering, and entrepreneurial endeavors afford great ways to branch out from coding!

For example, digital artists are critical for video games, movies, television, websites — basically any digital experience that has a visual component. It can be very important for digital artists to also have experience with coding in particular contexts. To support these creative activities outside of code, you might want to encourage your young coder to explore software such as Photoshop, Blender, Unity, and TinkerCad. The more artists understands how art interacts with the code, the better they can create integrateable art.

It's also important to have those young coders who do want to focus on code explore other fields that surround code. Understanding how usability, design thinking, aesthetics, and engineering intersect gives your young coder a better idea of how to create something useful for humans. Whether he's coding an app, planning software for a robot, or designing a drone (Unmanned Aerial Vehicle) and its autonomous control system, your coder can expand his thinking about the many applications of computer programming. Building these lateral skills serves your coder well as careers of the future will seamlessly integrate all these fields.

The effort of exploring technology outside of coding can give your young coder the inspiration to invent "the next big thing." One of Camille's students, Emily, created an adorable purple unicorn character (in Adobe Illustrator) for a GameSalad game she built as a freshman. It was such a hit, she combined the character with another passion of hers — squishies — and had it mass manufactured as a physical toy. She's now set up her own business entity and is selling huge quantities of scented squishy unicorns!

TIP

Exploration of the mathematical sides of coding, from cryptography and cybersecurity to big data and data analytics, are also great ways to "go lateral."

Language Tracking

Typically focusing on what languages a coder knows is not as important as the types of projects that they have built. However, for young coders, this can be a great way to start introducing them to other types of applications and give them a sense of accomplishment for starting to code in new languages. It isn't possible to master every single language, and it also isn't important to try. What is more important is to understand what languages are best suited for what types of applications.

A fun, ongoing project that you can have with your young coder is to track all the languages they have ever coded in. When doing this, you can mark down the types of projects they built using those languages, the benefits, and where problems might have arisen. Then, when a new project is being considered, you can take out the language tracking sheet and determine which language is probably best to tackle the project.

By talking about languages in this context, you can help your young coder realize that it's the projects, and the decisions about the projects, that are more important than just the number of languages you know.

Smart Home Projects

If you decide to get into some of the programmable hardware and electronics, you can help your young coder explore the world of smart homes. The benefit of projects like these is that they're always changing based on the interests and lifestyle of the coder. For example, at a young age, she might want to create an automatic night light that turns on when it gets dark, or turns on when she says "Night Light On." At an older age, she might want to create remotely operated mood lighting that adjusts in brightness and color according to the time of day.

Smart home projects can also be very motivating for young coders, because they can solve a lot of the chores that they don't enjoy doing! For example, if you have a pet that needs a water bowl filled when it gets below a certain amount, your young coder could create a device that measures the water levels and sends an alert to a phone when the water is low. Or, if he has a fish that needs to be fed every day at 5pm, they could create a small device to feed the fish on a timer! Little Bits even has a kit for smart home projects for kids; check it out at `https://shop.littlebits.cc/products/smart-home-kit`.

Include Outside Passions

One of the most important ways to keep coders interested and passionate about coding is to focus on the coder as a whole person — which includes non-technical or non-coding passions as well. Coding is considered "the 4th R" because it is similar to reading, writing, and arithmetic; it is a communications tool that is used to solve more complex problems. Not all professional writers like to write about the same topic, and if they were forced to just because they were "writers," they probably wouldn't enjoy their jobs, and would probably find a different passion. This is the same with coders. Coders not only like writing code, but they like solving problems that interests them.

Some of the most impressive coders have existed because they identified something that they loved, or a problem that they had, and they used their skill of coding to tackle it. Encourage conversations with your young coder about their lives outside of their coding adventure. What problems are they facing? Why do they think it's a problem? Why hasn't that problem been solved? How do they think they could solve the problem? Then try to help them solve the problem, or versions of the problem. You may not be able to solve every problem, but they could still brainstorm possibilities, including solutions that no one is actually able to build yet! This innovative conversation and thinking keeps your young coders interested in their coding adventure.

Leonardo da Vinci designed plans for a tank, and Star Trek posited a hand-held, wireless communication device long before either object could be built! New inventions start with new ideas — often to solve long-standing problems.

Open-Source Projects

Open-source projects are ones where someone has an idea for a project, starts it, and gives a description of where the project is heading. Then he opens the project to the entire world and asks for other coders to help complete the project. An example of an open-source project that became very successful is the Firefox web browser.

More relevant, perhaps, for your young coder are all the open-source projects related to Minecraft! Though Minecraft itself is developed by one company (Mojang, which was acquired by Microsoft), other developers can create *mods*. Mods are basically modifications to the original game so that you can do things in the game that weren't originally possible. The Minecraft modding community is very big and often the mods are open-source, meaning the original author of the mod is interested in sharing work products and collaborating with other coders.

Open-source projects might be more suited for older or more experienced coders, but knowing about the open-source world can be exciting for a lot of young coders. There are also ways to get involved in a similar community without the projects being explicitly open source. For example, Scratch (scratch.mit.edu) has over

28 million projects that have been shared publicly on the site. Each of these can be remixed, which means your young coder can make a copy of the project and make changes, or add to it. This is a very similar experience to contributing to an open-source project, but can be done by novice, young coders!

Group Projects

Contrary to what a lot of people believe, coding is a very social and collaborative activity. One way to keep your young coder interested and excited about coding is to engage him in group projects. Group projects can be difficult, if your coder is predominately working alone and has no coders at similar experience levels nearby. However, with sites like Scratch and applications like Skype or Google Hangouts, young coders can collaborate on code through remixing and video chats.

For group projects, you should encourage your young coders to design the overall concept and goal of the project first. This can prevent a lot of miscommunication or disagreements in the future. Some young coders who decide to collaborate on projects together have said that there is one "owner" of the project, and that the other young coders are just helping to make the project better. This can be an effective way to think about group projects, because disagreements most likely arise, and if one person is the "owner," then it's clear whose decision prevails. However, it's also important to establish clear roles for each group member, so that every contributor's voice is heard. (This also creates motivation for coders to continue working together and not just "drop out.") During this time, it's important to have conversations with your young coders about effective group work, communication, and listening to others ideas, even if you don't agree. These skills are critical for coders as they get older and join larger software teams.

Community Support

One way to encourage your young coder to keep exploring their passion is to create opportunities where they can collaborate within the community. This can be starting clubs at the local community center where they can find other young coders who might be interested in learning. You can encourage your young coder to start the clubs, or find other adults who can do it for them. The benefit of encouraging your young coder to start their own organizations and clubs is that you can also teach them a bit about entrepreneurship and leadership.

Another great way to get your coder involved in the community is to have them discover problems that the community is facing and design and develop solutions to solve those problems. For example, a young group of coders identified that their community was part of a food desert (fresh food was hard to come by within walking distance of a lot of homes). To help solve this problem, they started a community garden with sensors that would trigger automatic watering for their vegetables and fruits. Then they created an app for folks to update and receive updates regarding what foods were available. By encouraging your young coder to solve problems within their own community, you give them a larger sense of passion and determination. It also prepares them for solving larger community problems as they get older, and hopefully helps create a better world each generation!

Portfolios

One final idea for continuing to spark the passion of young coders is to encourage them to create a portfolio of all their work. This can be done by following some of the tips in Chapter 14, and creating a website on a simple webpage maker like Wix.com or Squarespace.com or even by using online coding communities and profiles with Scratch.mit.edu or GitHub.com for kids over 13.

There are several benefits for creating a digital portfolio. There is of course the benefit of your young coder realizing all the hard work that she put in, and what she has accomplished. Digital portfolios can also be very useful when looking for a job. For example, a lot of tech companies care significantly more about the projects you have contributed to or owned than the degrees and GPA that you possess. And although the projects that your young coder is starting out with might be novice, the history of their development and learning is worthwhile. Another benefit is that they can find collaborators and other young coders through these same platforms and create something even more amazing together!

Aside from the code aspect of digital portfolios, there is also a communication benefit for young coders. Being able to concisely explain a project, introduce it to users, and communicate in comments about feedback and iterations of their code improve their written communication skills. You can also help your young coder start a YouTube channel where she describes all the projects that she's built! There are a lot of ways for young coders to show off what they have done. Helping them discover the medium they're most excited about fosters their continued interest in improving their portfolios, giving them inspiration and dedication to continue their coding journeys.

Index

Symbols

dice game, 335

`digital write pin P0 to` command, 330–331

`direction` command, 96

`<div>` tag, 263, 265

DNS (domain name system), 261

Don't Wake Baby device

  coding

    "all good" status, 326–327

    forever loop, 332–333

    sideways motion decisions and consequences, 327–331

    up-or-down motion decisions and consequences, 331–332

  downloading code to micro:bit, 333

  flowcharting program, 324–326

  hardware components, 318–320, 333–334

  IDE interface, 320–321

  overview, 324

  testing, 322, 333–334

  variations, 335–336

`do–while` loops

  overview, 187

  using pseudocode, 189

  using Python, 193–194

Draw.io, 30

dynamic type, 50

E

EarSketch, 345

efficiency, 221

electronics

  coding

    "all good" status, 326–327

    forever loop, 332–333

    sideways motion decisions and consequences, 327–331

    up-or-down motion decisions and consequences, 331–332

  downloading code to micro:bit, 333

  flowcharting program, 324–326

  hardware components, 318–320, 333–334

  IDE interface, 320–321

  overview, 324

  testing, 322, 333–334

  variations, 335–336

emulators, 39, 67, 294–295, 299–300, 314

`.equals( )` method, 181–182

event handlers, 74, 105

exponents

  using Python, 154

  using Scratch, 152–153

F

Fibonacci Sequence, 199–200

final score, coding, 314

floats, 150

flowcharts, 28–30

The Foos, 14, 42–43, 346

For Loop Fun puzzle, 186–187

`for` loops

  nesting, 197–198

  overview, 187

  using pseudocode, 190

  using Python, 193, 195

  using Scratch (repeat loop), 191–192

`for–each` loops

  nesting, 196–197

  overview, 187–188

  using pseudocode, 190

  using Python, 193, 195

foreign languages, 9

`forever` command, 38, 99, 102–103

forever loop, 332–333

FORTRAN, 9–10, 16, 92

fractals, 196

functions, 154, 227

G

GameSalad, 14, 58–59, 96

Gates, Bill, 323–324

geolocation, 84

geometry

  acting out, 83–84

  Asteroid Blaster game, 104–105

  coordinates, defined, 82

  general discussion, 81

  movement, 100–104

Mad Lib program, 79–80
math operations
    advanced operations, 153–156
    basic operations, 149–150
    mod operations, 157
    PEMDAS order of operations, 158–159
    random numbers, 163
    rounding, 161
origin of, 52–53
overview, 50–51
setting and finding direction, 96
text
    concatenation, 75–76
    formatting, 77
    input/output, 71
    showing onscreen, 65–66
variables
    changing type, 135
    creating, 134–135
    declaring, 128
    incrementing and decrementing, 141–142
Python Tutor, 51, 71

Q

QR codes, 316
queries, 34

R

R, 10
randint function, 163
randomness
    defined, 38–39
    random numbers, 162–163
    random placement of items, 309–311
    random positioning, 93–95
    setting direction randomly, 97
raster file types, 110
rational actor personality type, 18
reaction time game, 335–336
repeat command, 36, 38
repeat until command, 38, 103
repetition, 36, 38

reserved words, 129
resilience, 9
return command, 236
reusability, 221
Rock, Paper, Scissors game, 182–184
Ruby, 10

S

Safe Search feature (Google Images), 112
say command, 64
scope, 133
scoping errors, 242–243
Scratch
    Asteroid Blaster game, 104–105
    commenting, 31–32
    concatenation, 75
    crypto code maker project, 163–166
    debate over starter languages, 42
    debugging
        infinite loops, 246
        off by one errors, 247
        typing errors, 243–244
    entry level, 14
    general discussion, 3–4
    geometry
        random positioning, 93–94
        setting and finding direction, 96–97
        setting and finding position, 86–87
        setting direction randomly, 97
        turning, 98–99
    importing GIF images, 116
    importing JPEG images, 114–115
    importing PNG images, 114–115
    lists
        adding items to, 206–207
        creating, 205–206
        getting items or positions in list, 207–208
        getting size of, 207–208
        iterating through, 208
        removing items from, 207
    logic operations
        compound conditionals, 177–179
        if–then statements, 169–170

About the Authors

Camille McCue earned her PhD in Curriculum and Instruction at UNLV, investigating how youth learn math through designing and coding video games. She began her career at IBM before serving as the Educational Television Anchor-Producer for NASA HQ, connecting kids with STEM experts, from orbiting ISS astronauts to Antarctic researchers. Camille then led the Ready to Learn initiative for Vegas PBS, as well as served as Founding Director for Dawson College Bound. For the past several years, she has developed and taught engineering, enriched math, and computer science courses to youth of all ages in independent schools. Camille currently serves as Director of Curriculum Innovations for the Adelson Educational Campus in Las Vegas, where she directed the creation of a multimillion dollar Startup Incubator (startupincubator.site) and implements innovative instructional initiatives. She teaches Systems Modeling and AP Computer Science, and presents and publishes extensively, including writing nine technology books for John Wiley & Sons. Camille was recently awarded the Tech Exec Lifetime Achievement award from VEGAS, Inc. and Cox Business. During the summer she serves as the Curriculum Director for Spark Skill (sparkskill.com), an education startup providing cutting-edge STEM summer camps in programming, 3D printing, drone development, animation, cybersecurity, and IoT prototyping for tweens and teens. Camille is an active voice for evolution of the education system, blogging about this critical theme at camillemccue.com.

Sarah Guthals received her PhD from UCSD in Computer Science specializing in CS Education in 2014. During graduate school she built the beta version of CodeSpells, a 3D immersive video game designed to teach children to code through playing a wizard and writing "spells." She went on to co-found ThoughtSTEM, a company that builds software (for example, LearnToMod), curriculum, and pedagogies for teaching children to code and empowering K-12 teachers to teach their students. She has written four books around Minecraft, one on mobile app development, and one on making digital games, launched a Coursera and EdX course for teachers interested in teaching coding, was recently named Forbes 30 under 30 in Science and UCSD's 40 under 40 Alumni, and founded We Can — a company dedicated to encouraging ALL kids to do anything. She is currently a lecturer at UCSD for the department of Computer Science and the department of Educational Studies and is an Engineering Manager at a tech company. Her passion is making coding accessible to everyone, with the goal of making it a basic literacy.

Dedications

Camille: I dedicate this book to the many, many teachers and mentors who have taught me, inspired me, challenged me, and pushed me to "lean in" throughout my life. My parents, Beverly and Eric; my exceptional teachers; my husband,

Michael, and our children, Ian and Carson (who keep me on my toes in tech!); and my colleagues and students who have all been the engines that keep me fired up.

Sarah: I would like to dedicate this book to my close friends and family members who have supported me, not only in writing this book, but in becoming who I am today. I'd like to specifically dedicate this book to my husband Adrian who has always helped me to see that, with passion and dedication, I can really do anything I want. And finally to my daughter Ayla who gives me the drive to keep pushing forward!

Authors' Acknowledgments

Camille: What would we do without Dummies?! First, I'd like to acknowledge the Wiley team — especially my longtime friend, Acquisitions Editor, Steve Hayes; and our Project Editor, Rebecca Senninger, for their work in developing this book for parents and teachers as we promote STEM education around the world. And second, I'd like to thank Sarah Guthals for her expertise, educational savvy, and can-do mindset in co-authoring this book. We did it!

Sarah: I would like to acknowledge all the hard work that went into making Scratch, Java, JavaScript, Python, micro:bit, Android, App Inventor, and every programming language, coding application, and effort to improve the field of computer science — without these, coding would be so much harder. I would also like to acknowledge the teachers and parents around the world who have recognized the importance of coding in learning so many valuable lessons to our next generation of makers. Finally, I would like to acknowledge Camille for inviting me to co-author this book with her, and Steve and Rebecca and the folks at Wiley for making it a great experience as always!

Publisher's Acknowledgments

Executive Editor: Steven Hayes

Project Editor: Rebecca Senninger

Sr. Editorial Assistant: Cherie Case

Production Editor: Tamilmani Varadharaj

Front Cover Image: © FatCamera/iStock Photo